GOTHIC NOVELS OF THE TWENTIETH CENTURY

An Annotated Bibliography

by

Elsa J. Radcliffe

The Scarecrow Press, Inc.
Metuchen, N.J. & London
1979

Library of Congress Cataloging in Publication Data

Radcliffe, Elsa J., 1935-
Gothic novels of the twentieth century.

Includes index.
1. American fiction--20th century--Bibliography. 2. English fiction--20th century--Bibliography. 3. Gothic revival (Literature)--Bibliography. I. Title.
Z1231. F4R32 [PS379] 016. 823'0872 78-24357
ISBN 0-8108-1190-1

Manufactured in the United States of America

Dedicated to all lovers of castles, ghosts,

heroines, heroes and quests;

and to my hero, Jim.

CONTENTS

FOREWORD

> Let those who smile at me, ask themselves whether they have been indebted most to imagination or reality for all they have enjoyed in life, if indeed they have ever enjoyed anything.
>
> C. R. Maturin, in Melmoth the Wanderer

Due to opinions instilled in me throughout my education, it was rather late in life that I came upon, via detective fiction, the literature called "Gothic." I found, somewhat to my surprise, that these tales held a great appeal. The more I read, however, the more I became aware that between the covers of a book labeled "Gothic" one could find anything from a tale of mystery and detection, or sentimental and historical romance, to a "pure" Gothic, and any quality from superb to utter nonsense. I further discovered that Gothic fiction in paperback editions is only a fraction of a huge body of literature which has been written ever since the 1760's by authors of greatly varied backgrounds and skills. For lovers of the Gothic genre, there is available an almost limitless amount of reading pleasure if one has some way to discover it.

Thus, it seemed that it could be most helpful to make available to the reading public a fairly comprehensive bibliography and to give some indication of relative quality to help the reader and librarian select from the mind-boggling quantity.

This bibliography may be of use some day in the distant future to scholars who, from my observations, appear to be interested in this type of literature only in retrospect, when it achieves the distinction of antiquity, if nothing more.

I wish to express my appreciation to the Shippensburg State College Library and in particular to Dr. Scott Bruntjen, whose technical help and moral support were invaluable; and to Mrs. Barbara Taylor, whose help with interlibrary loans went far beyond any routine library service. I am also indebted to the Shippensburg, Pennsylvania Public Library's extensive paperback book collection, to the Coyle Free Library of Chambersburg, Pennsylvania and to the Public Library of Alexandria, Virginia.

E. J. R.

INTRODUCTION

> You serious people must not be too hard on human beings for what they choose to amuse themselves with when they are shut up as in a prison, and are not even allowed to say that they are prisoners. If I do not soon get a little bit of fun, I shall die.
>
> Pierre Andrezel, Introduction to The Angelic Avengers

When I first began reading contemporary Gothic fiction, the question, What is a Gothic? did not seem particularly complicated. Lovers of the form will know what I mean when I say that I came to "sense" Gothics without having to define them. But that explanation really won't do when one is trying to defend the inclusion or omission of works in a bibliography, so I went to the scholars of English literature to see what I could find.

It seems to be generally agreed that the first work to be called "Gothic" was Horace Walpole's Castle of Otranto, written in 1765. That book apparently began a fad and served as the direct model for an enormous number of stories, increasingly varied in theme, thereafter. The term "Gothic" was used to describe these books because they tended to romanticize the medieval period. These Gothic stories were the first to use suspense, the supernatural and romanticism of the medieval. Later, "the term [Gothic] lost all connotation of 'medieval,' and became synonymous for the grotesque, ghastly, and violently supernatural or superhuman in fiction. Gothic romance became the romance of the supernatural."[1] According to Devendra Varma, science fiction, mystery-detective and spy fiction all had their origins in the Gothic era.[2]

1. Devendra Varma, The Gothic Flame: A History of the Gothic Novel in England, p. 13.
2. Ibid., p. 158.

Some of the earliest, most influential and best known of the dozens of Gothic writers were Ann Radcliffe, Matthew Gregory (Monk) Lewis, Mary Wollstonecraft Shelley and Charles Maturin. The List of References following this introduction includes works with comprehensive information on the lives and works of these and other early authors. With a few exceptions, these early Gothics are of interest only academically as they were written for the popular entertainment of the time and today seem verbose and quaint.

Where the real confusion and disagreement seem to begin is in deciding what happened to the Gothic novel after about 1850. With but little exception, the scholars of the Gothic novel tell us that the genre died out about that time. To me, there seems little evidence to substantiate that theory. I think what died out was scholarly interest. Antiquity seemed the only justification for seriously studying such blatantly popular literature. Furthermore, the enormous proliferation of works and the expansion of themes and formulas in the literature have made the whole subject quite complex.

It is my view that from the seeds sown by Walpole, Radcliffe, Maturin, Lewis and so many others has grown an immense garden of literature which, by the twentieth century, has diverged into a rich variety of sub-species. In spite of some cross-breeding, there are to this day a large number of books being written which are identifiable as Gothic.

The key to an empathy for Gothic fiction is, to my mind, the idea that from the very beginning to the present day, these writers have not been "novelists" in the literary sense, but storytellers, in the most ancient and venerable of traditions. They have written about and elaborated on the everyday fairy tales, myths, fantasies and dreams that were once told around campfires and hearths and are basically as old as humankind on earth. They are not attempting to edify, enlighten, impress or persuade. Their sole *raison d'être* is *to entertain*. Such a humble goal has not particularly impressed the literary establishment which seems to have done its best to relegate this literature, surely in the twentieth century, to oblivion by neglect. But the storytellers and their devoted reading public tend to ignore all that and happily go their way, writing and reading what pleases and entertains. And what pleases a great many readers (including some closet readers of Gothics among the "intellectuals") are tales of ghosts, witches, terrors of the Unknown, quests, castles, heroines and villains.

In many ways it seems a spurious effort to try to separate literature into categories for, like the desert sands, it is in continual flux, inventing new themes, combining old themes in new ways and, in general, artfully evading the efforts of the conscientious analyst. To separate the Gothic from the general body of fiction is much like attempting to rope off and analyze one sand dune in the Sahara. One will never get it to remain static long enough to determine its make-up with any real assurance.

With this reservation in mind, and using the eighteenth-century Gothic novel as a prototype, I have found it helpful, using Montague Summers' idea,[3] to divide Gothic works into five general categories based on the overall emphasis given to particular elements.

1) Historical Gothic: those which are essentially historical novels but which also include such Gothic elements as mystery, suspense and the supernatural. Examples of excellent works in this group include: Barbara Michaels' _Greygallows_, Anya Seton's _Green Darkness_, Sandra Shulman's _The Brides of Devil's Leap_ and Sylvia Thorpe's _Stranger on the Moor_.

2) Sentimental Gothic: the group most associated today with the term "Gothic novel." It is the predominant form used for the enormous paperback Gothic phenomenon begun in the 1960's and is distinguished by its emphasis on the love fantasy element. Such works as Elsie Cromwell's _Ivorstone Manor_, Cecily Crowe's _Northwater_, Glenda Carrington's _Master of Greystone_, and Erica Lindley's _The Brackenroyd Inheritance_ are examples of superior works in this category.

3) Horror Gothic: the emphasis here is upon the supernatu-

3. Montague Summers, _The Gothic Quest: A History of the Gothic Novel_. New York: Russell & Russell, Inc., 1938; reissued, 1964.

ral, the occult and the ghastly. These were a significant part of the seventeenth-century Gothics and are still written and popular to-day. Examples include: David Case's Fengriffin, Eleanor Ingram's The Thing from the Lake, Richard Matheson's Hell House and Marlys Millhiser's Nella Waits.

4) Exotic Gothic has become rather out of fashion in the latter part of the twentieth century. The form is represented by tales of the "Dark Continent" or the "mysterious East." Some remnants of this type of fiction are seen in the Voodoo cult tales. For the most part, it seems to me that with our greater knowledge of this world these themes have been taken over by science fiction and the tales of other worlds. Twentieth-century examples of what I would term Exotic Gothic include: E. F. Benson's The Image in the Sand, George Griffith's The Mummy and Miss Nitocris, and Henry Rider Haggard's The Ghost Kings.

5) Whimsical Gothic may have begun with the early satires on the Gothic. Whatever the case, in contemporary fiction there has been a small but delicious group of tales using Gothic themes in either cynical or playful ways which can be thoroughly enchanting. I have included here, with some reservations, such adult fairy tales as Thurber's The 13 Clocks and Peter Beagle's The Last Unicorn. Examples of whimsical Gothic include Richard Brautigan's The Hawkline Monster, Dora Shattuck's The Half-Haunted Saloon and Michael Innes' Christmas at Candleshoe. Elizabeth Cadel and Maggie Waddleton have also written delightful tales in this form.

What ties all these groups together under the common title "Gothic" is, I believe, their use of several, if not all, of the following which I consider the "elements" of a Gothic tale: 1) the supernatural; 2) a quest or a wrong to be righted; 3) a setting that includes an old dwelling, traditionally a castle; 4) a fantasy of wealth suddenly acquired, or inheritance; 5) mystery, suspense and intrigue; 6) a fantasy of romantic love in some form, often including a love-hate, trust-fear ambivalence between men and women; 7) romanticism of the past and an historical setting--no longer necessarily medieval, but of a generation past or more; and 8) confrontations between the Forces of Good and Evil.

Although none of the individual elements are absolutely essential, the closer one comes to having all eight, the "purer" the Gothic. Using the eighteenth-century prototype, one must see that Gothic literature is a much broader field than simply the "damsel-in-distress" tale, popular and appealing though that still may be. The horror story, the ghost story, the tales of the occult, are all part of the Gothic tradition and are all viable forms in the 20th century.

After reading a few hundred of these stories it has become evident to me that relatively few allow themselves to be fitted into rigid categories. There are a great number of tales that some would call murder-mysteries and others call Gothics, or that some would call psychological melodrama or suspense and others call Gothic. I believe my own decisions in many cases have been essentially arbitrary and apologize to those who find that troublesome.

In the past fifteen years or so, a large number of books have been written which do not entirely qualify as Gothic and yet are both closely related to and often labeled as Gothic by their publishers. Romantic-Suspense novels comprise this group and I distinguish them by their use of only elements 2, 5, 6, and occasionally 4, from the list. The element of the supernatural is eliminated, romanticism of the past wanes, and the love fantasy element outweighs or equals that of suspense. Not fitting the definition of Gothic, I feel them to be a separate category--but because they seem so closely related to the genre, they are included and so identified in this bibliography. Authors who seem to me to best exemplify this type of story include Elsie Cromwell, Helen Maxwell and Madeleine Brent.

In general, I have not chosen to include authors whose work might be described as having "Gothic themes" or "Gothic tendencies." This is a purely practical decision. I found as I dipped into the scholars' studies of the Gothic that the whole of English literature is awash with what someone or other might interpret as a "Gothic theme or tendency." Irving Malin, for example, in his New American Gothic, attempts to show that Truman Capote, Carson McCullers, John Hawkes, James Purdy, Flannery O'Connor, and J. D. Salinger are writers of Gothic fiction. I have read some of these authors' works and have decided that Mr. Malin's criteria for what constitutes a Gothic are, for the most part, not mine.

As can be seen from this bibliography, the writers of Gothic fiction are from quite varied backgrounds. A few have concentrated their efforts primarily on Gothic-type fiction, but a great many more have produced only one or two Gothic works from a very diversified output. Some very scholarly folk seem to have had "one or two good Gothics in them," for example, Laurence Lafore (The Devil's Chapel, 1964) and Russell Kirk (Old House of Fear, 1961). Writers of mystery-detective fiction (certainly first cousin to the Gothic) have frequently produced works either Gothic or very nearly so: Mary Roberts Rinehart, Mabel Seeley, John D. Carr and Patricia Wentworth, for example. I have tried to at least make mention of such authors who seem to qualify.

This is very much a literature of the pseudonymous writer. Because so many of the authors write under several fictitious names, I felt clarity would best be achieved by listing all works under the author's given name whenever possible. All verified pseudonyms are also listed alphabetically within the bibliography and cross-referenced to the author's given name. This listing of all works by an author under one name will enable readers to "devour" all works written by one author and facilitate comparison and/or contrast of works written under different pseudonyms. In a few cases, when I suspect a pseudonym but have been unable to verify it by means of NUC, Contemporary Authors or the publisher, I have bracketed the probable real name along with a copyright symbol (©). I did not feel justified in listing the entries under a merely suspected real name.

I have speculated on the motivation behind this wide use of pseudonyms. Fad seems as likely a reason as any. There are too many good stories written under pseudonyms for embarrassment to be a motive, although in some cases I suspect it likely. In some cases it seems largely mercenary as with W. E. D. Ross, who turns out a mind-boggling number of books per year and writes under more than ten pseudonyms. I assume he could never get them all published under one name, and the reader of any discrimination whatsoever would very soon recognize and avoid his name. Some writers seem to use pseudonyms to categorize their various story forms. Eleanor Hibbert, for example, uses the name Victoria Holt for her so-called "Gothic" tales and the names Jean Plaidy and Philippa Carr for her historical novels. In general, I have found no real relation between the use of pseudonyms and the quality of the work. Even prodigious output is not a guarantee of poor quality although it can be a good clue.

The choice of which works to annotate has been made essentially on the basis of which books I have been able to obtain. Some of these books, published only in paperback or by small publishers, are very hard to track down. The recent trend in public libraries to keep paperback book collections is a great boon to the fans of Gothic fiction. I regret for other readers that this could not be a completely annotated work. For my own sake, I'm quite satisfied since it means that I too still have a great deal of pleasurable reading to anticipate.

Following most titles I have "graded" these works for quick reference as to my opinion of their relative merit; (A) indicates superiority in the genre; (B) means better than average; (C) means stock formulas and characters, but still not too bad; (D) means barely acceptable; and (F) means, in my opinion, the work is essentially unfit for human consumption--alas, there are a number thereof. My criteria for these judgments are very modest indeed. I expect readable English. I expect some skill in character development--the plots are so similar in format that without three-dimensional characters it is almost impossible to keep interest alive. The plot must be consistent--the author may pursue whatever flight of fancy imagination allows but the story must follow sensibly from one event to the next. (Alice Campbell's With Bated Breath is an example of utter failure in this respect.) The author must create an interesting situation and arouse and sustain the reader's curiosity concerning the outcome. Anything other than the comfort of a "happy ending" must be handled with care. A shocking, unpleasant ending must have more to it than just shock. Joan Aiken's An Embroidered Sunset and John Latimer's Border of Darkness both manage very skillfully to sustain unpleasant endings.

As the preceding implies, a good deal of the so-called Gothic literature published does not meet even these modest standards. The main purpose of this bibliography is to help the reader find the many wonderful books that do meet these standards or exceed them.

There are included in the bibliography a number of books which are not Gothic. These are principally works that someone--a reviewer, critic or publisher--has said were Gothic but with whom I disagree and think the information will be helpful in the reader's selections. And I, of course, cannot guarantee that the books I have not read will be Gothic. In those cases, I have had to rely on other works of the author that I have read and, in many instances, by the suggestion given by the title which can, admittedly, be very deceiving.

A note to the librarian: I have checked every book herein listed in the National Union Catalogue and/or Library of Congress Card Catalogue through 1974, and have noted the verification of each book along with its imprint.

> If man had not his dreams the world would become hideously real, and man himself an intellectual automaton. We call our dreams Romance, and it was just this that the Gothic novelists gave to their readers.[4]

4. Varma, op. cit., p. 229.

LIST OF REFERENCES

Barnhart, Clarence L., ed. The New Century Handbook of English Literature. New York: Appleton-Century-Crofts, Inc., 1956.
Has about as concise a summary of the "establishment" definition of the Gothic novel as I have come upon.

Barzun, Jacques and Wendell Hertig Taylor. A Catalogue of Crime: Being A Reader's Guide to the Literature of Mystery, Detection & Related Genres. New York: Harper & Row, 1971.
Includes a few writers of Gothic-type fiction but, more important here, has a fair bibliography of ghost stories and anthologies. These fellows call Victoria Holt's work "garden club gothic," which I thought was rather choice.

Birkhead, Edith. The Tale of Terror: A Study of the Gothic Romance. New York: E. P. Dutton, 1921.
Includes a chapter on the American tales of terror.

Bleiler, E. F., ed. The Castle of Otranto by Horace Walpole, Vathek by William Beckford, The Vampyre by John Polidori--Three Gothic Novels. New York: Dover Press, 1966.

A Catalogue of Books Represented by Library of Congress Printed Cards Issued to July 31, 1942. New York: Pageant Books, Inc., 1960.
(Herein referred to as LCPC pre '42.)

A Catalogue of Books Represented by Library of Congress Printed Cards--Supplement Aug. 1, 1942-Dec. 31, 1947. Paterson, N.J.: Pageant Books, 1960.
(Herein referred to as LCC supp.)

Ethridge, James M. and Barbara Kopola, eds. Contemporary Authors: A Biobibliographical Guide to Current Authors and Their Works. rev. ed. Detroit, Mich.: Gale Research Co., The Book Tower, 1967.

Kennedy, Arthur G. and Donald B. Sands. A Concise Bibliography for Students of English--1940. 4th ed. Stanford: Stanford University Press, 1960.

The Library of Congress Author Catalogue. A Cumulative List of Works Represented by Lib. of Cong. Printed Cards 1948-1952.

N. J.: Pageant Books, 1960.
(Herein referred to as LCAC.)

Library of Congress Catalogues National Union Catalogue. Washington, D. C.: Library of Congress, 1974.
(Herein referred to as NUC 1973.)

Library of Congress Catalogues National Union Catalogue 1974. Washington, D. C.: Library of Congress, 1975.
(Herein referred to as NUC 1974.)

McNutt, Dan J. The Eighteenth-Century Gothic Novel. An Annotated Bibliography of Criticism and Selected Texts. Foreword by Devendra Varma and Maurice Lévy. New York: Garland Pub., 1975.
Appears to me to be the comprehensive, primary resource on the 18th-century Gothic novel.

Malin, Irving. New American Gothic. Preface by Harry T. Moore. Carbondale: Southern Illinois University Press, 1962.
See listing in McNutt for a summary of this book.

The National Union Catalogue Pre-1956 Imprints. London & Wisbeck: Mansell, 1969.
(Herein referred to as NUC pre '56.)

The National Union Catalogue 1953-57. Paterson, N. J.: Rowman & Littlefield, 1961.
(Herein referred to as NUC 1953-57.)

The National Union Catalogue 1956 through 1967. Totowa, N. J.: Rowman & Littlefield, [1970].
(Herein referred to as NUC 1956-67.)

The National Union Catalogue 1968-72. Ann Arbor, Mich.: J. W. Edwards Publisher, Inc., 1973.
(Herein referred to as NUC 1968-72.)

Railo, Eino. The Haunted Castle: A Study of the Elements in English Romanticism. New York: E. P. Dutton, 1927.

Scott-James, R. A. Fifty Years of English Literature 1900-1950. London, N. Y. & Toronto: Longmans, Green & Co., 1951; 2nd ed., 1956.
Some discussion of trends in romance literature.

Siemon, Fred. Ghost Story Index. San Jose, Calif.: Library Research Assoc., 1967.
A good listing of short stories but very incomplete for longer works.

Summers, Montague. The Gothic Quest: A History of the Gothic Novel. New York: Russell & Russell, Inc., 1938; reissued,

1964.

Summers is probably the least objective of all the students of the Gothic novel I have found. His enthusiasm is unscholarly but lovable. I found his categorizations of the Gothic novel very helpful.

Varma, Devendra P. The Gothic Flame: A History of the Gothic Novel in England. New York: Russell & Russell, 1957; reissued, 1966.

This was the most useful and the most objective of the works I have read. Varma was one of the few to imply the possibility that the Gothic did not actually end in the nineteenth century.

THE BIBLIOGRAPHY

ABBEY, Kieran

1. And Let the Coffin Pass. New York: Scribner's, 1942. (NUC pre'56 1-18)

2. Beyond the Dark (B). New York: Scribner's, 1944. (NUC pre'56 1-18)

A fast-paced suspense tale about a young man and woman, unknown to each other, who happen to overhear a conversation between some very bad men, are spotted and flung into a three day flight from assassination through the city of New York. Well plotted and written although the resolution to the whole thing is not as dramatic as the events leading to it. This is certainly a forerunner of the popular romantic suspense stories of the 60's and 70's.

3. Run with the Hare. New York: Scribner's, 1941. (NUC pre'56 1-18)

ABBEY, Ruth

4. Evil at Nunnery Manor. New York: Acė (21855), 1973.

5. The Shadow Between (F). London: Hale, 1970; New York: Ace, 1974. [© Ruth Pattison].

The first half of the book is pure and dull romance in which Sarah goes as governess to Grangers Hall and deals with the Lady, her daughter and two stock-character eligible sons--yes, dark and fair, friendly and remote, naughty and nice and ho hum and so what. If the second half be Gothic, it wasn't worth reading to find out.

Other works of Ruth Abbey include: Portrait of Doubt (Ace) and Prisoner of the Manor (Ace).

ABBOTT, Alice (pseud.) see BORLAND, Kathryn Kilby

ABBOTT, Sandra

6. Castle of Evil. New York: Avon (18044), 1974.

7. The River and the Rose (F). New York: New American Library (Signet P3199), 1967.

An action-packed tale that carries little logic between one action and the next. Suzanne goes to Belle Rose, a Southern Plantation, supposedly to be hostess and help renovate the place after the Civil War. She walks into an absurd situation and behaves in an absurd manner. Surely this heroine ranks as first runner-up for the top ten twits in neo-Gothic literature.

8. Whispering Gables (D). New York: Paperback Library (52-624), 1968.

Eleanor is invited by her long-lost aunt to visit Whispering Gables and becomes immeshed in a plot for her destruction. A trivial and hyperdramatic tale.

ADAMS, Doris Sutcliffe

9. No Man's Son (C). London: Hale, 1961; New York: Walker, 1969. (NUC 1956-67 1-357)

It is the time of the Third Crusade, 1192, and the story of Rodriga de Perolles, a high-spirited daughter of an aging knight who accepts the quest of retrieving the lost inheritance of a young, handsome knight, Piers. Rodriga saves the life of the mysterious and infamous Marco and wins his allegiance through the trouble and turmoil to follow. This is truly a Gothic, according to all the definitions, but I found it rather hard going--partly because of the printing in the Walker edition. The prose is dense but worth the extra time for a Gothic tale and lots of colorful description of the life and times of 1192.

10. Power of Darkness (B). London: Cassell, 1967; New York: Walker, 1968; New York: Belmont-Tower, 1970. (NUC 1968-72 1-360)

About as Gothic as one can get. A Medieval setting and witchcraft, heroics, romance and melodrama. Hélie de Trevaine returns to his inheritance in the dark and troubled England of King John. He refuses a marriage arranged by his mother and champions a spirited heiress accused of witchcraft and murder. Even the prose is "Gothic."

11. The Price of Blood. New York: Scribner's, 1966. (NUC 1956-67 1-357)

ADDISON, Gwen

12. Storm over Fox Hill (A Ravenswood Gothic) (B). New York: Pocket Books (77716), 1974.

Frustrating only in the sense that if some craftsmanship had been used on this barebones of a tale, it might have been a superb Gothic novel. As it is, it is not a bad story of Rosalind who is called to the family estate of Fox Hill for a visit and finds all not well with her kin. Attempts are made on her life but a handsome stranger and a few family ghosts help out.

AIKEN, Joan

Born 9/4/24 in Rye, Sussex, England, her home is now in Pentworth, Sussex, England. She has been a full-time writer since 1961 but before that held a variety of jobs with the B. B. C., the UN Information Office, Argosy magazine and an advertising agency. Aiken has written a large number of juvenile mysteries and Gothics. She says of herself: "Widowed at 30 with two small children, I have not had much time or money for hobbies or travel. My chief pleasures are reading, meeting friends, painting, gardening, listening to classical music. Vocational interests are cooking and housewifery .... I enjoy writing. At least I suppose I must, or I wouldn't keep on doing something so utterly consuming and exhausting. While I am at work on one kind of piece I am feverishly longing and planning to write something else in a different idiom.... Thinking back over my children's books and my adult thrillers ... I honestly can't recall any difference in the writing process...." Contemporary Authors, Vol. 9-10, p. 14.

13. Beware of the Bouquet (C). Garden City, N. Y.: Doubleday (Crime Club), 1966. (NUC 1956-67 2-109)
Not one of Aiken's best, but good characterization and style along with some innovation of the neo-Gothic formula made this enjoyable reading.

14. A Cluster of Separate Sparks. Garden City, N. Y.: Doubleday, 1972. (NUC 1968-72 2-56)

15. The Crystal Crow (D). Garden City, N. Y.: Doubleday, 1968. (NUC 1968-72 2-57)
Aulis finds trouble in Cornwall. Unusual characters and plot--almost too unusual. Slow paced.

16. Dark Interval (F). Garden City, N. Y.: Doubleday, 1967. (NUC 1956-67 2-109)
Caroline goes through unbelievable tragedy and trauma and comes out smelling like a rose with her horrid family a series of corpses. This is "juvenile Aiken" in transition. Too much!

17. The Embroidered Sunset (B). Garden City, N. Y.: Doubleday, 1970; New York: Ace, 1970. (NUC 1968-72 2-57)
This story breaks all the rules of the damsel-in-distress formula, but beautifully. Clever, involved plot and 3-D characters. The style is elegant and witty.

18. The Fortune Hunters (C). Garden City, N. Y.: Doubleday (Crime Club), 1965. (NUC 1956-57 2-109)
Annette tangles with a mad painter and his mad relatives. A bit too melodramatic for my tastes.

19. Hate Begins at Home. London: Gollancz, 1967. (NUC 1956-67 2-109)

20. Midnight Is a Place. New York: Pocket Books, 1975.

21. The Ribs of Death. London: Gollancz, 1967. (NUC 1968-72 2-57)

22. The Silence of Herondale (B). Garden City, N.Y.: Doubleday (Crime Club), 1964; Ace, n.d. (NUC 1956-67 2-108)

Deborah takes a job as governess to a 13-year-old playwright. Fairly conventional neo-Gothic plot but cleverly done and well written.

23. Trouble with Product X. London: Gollancz, 1966. (NUC 1956-67 2-109)

24. Voices in an Empty House (A). Garden City, N.Y.: Doubleday, 1975.

This is not a Gothic, but those who like Joan Aiken, or a very good suspense story with wonderful characters, shouldn't miss this.

25. The Windscreen Weepers, and other tales of horror and suspense. London: Gollancz, 1969. (NUC 1968-72 2-57)

AINSWORTH, Harriet (pseud.) see CADELL, Elizabeth

ALBRAND, Martha (pseud.) see LOEWENGARD, Heidi Huberta

ALCOTT, Cynthia

26. The Dungeons of Crowley Hall (F). New York: Ace (17230), 1973.

Dianne goes to Crowley Hall to take over an inheritance and runs into a houseful of people out to get her. This is a slap-dash effort, full of flaws and empty of anything except one horrible catastrophe after another.

27. Storm over Windmere. New York: Ace, 1973.

ALEXANDER, Jan

28. The Bishop's Palace. New York: Popular Library, n.d.

29. Blood Ruby. New York: Ballantine, 1975.

30. Darkwater. New York: Pocket Books, 1975.

31. Green Willows. New York: Pocket Books, 1975.

32. The Haunting of Helen Wren. New York: Pocket Books, 1975.

33. House of Fools. New York: Lancer (74-745), n.d.

34. The Second House (D). New York: Ballantine, 1971.
Liza Durant came to La Deuxieme and found herself caught in a strange masquerade--pretending to be the wife of Jeff Forrest, master of the house and family fortune. Rather poorly written. The heroine is miraculously and unbelievably saved from perpetual disasters.

35. White Jade. New York: Popular Library, 1972.

ALLAN, Dennis (pseud.) see DENNISTON, Elinore

ALLARDYCE, Paula (pseud.) see TORDAY, Ursula

ALLEN, Barbara (pseud.) see STUART, Vivian

ALLEN, Erika Vaughn

36. Voices in the Wind (C). New York: New American Library (Signet P3189), 1967.
The beginning of this story, set in the Ozarks, seems to hold more promise than is ever fulfilled. The setting, house and local characters hold possibilities the author never realizes and what results is a mediocre tale of romantic suspense.

ALLYSON, Kym (pseud.) see KIMBRO, John M.

AMES, Jennifer (pseud.) see GREIG, Maysie

AMES, Leslie (pseud.) see ROSS, William Edward Daniel

AMES, Norma (pseud.) see NORMAN, Ames

AMOS, Alan (pseud.) see KNIGHT, Kathleen Moore

ANDERSON, Jan

37. Storm Castle (B). New York: Pyramid Books (X1610), 1967.

"1st prize winner in Pyramid Book's Gothic Romance Contest." And rightly so, I think. Anderson has taken a fairly formula idea--young girl goes to France to trace her long-lost kin and to try to right a past wrong--and breathes fresh life into it with skilled narrative, innovations of plot and some very solid characterizations. A very entertaining and satisfying neo-Gothic.

ANDRIZEL, Pierre (pseud.) see BLIXEN, Karen

ANSLE, Dorothy Phoebe

(Laura Conway, Hebe Elsna, Lyndon Snow; the Hebe Elsna books appear to be historical novels and are not included here.)

38. The Abbot's House, by Laura Conway. New York: Saturday Review Press, 1974; New York: Popular Library (00328), 1975. (NUC 1968-72 2-420)

39. A Butterfly's Hour, by Laura Conway. New York: Saturday Review Press, 1973. (NUC 1974 1-549)

40. Francesca, by Laura Conway. New York: Saturday Review Press, 1973; New York: Bantam (8634), 1975. (NUC 1973 1-592)

41. Francesca, by Lyndon Snow. London: Collins, 1970.

42. Heiress Apparent (D), by Laura Conway. New York: McCall, 1970. (NUC 1974 1-549)

A boring and slow-paced tale of Arabel, daughter of a housekeeper, who inherits from her mother's employer only to find her life threatened. A paranoiac's delight, but I found little else to commend it. The plot was fully predictable, characters tiresome, etc.

Other works include: Living with Paula (Collins, 1972), The Night of the Party (McCall, 1971) and The Unforgotten (Sat. Rev. Press, 1972), all by Laura Conway.

ANTHONY, Evelyn

Writer of historical romances and not included herein. I do recommend her Stranger at the Gates (Coward-McCann, 1973), however.

ARCH, E. L. (pseud.) see PAYES, Rachel Cosgrove

ARKHAM, Candice

43. Deadly Friendship (C). New York: Avon, 1973. [© Alice

Ramirez].

Cary goes to the Louisiana plantation of St. Anne Manor following a cryptic and urgent summons from its mistress, her old college roommate, Charon. Cary finds some mysterious goings on. Standard "Louisiana Gothic." No worse than most and a good deal better than many.

ARMSTRONG, Charlotte [Lewi]
(Jo Valentine)

Born in Vulcan, Michigan, in 1905, married to Jack Lewi and mother of three children, Armstrong received a B.A. from Barnard College in 1925. Her home is in Glendale, California. Her career has always been that of writer and she began by writing plays. In spite of the publishers' categorizations, Armstrong's work does not, in general, fit my criteria for Gothic fiction. I would classify it as mystery and detection and occasionally romantic suspense. Some examples are as follows:

44. A Dram of Poison. New York: Coward-McCann, 1956. (NUC 1956-67 6-13)
Mystery Writers of America Award for best novel of 1956.

45. The Innocent Flower (A MacDougal Duff Mystery). New York: Coward-McCann, 1945; New York: Berkley Medallion, 1970. (NUC pre'56 21-422)
Romantic-detective-mystery and moderately entertaining.

46. Lemon in the Basket (C). New York: Coward-McCann, 1967; Greenwich, Conn.: Fawcett-Crest (T1491), 1967. (NUC 1956-67 6-13)
The lives of the rich and talented Tyler family are put in crisis when one son, a famous heart surgeon, is called upon to operate on the crown prince of a tiny anti-American monarchy. Those who prefer romantic suspense to Gothic may enjoy this tale more than I did. Armstrong can craft her work.

47. Seven Seats to the Moon. New York: Coward-McCann, 1969; Greenwich, Conn.: Fawcett-Crest (M1399), 1970. (NUC 1968-72 5-266)
Evidently science fiction suspense. Certainly not Gothic. Partial reading inspired no interest.

48. Something Blue (B). New York: Ace, [© 1959].
Johnny Sims endeavors to prove the guilt or innocence of his childhood girl friend's new fiancé from suspicion of murder. Well written and suspenseful tale, more a murder mystery than a Gothic.

49. The Turret Room (F). New York: Coward-McCann, 1965. (NUC 1956-67 6-13)
Paranoiac's Paradise once again. Harold gets out of the psychoward following a false rap by former wife and family only to

go right back to being accused of all kinds of horrendous things. I see no point in these stories where one pretty well knows the plot from the first chapter. No Gothic elements other than those used as props.

50. The Witches' House (B). New York: Coward-McCann, 1963; Greenwich, Conn.: Fawcett-Crest, 1963. (NUC 1956-67 6-13)

Two college professors disappear. One is injured and held captive by a mad woman. The other is running from trouble. Will they be found in time? A well-wrought tale of suspense. Not Gothic.

ARVONEN, Helen

51. A Choice of Angels. New York: Ace, 1973.

52. Doorway to Death. New York: Ace, 1973.

53. Garden of Grief. New York: Ace, 1974.

54. The Least of All Evils. New York: Ace, 1975.

55. Remember with Tears (F). New York: Ace (71331), 2nd printing, 1972.

A clumsily written orgy of paranoia. Somebody's trying to kill sweet, rich, naive Leslie. Could it be her husband whose first wife died violently a year before? Could it be another of the four or five other nasty folk around her? First two chapters and the last tell the story and it's not worth even that--and not Gothic.

56. Rickshaw Bend. New York: Ace (72180), 1973.

57. A Sorrow for Angels. New York: Ace (77560), 1973.

58. Stranger in Her House (D). New York: Pocket Books, 1970.

"Patricia was the second Mrs. LaSalle. Was she fated to become the late Mrs. LaSalle?" Romantic suspense with no Gothic elements worth mentioning. The heroine is likeable but the plot is clumsy, the red herring "bad guys" are much too bad, and all-in-all the effort is disappointing.

59. Summer of Evils. New York: Ace (79081), 1972.

60. Whistle at My Window. New York: Ace (88540), 1971.

Also by Helen Arvonen: Circle of Death (Ace) and Shadow of the Truth (Warner Paperback).

ASHBY, Kay

61. Climb a Dark Cliff (D). New York: Dell (1247), 1972.

Leah goes to visit a long-lost uncle at his remote estate in Southern California and finds her uncle's life threatened by his young and nasty wife and her two weird brothers--all of whom are searching for the uncle's supposed hoard of hidden wealth. The plot and characters in this tale are very weak. Some of the action is simply not logical. Romantic suspense of a less than mediocre sort.

ASHE, Douglas

63. The Longstreet Legacy. New York: Scribner's, 1951; New York: Paperback Library, 1970. (Orig. title: A Shroud for Grandma)

An amusing tale, full of bizarre characters with a sentimental Gothic setting and heroine but otherwise primarily a murder mystery.

ASQUITH, [Lady] Cynthia Mary Evelyn (Charteris) 1887-1960

64. This Mortal Coil. Sauk City, Wisc.: Arkham, 1947. (NUC pre'56 23-689)

Short stories. The first one is a nicely written, horrid little tale. Asquith has written numerous volumes of ghost stories and various novels which do not appear to be Gothic.

ATKINS, Meg Elizabeth

65. By the North Door (A). New York: Harper & Row, 1975; New York: Ballantine, 1976.

This delightfully conceived and written story is a good example of the fine line between the literature of mystery-detection and that which is Gothic. There are here strong elements of both and fans of either form should not be disappointed.

ATWOOD, Drucy (pseud.) see MORRISON, A(twood) Eula

AVALLONE, Michael (Angelo, Jr.)

(Priscilla Dalton, Mark Dane, Steve Michaels, Dorothea Nile, Ed Noone, Edwina Noone, John Patrick, Sidney Stuart; see also Jean-Anne De Pré)

Born 10/27/24 in New York City. His career has been that of a free-lance writer and editor. He terms himself a "paperback novel specialist." His Ed Noone series, about seventeen mystery-detective Nick Carter novels, is not included herein. He has also written (under pseudonym John Patrick): The Main Attraction (a movie novelization) Belmont 1963; Tales of the Frightened, Belmont 1963; Shock Corridor (a movie novelization) Belmont 1963; (under the pseud. Sidney Stuart): The Night Walker (movie novelization) Popular Library 1964; The Man from U.N.C.L.E., Ace 1965; Madam

X, Popular Library 1965; Kaleidoscope, Popular Library 1966; Felony Squad, Popular Library 1967; Mannix, Popular Library 1968; Hawaii Five-O, Signet 1968 and many others.

66. Corridor of Whispers, by Edwina Noone. New York: Ace, 1966.

67. The Craghold Legacy, by Edwina Noone. New York: Ballantine, 1971.

68. Dark Cypress (D), by Edwina Noone. New York: Ace, 1965.
Stella goes to Hawk House as tutor for Todd Hawk and finds a boy haunted by his dead brother. A poorly written story. Gothic elements are used but are disappointing in their development.

69. Darkening Willows, by Priscilla Dalton. New York: Popular Library, 1966.

70. Daughter of Darkness, by Edwina Noone. New York: New American Library (Signet), 1967.

71. Felicia, by Mark Dane. New York: Belmont, 1964.

72. Gothic Sampler, by Edwina Noone. New York: Award Books, 1966.
Includes Avallone's opinion as to what constitutes a Gothic.

73. Heirloom of Tragedy, by Edwina Noone. New York: Lancer, 1966.

74. The Living Bomb. London: W. H. Allen, 1963. (NUC 1956-67 7-148)

75. Mistress of Ferrondale, by Dorothea Nile. New York: Tower, 1966.

76. 90 Gramercy Park, by Priscilla Dalton. New York: Paperback Library, 1965.

77. Seacliffe, by Edwina Noone. New York: New American Library (Signet), 1968.

78. The Second Secret, by Edwina Noone. New York: Belmont, 1966.

79. Silent Silken Shadows, by Priscilla Dalton. New York: Paperback Library, 1965.

80. Terror at Deepcliff (D), by Dorothea Nile. New York: Belmont (BT50243), 1972.
"What I Did on My Summer Vacation." On leave from Miss Slocum's Ladies Academy, Alice meets and marries the dashing Charles Manning, goes home with him to Deepcliff Manor and finds

he married her only to fulfill the terms of his father's will. By the time she's to return to the Academy, two people are dead, Deepcliff is burned to the ground and she has another romance in the offing. Neo-Gothic of a less than mediocre quality.

81. The Third Shadow, by Dorothea Nile. New York: Avon, 1973.

82. Vampire Cameo, by Dorothea Nile. New York: Lancer, 1968.

83. The Victorian Crown, by Edwina Noone. New York: Belmont, 1966.

84. Violence in Velvet (An Ed Noone Novel of Suspense). New York: New American Library (Signet 1294) 1956. (NUC 1956-67 7-148)

85. The Voodoo Murders. Greenwich, Conn.: Fawcett (Gold Medal 703), 1957. (NUC 1956-67 7-148)

AVERY, Lynn (pseud.) see COLE, Lois Dwight

BAER, Jill

86. House of Whispers. New York: Pocketbooks, 1971.

BAKER, Betty D(oreen Flook) 1916-
(Elizabeth Renier)

Works appear to be historical romance rather than Gothic.

BALL, Doris Bell [Collier]
(Josephine Bell)

Born in Manchester, England in 1897. She is a qualified physician and practiced with her husband until his death in 1935 and then alone until 1954. Has been a novelist since 1937, producing numerous works of mystery and detection which are listed in the Catalogue of Crime. Her avocations are theater, sailing and gardening. The three works listed here represent first, one of her better works, and, second and third, the only ones that may have Gothic elements.

87. To Let, Furnished (B), by Josephine Bell. London: Methuen, 1952. (NUC pre'56 32-310). Also pub. in U.S. as: Stranger on a Cliff (New York: Ace Star, 1952).

No Gothic elements to speak of but an engrossing murder mystery with the heroine a 40-year-old wealthy matron staying temporarily alone in a rented mansion. The story is good if you can swallow the major coincidence of the heroine finding this particular house. This 40-year-old reader was heartened by a 40-year-old heroine and also delighted with her chauffeur-bodyguard, Peck.

88. The Upfold Witch, by Josephine Bell. London: Hodder & Stoughton, 1964; New York: Macmillan, 1964. (NUC 1956-67 8-95)

89. The Wilberforce Legacy, by Josephine Bell. London: Hodder & Stoughton, 1969; New York: Walker, 1969. (NUC 1968-72)

BANVILLE, John

90. Birchwood (B). London: Secker & Warburg, 1973; New York: Norton, 1973. (NUC 1973 2-61)

The publisher calls this a "Gothic novel" but it fits too few of the criteria except in its grotesque atmosphere and some elements of suspense. Malin (see Introduction) would probably call this a Gothic. A very strange, almost surrealistic tale of Gabriel Godkin, heir apparent to the decaying estate of Birchwood. Set in Ireland during the 1850's and the Great Famine. Worth reading for imaginative style and beautiful imagery but it is a savage little tale and will be a shock to those expecting "classic Gothic" in any sense.

91. Long Lankin. London: Secker & Warburg, 1970. (NUC 1968-72 7-331)

92. Nightspawn. London: Secker & Warburg, 1971; New York: Norton, 1971. (NUC 1968-72 7-331)

BARRETT, Mary Ellin

Born 11/25/27 in New York City and daughter of the composer Irving Berlin. Married Marvin Barrett in 1952 and has four children. Received a B.A. (cum laude) from Barnard College in 1949. She has had a career mostly centered in the magazine business and has worked for several well known magazines.

93. Castle Ugly. New York: Dutton, 1966. (NUC 1956-67 9-9)

This is Barrett's first novel and her own comments in Library Journal do not indicate she intended it as a Gothic. She wanted "to say something about the traps people lay for themselves when they play games with love." Paul Zimmerman, in a review, says: "Her book belongs in the tradition of Gothic romance...." In my opinion, the only Gothic element in this psycho-social drama is a summer home called by the family "Castle Ugly."

BARRON, Ann Forman

94. Serpent in the Shadows (C). New York: Berkley Medallion, 1973.

Nicole marries childhood sweetheart Shannon following her sister's/his wife's death by accident. When they return from their honeymoon to Shadow Oakes, troubles continue. Standard "Louisiana Gothic" and not bad if you haven't read so many as I have.

95. Strange Legacy. Greenwich, Conn.: Fawcett, 1969, 1972.

Has also written: Spin a Dark Web (Pocket Books).

BARRY, Iris 1895-

96. The Darkness at Mantia (C). New York: Berkley Medallion, 1974.

The Daventrys assemble at Mantia, the family mansion, three years after the tragic disappearance of Patrice, wife of Ranson Daventry. Heather is along as secretary to Dr. Drake Daventry and she is the heroine of this very standard neo-Gothic.

97. House of Deadly Night. Indianapolis: Bobbs-Merrill, [1929]; New York: Belmont-Tower, 1972. (NUC pre'56 37-187)

98. The Mandura Mystery. London: Hale, 1966. (NUC 1968-72 7-598)

99. Seven Guests of Fear. London: Hale, 1970. (NUC 1968-72 7-598)

Has also written: The Unprotected (Berkley); The Last Enemy (Bobbs-Merrill) and several histories of the motion picture industry.

BARRY, Loretta

100. Sudden Silence (D). New York: Kensington Pub. Corp. (Zebra Books), 1975.

I gave up on this book when, by page 90, the author was still introducing characters, filling in background and describing scenery--an undue infringement on the reader's patience. Becky goes to Japan for some complicated reason not yet clear by page 90. Buffs of Japanese culture may enjoy. I found it a great bore.

BARTH, Lois (pseud.) see FREIHOFER, Lois Diane

BAUMAN, Carolyn

Born in Oakland, California and attended UCLA. She has won a number of poetry prizes and has contributed short stories and articles to various magazines. Mrs. Bauman, a widow, has five daughters, four granddaughters, seven grandsons and one great-grandson. (Information from Bantam ed. of Haverly.)

101. The Secret of Haverly House (D). New York: Bantam (N6447), 1966, 1975.

The skill of this author is not sufficient to sustain the enormous coincidence that is the crux of her plot. Every event is cushioned in pages of rhetorical questions and the heroine's internal dialogue which is banal and boring. Standard Gothic format without life.

BAWDEN, Nina (pseud.) see KARK, Nina Mary

BEAGLE, Peter S(oyer)

Born 4/20/39 in New York, N.Y. Education included a B.A. from the University of Pittsburgh in 1959 and graduate study at Stanford University 1960-61. His career has always been that of writer.

102. A Fine and Private Place: A Novel. New York: Viking, 1960. (NUC 1956-67 9-440)

103. The Last Unicorn: A Fantastic Tale (A). New York: Viking, 1968; New York: Ballantine, 1968. (NUC 1968-72 8-328)

An adult fairy tale. I'm not sure whether this type of story is Gothic or not. It certainly has all the elements and they are here skillfully woven together and sprinkled with dream dust to create a perfectly enchanting tale.

BELL, Josephine (pseud.) see BALL, Doris Bell

BELLAMANN, Henry 1882-

Author of several popular novels including King's Row (Simon & Schuster, 1940), only two of which seem to qualify here.

104. The Grey Man Walks. Garden City, N.Y.: Doubleday (Crime Club), 1936. (NUC pre'56 45-79)

105. Victoria Grandolet (C). New York: Simon & Schuster, 1943; New York: Ace, 1943. (NUC pre'56 45-80)

Victoria marries the dashing Niles Grandolet and comes under the spell of his Louisiana ancestral home, White Cloud. This is tame stuff compared to later works of similar theme but the mystical and malevolent influence of the great house is surely Gothic. May be the first of the now large "Louisiana Gothic" genre.

BELLAMY, Jean

106. The Prisoner of Ingecliffe (D). New York: Dell (7138), 1971.

I found this a dull tale--essentially historical romance and annoying to read because of the author's inconsistent use of period dialect. Set in 16th-century England, it is the story of conspiracy and political intrigue. Historical Gothic, maybe, but with the emphasis on the historical.

Has also written: Ghost of Coquina Key (Lancer).

BENEDICT, Lynn

107. The Fatal Flower (F). New York: Avon (15909), 1973.
This story is based on a supposed story by Hawthorne called "Rappaccini's Daughter" and involves a girl engulfed by a carnivorous plant in early childhood and thereafter able to live only by siphoning off the "vital essences" of her fellow humans or wild animals. It would take a darn fine writer to carry off this wild plot and Benedict doesn't make it. Juvenile horror Gothic.

Other works include: Bloodstone, Family Affair, Moon Fire and The Twisted Tree.

BENNETT, Arnold 1867-1931

Out of a very large number of works, Bennett's "fantasias" seem to be the only ones with Gothic qualities. Some of the others are included here due to the appellations of Gothic made by various critics or publishers.

108. Buried Alive: A Tale of These Days. Garden City, N.Y.: Doubleday, 19(08?) (NUC pre'56 46-625)
A reclusive artist trades identities with his just dead valet. A witty and charming tale but in no way Gothic.

109. The Ghost (C). Boston: H. B. Turner, 1907. (NUC pre'56 46-630)
Carl, newly graduated from medical school falls in love with a beautiful opera singer and simultaneously falls under the curse of her former lover. It's a ghost story all right, but mediocre.

110. The Glimpse: An Adventure of the Soul. New York: Appleton, 1909. (NUC pre'56 46-630)
On the fly leaf of the Shippensburg State College Library copy is the following, erased but readable, comment: "Absolutely horrible and unsatisfactory with a Damned poor ending. A. H. B., Norwich, Conn. May 19, 1912." Evidently "B." and I are very different people. I thought the book quite lovely and very much tuned in to the mysticism of the 60's and 70's. Beautifully written and conceived. No Gothic elements.

111. Hugo: A Fantasia on Modern Themes. New York: F. M. Buckles, 1906. (NUC pre'56 46-634)

112. The Strange Vanguard: A Fantasia. London: Cassell, 1928. (NUC pre'56 46-648)

Also worth checking might be: Teresa of Watling Street (Chatto & Windus, 1910) and The Vanguard (Doran, 1927).

BENNETT, Janice N.

113. The Haunted. New York: Ace, 1974.

114. House of Athena (B). New York: Ace, 1970.
A well written, fast paced neo-Gothic. Chris Shaw takes a job as companion to the crippled niece of a wealthy Greek tycoon and finds herself involved in a family torn by strife. Another innovative and skillful treatment of a cliché theme.

115. To the Castle. New York: Ace, 1975.

BENSON, Edward Frederic

Born in Berkshire, England in 1867, he produced an enormous number of popular works, the best known probably being the series of satires centered around the heroine Lucia. He died in 1940.

116. The Image in the Sand (B). Philadelphia: Lippincott, 1905. (NUC pre'56 47-226)
Mentioned in Varma's book as being "of Gothic lineage" and I quite agree--probably kin to the exotic or "Dark Continent" Gothics. Anyone interested in stories of the occult, or parapsychology should find this dramatic story of great appeal. Be prepared to wade through pages of description that gets to be a bit much--six pages on Mrs. Desmond's garden, for example.

117. Raven's Brood. New York: Popular Library, 1961.
Popular Library published this 1934 work of Benson's as Gothic but although there are Gothic elements toward the end, I believe most readers would find this tale a tedious disappointment.

BENTLEY, Joyce

118. Secret of Strangeways (C). New York: Pocket Books, 1976.
It would take a better story and more skillful writing to sustain the backbone of this work--a description of political corruption and the practice of medicine in an 18th-century English town. This is really a second-rate historical novel rather than Gothic.

BERCKMAN, Evelyn Domenica
(Joanna Wade)

Born 10/18/1900 in Philadelphia and currently living in

England. She has had a career as both a writer and a musician (her compositions have been performed by the Philadelphia Orchestra, the Rochester Symphony and others). Her avocational interests include the protection of animals, bridge and two-piano playing.

119. The Beckoning Dream. New York: Dodd, Mead, 1955; New York: Dell, 1957. Pub. also as: Worse than Murder. (NUC pre'56 47-618)

120. Blind Girl's Buff: A Novel of Suspense. New York: Dodd, Mead, 1962. (NUC 1956-67 10-537)

121. The Blind Villain. New York: Dodd, Mead, 1957; New York: Dell, 1960. Pub. also as: House of Terror. (NUC 1956-67 10-537)

122. A Case of Nullity. London: Eyre & Spottiswoode, 1967; Garden City, N.Y.: Doubleday, 1968. (NUC 1968-72 9-271)

123. The Evil of Time. New York: Dodd, Mead, 1954. (NUC pre'56 47-618)

124. A Finger to Her Lips (B). Garden City, N.Y.: Doubleday, 1971; New York: Dell, 1972. (NUC 1968-72 9-271)

A Gothic tale very much in the 18th-century tradition. Berckman seems fascinated by the real story from whence arose the legend of a ghost. A very good story, well told.

125. The Fourth Man on the Rope (B). Garden City, N.Y.: Doubleday, 1972. (NUC 1968-72 9-271)

Not a Gothic, but a nicely written little romantic-suspense story. Archivist Alison takes a job at a library in rural England and goes to live with an old chum. Intrigue develops at the library.

126. The Heir of Starvelings (A). Garden City, N.Y.: Doubleday, 1967; London: Eyre & Spottiswoode, 1968; New York: Dell, 1967. (NUC 1956-67 10-537)

I enjoyed this story enormously. The plot is graced with originality and the work is well crafted. Many Gothic elements. A touching story.

127. The Hovering Darkness (D). New York: Dodd, Mead, 1957. (NUC 1956-67 10-537)

This story does not live up to its title. A dreary little tale of a young girl's voyage to Europe on an ocean liner and her involvement with a fabulously rich couple who are threatened with the kidnapping of their child. The plot is contrived and the characters shallow.

128. Lament for Four Brides. New York: Dodd, Mead, 1959. (NUC 1956-67 10-537)

129. The Nightmare Chase (F). Garden City, N.Y.: Doubleday, 1975. Pub. in England as Indecent Exposure.

Jacentha is engaged as a companion to a rich, aged and formerly famous lady. The pace of this tale is maddeningly slow, the dialogue unbelievably boring and the characters faceless and mindless. The plot is dull and events are not consistent with the character's behavior. It is hard to believe that this is by the author of Starvelings (no. 126 above).

130. No Known Grave. New York: Dodd, Mead, 1958. (NUC 1956-67 10-537)

This book is listed in the Catalogue of Crime and rated average.

131. She Asked for It. Garden City, N.Y.: Doubleday, 1969. (NUC 1968-72 9-271)

132. A Simple Case of Ill-Will: A Novel. London: Eyre & Spottiswoode, 1964; New York: Dodd, Mead, 1965. (NUC 1956-67 10-537)

133. Stalemate. Garden City, N.Y.: Doubleday (Crime Club), 1966. (NUC 1956-67 10-537)

134. The Strange Bedfellow (C). London: Eyre & Spottiswoode, 1956; Pub. in U.S. as: Jewel of Death. New York: Dodd, Mead, 1956; New York: Pyramid, 1968. (NUC 1956-67 10-537)

Mart, an historian, goes to Germany in search of a lost and historic ruby. Not too bad a "quest-type" tale or mystery but there are few traditional Gothic elements.

135. A Thing That Happens to You. New York: Dodd, Mead [1964]. (NUC 1956-67 10-537)

136. Victorian Album. New York: Dell, 1975.

137. The Voice of Air. Garden City, N.Y.: Doubleday, 1970. (NUC 1968-72 9-271)

Has also written: Nelson's Dear Lord (Dodd, Mead); The Stake in the Game; and Wait, Just You Wait.

BEVERLY, Linda (pseud.) see QUENTIN, Dorothy

BIRKIN, Charles

Writer of a large number of short stories of the supernatural and occult but of no novel-length tales of which I am aware.

BIRKLEY, Dolan (pseud.) see HITCHENS, Dolores

BISHOP, Sheila

138. The Durable Fire. New York: Ace (17321), 1972.

139. The House with Two Faces (D). New York: Ace (K192), 1971.

Within the first fifty pages the reader is introduced to a mind-boggling cast of characters--nearly an entire English village--who are in the process of putting on a festival. Neither a main character nor the point of the story seemed at all clear and there was nothing to inspire further reading.

BLACK, Veronica (pseud.) see PETERS, Maureen

BLACKBURN, John Fenwick

Born 6/26/23 in Northumberland, England. Had a career as schoolmaster and director of Red Lion Books. Currently owns and operates a second-hand bookstore with his wife in a suburb of London. He is the brother of poet Thomas Blackburn.

140. Blow the House Down. London: Cape, 1970. (NUC 1968-72 10-560)

141. Blue Octavo. London: Cape, 1963; pub. in U.S. as: Bound to Kill. New York: Mill & Morrow, 1963. (NUC 1956-67 12-424)

142. Broken Boy. London: Secker & Warburg, 1959; New York: Mill & Morrow, 1962. (NUC 1956-67 12-424)

143. Bury Him Darkly. London: Cape, 1969; New York: Putnam, 1970. (NUC 1968-72 10-560)

144. Children of the Night (C). London: Cape, 1966; New York: Putnam, 1969. (NUC 1956-67 12-424)

The Yorkshire village of Donstonholme is threatened by a mysterious series of deaths and disasters. Several village folk work to discover the source of the trouble. A fairly well written tale, paced fast enough to keep one's interest. Horror Gothic.

145. The Gaunt Woman. New York: Mill, 1962; London: Cape, 1962. (NUC 1956-67 12-424)

146. The Household Traitors. London: Cape, 1971. (NUC 1968-72 10-560)

147. Nothing But the Night. London: Cape, 1968. (NUC 1968-72 10-560)

148. A Ring of Roses. London: Cape, 1965. (NUC 1956-67 12-424)

149. A Scent of New-Mown Hay (C). London: Secker & Warburg, 1958; New York: Mill & Morrow, 1958. (NUC 1956-67 12-424)

Horror Gothic. A ghastly fungus invades Russia and threatens the world. Ho hum.

150. A Sour Apple Tree. London: Secker & Warburg, 1958; New York: Mill & Morrow, 1959. (NUC 1956-67 12-424)

151. The Young Man from Lima. London: Cape, 1968. (NUC 1968-72 10-560)

BLACKMORE, Jane

152. Angels' Tear. New York: Ace (022848), 1974.

153. Beware the Night. New York: Ace (055525), 1958, 1975.

154. Bitter Love. New York: Ace (063602), 1973.

155. Bridge of Strange Music. New York: Ace (080110), 1974.

156. Broomstick in the Hall. New York: Ace (082016), 1974.

157. The Cresselly Inheritance (C). New York: Ace (121707), 1974.

I applaud the effort here to break away from the Gothic formulas. Unfortunately it doesn't come off too well in this rather disjointed tale of a family curse coming to crisis with the arrival of the long-lost heir. The idea is good but the execution clumsy.

158. The Dark Between the Stars. New York: Ace (137612), 1972.

159. Deed of Innocence. New York: Ace (142018), 1972.

160. The Deep Pool (C). New York: Ace (142083), 1972.

Emma returns to her ancestral estate as a governess under an assumed name to find a way to reclaim her inheritance. She finds a family full of unhappiness and threatened by evil. Her efforts solve the dilemma. Fairly well written story. Interesting to compare this tale with Edwina Noone's Dark Cypress (Ace, 1965) and Patricia Wentworth's The Alington Inheritance (Lippincott, 1958). The story lines are very similar but Blackmore's superior skill is strongly evident. This tale, unfortunately, has a very weak ending.

161. It Happened to Susan. New York: Dell, 1973.

162. Joanna (B). New York: Dell, 1972.
Jo goes to spend a week in the home of a decreased relative with all the rest of the clan to see who will inherit. As days pass, tension mounts and bad things happen. Romantic-suspense.

163. Miranda. New York: Dell, 1973.

164. The Missing Hour (C). New York: Ace (53485), 1959.
Lisa is accused of the murder of a beautiful woman who had been chasing her T.V. personality husband. Mediocre murder-mystery.

165. My Sister Erica. New York: Ace, 1975.

166. Night of the Bonfire. New York: Ace (575548), 1974.

167. Night of the Stranger. New York: Ace (578526), 1974.

168. The Other Mother. New York: Ace (632819), 1972.

169. The Other Room. London: Collins, 1968. (NUC 1968-72 10-567)

170. Raw Summer. London: Collins, 1967. (NUC 1968-72 10-567)

171. Room in the Tower. New York: Ace (734608), 1973.

172. The Square Root of Many Colours. New York: Ace (779066), 1975.

173. Stephanie. (Orig. title: Return to Love). New York: Ace, 1972.

174. Tears in Paradise. New York: Dell (08565), 1973.

175. Three Letters to Pan. New York: Ace (808279), 1972.

176. The Velvet Trap. New York: Ace (860916), 1972.

177. A Woman on Her Own. New York: Ace (908152), 1974.

BLACKSTOCK, Charity or Lee (pseuds.) see TORDAY, Ursula

BLACKWOOD, Algernon

Born in Kent, England in 1869, he was a farmer in Canada, operated a Toronto motel, was a newspaperman and worked in the dried milk industry before adopting a writing career in 1906. Although mentioned by critics as a writer of Gothic literature, the works I have read seem more mystical than Gothic, with the exception of several works of short stories on ghosts, psychic phenomena and such. He died in 1951. The NUC lists his works in the pre 1956 volume 59, pages 683-7.

178. The Empty House. London: Nash, 1906. (NUC pre'56 59-684)
Short stories, and the first one very poor indeed.

BLACKWOOD, Joy Ann

179. The Ghost at Lost Lovers Lake (A). New York: Popular Library (00491), [1973]. [© Evan L. Heyman; see also Hayworth, Evelyn.]
Kind of a dumb title for a very interesting story and a most innovative plot. Leandra goes to a Maine lake cottage to rest following the plane-crash death of her husband. Episodes of harassment begin and Lee has a tough time coping. There's a lot to this book, a complicated heroine and plot, and all are handled well. A very "grown-up" Gothic.

BLACKWOOD, Stephanie

180. Lamontane (F). New York: Popular Library, 1972. [© Sigmund Miller]
Dull, dreary story. Began with some promise as Amy goes to South Carolina to claim an inheritance of a huge old mansion and a fortune. What follows is so obvious and such a "perils of Pauline" cliché and so overdone that the reader soon sickens. The heroine is also particularly stupid.

BLAKE, Alfred or Andrew (pseuds.) see JANIFER, Laurence

BLAKE, Katherine or Kay (pseuds.) see WALTER, Dorothy Blake

BLAKE, Vanessa

181. The Dark Guardian (B). London: Hale, 1973; New York: Pocket Books, 1974.
Kate, a wealthy heiress, befriends sick, pregnant and possibly abandoned Anne. When Kate learns that Anne's missing husband is apparently announcing his engagement to someone else, Kate decides to take matters in hand and see justice done. A nicely plotted and written tale with sufficient elements to be Gothic. I especially liked the characterization of the heroine which avoided a lot of the less attractive "formula characteristics" of the literature.

BLATTY, William Peter
(Terence Clyne)

A native of New York City since his birth in 1928, he is now living in Encino, California. He holds an M.A. from George Washington University and worked in publicity and publications until becoming a full time writer about 1960. He has written several popular novels including John Goldfarb, Please Come Home.

182. The Exorcist (B). New York: Harper & Row, 1971; New York: Bantam (X7200), 1972. (NUC 1968-72 10-648)
A fairly well written and conceived horror-Gothic tale of demonic possession. Probably the least offensive of the child-demon-type tales which keep cropping up and which, in general, I find in very poor taste.

BLIXEN, Karen 1885-
(Pierre Andrèzel, Isak Dinesen)

183. The Angelic Avengers (B). London: Putnam, 1946; New York: Random House, 1946; New York: Ace, 1947. (NUC pre-56 61-315)
Lucan and Zosine join forces to seek their fortunes through great trials and tribulations. Well written, fast-paced--and dated.

184. Seven Gothic Tales (B). London: Putnam, 1934; New York: Smith & Haas, 1934. (NUC pre'56 61-316)
These are not so much "Gothic" in the sense herein defined but certainly have the involved plot structure, the tale-within-a-tale style, of many of the 18th-century Gothics. There are some very nice stories here.

BLOOM, Ursula
(Sheila Burns, Mary Essex, Rachel Harvey, Deborah Mann, Sara Sloane; Lozania Prole, a joint pseudonym)

Born in Chelmsford, Essex, England, twice married and "no education save reading," Ursula Bloom first appeared in print with an 11-page book, Tiger, at the age of seven. She has been writing continuously as both author and journalist since the early 1920's, producing more than 420 books ("the most of any English writer,") she claims. Some of her works may have Gothic elements. The largest portion appear to be sentimental romances, domestic romances and so on. A large listing of her works can be found in Contemporary Authors, Vols. 25-28, pp. 85-6.

BOLAND, John 1913-

185. The Catch (C). New York: Holt, Rinehart & Winston, [1964]. (NUC 1956-67 13-378)

This tale is borderline between Gothic and mystery-suspense but I think, in spite of the castle setting and some bizarre events, that it is less Gothic than fans of the genre would hope for. The tale is also largely predictable and not particularly engrossing.

186. The Shakespeare Curse. London: Cassell, 1969; New York: Walker, 1970. (NUC 1968-72 11-352)

BOMBAL, Maria Luisa 1910-

187. House of Mist (B). New York: Farrar, Straus, 1947. (NUC pre'56 64-148)

A fantasy-type, almost fairy tale, of Helga's love for Daniel which begins in their childhood and continues through Daniel's marriage to Helga's beautiful cousin, his eventual loveless marriage to Helga, and, at long last, a happy ending. A "Beauty and the Beast" theme and Gothic in mood, the use of the supernatural and the male-female, and love-hate conflicts. The setting is nonspecific but probably 19th-century South America.

188. The Shrouded Woman (C). New York: Farrar, Straus, 1948. (NUC pre'56 65-148)

A dead woman reflects back over her past life, particularly her loves and her family's and friend's loves. Moderately interesting and very pathetic. More mystical than Gothic.

BOND, Evelyn (pseud.) see HERSHMAN, Morris

BONNER, Paul Hyde

Born 2/14/1893 in New York City. Bonner worked for the Stehli Silks Corp. 1919-31, rising to vice-president. Between 1946 and 1952 he worked for the U.S. State Department with posts in Paris and Rome. He served in the U.S. Army 1917-19 and the U.S. Air Corp 1941-45, becoming a Colonel. He has written several novels, the one listed below being the only one of Gothic genre.

189. Amanda (B). New York: Scribner's, 1957. (NUC 1956-67 13-547)

A ghost saves the living man she loves. Nice.

BOOTON, (Catherine) Kage 1919-

Works appear to be murder mysteries and dramas--for example:

190. The Troubled House. New York: Dodd, Mead, 1958. (NUC 1956-67 14-42)

Beth goes to the home of famous author Stanley King to work as secretary and as companion to King's daughter and wife. The family seem strangely hostile to Rika, Stanley's second wife, and Beth befriends her only to begin to discover that all is not right. One of the "evil women" stories and a version of "the sweet innocent heroine who protects the cruelly mistreated husband of a harpy" fantasies which I find adolescent at best and loathesome when done less well than Booton manages. Not Gothic.

BORDEN, Lee (pseud.) see DEAL, Borden

BORLAND, Kathryn Kilby
(Alice Abbott, Jane Land, Ross Land)

Born 8/14/16 in Pullman, Michigan. Married James Borland in 1942. They have two children. Home: Frankfort, Indiana. She has been a free-lance writer for her entire career. Her writings (all with Helen Speicher) are mostly books for children and juveniles. Borland commented to Contemporary Authors on her association with Speicher: "We are often asked how two people can write together, and it probably does require special circumstances--in our case friendship since childhood, similar viewpoints, and insatiable curiosity about people, events and places. It is our hope that whatever we write will reinforce the positive values of integrity, love and responsibility for one another." C.A. Vol. 53-56, p. 59.

191. Goodbye Julie Scott, by Alice Abbott. New York: Ace, 1975.

192. The Third Tower (B), by Alice Abbott. New York: Ace, 1974.

Ruth Hood hires on as a teacher to blind Sheila at Dunrovin off the coast of Maine. This story sticks to the rules and is fairly well done. Characters are better than average. The mystery is a puzzler and the solution believable.

BOURNE, Hester

193. Haunted Island (D). New York: Pyramid, 1971; pub. in England as After the Island. London: Hutchinson, [© Molly Troke].

Alison takes a job as nurse, companion and chaperone to the wealthy Teresa who is apparently dying of heart disease and has only a year to live. When they travel to Teresa's estate where she is to spend her remaining days near her betrothed, Piers, some intrigue develops. Not a bad, if not a new, idea, but this effort is too clumsy to make much of it. The plot is barely credible, the heroine is the victim of very mundane emotions, and the characters do not come to life as they should.

194. In the Event of My Death. Garden City, N.Y.: Doubleday (Crime Club), 1964. (NUC 1956-67 14-335)

Has also written: The Spanish House (Pyramid).

BOWEN, Marjorie (pseud.) see LONG, Gabriella Margaret

BRADLEY, Marion Zimmer

Born 6/3/30 in Albany, N.Y., she was married to Walter H. Breen in 1964 and has three children. She now lives in Berkeley, California and is a musician as well as a writer of science fiction and Gothic fiction. Her science fiction, including the "Darkover Series" are not included here. Bradley is quoted in Contemporary Authors: "I consider myself basically a musician, and my writings of science fiction and fantasy are largely an extension of my original interest in folklore and folk music. I have also done serious work in parapsychology, believe in it, and almost all of my serious writings embody a deep and basic belief in the paranormal powers of the human mind, and in forces which transcend humanity as such." C.A. Vol. 51-60, p. 79.

195. Bluebeard's Daughter. New York: Lancer, 1968.

196. Can Ellen Be Saved? New York: Tempo Books, 1975.

197. Castle Terror. New York: Lancer (74-534), 1965.

198. Dark Satanic. New York: Berkley (S2231), 1972.

199. Souvenir of Monique (B). New York: Ace (G616), 1967.
Laura accepts a proposal by Count Etiènne de Montigny to return as his wife (Laura's cousin and lookalike) in an attempt to foil the devious machinations of his greedy in-laws who Etiènne feels are responsible for his wife's disappearance and probable demise. A good story, well told.

BRAMWELL, Charlotte (pseud.) see KIMBRO, John M.

BRANDON, Beatrice

200. The Cliffs of Night (B). Garden City, N.Y.: Doubleday, 1974; New York: New American Library (Signet W6575). (NUC 1974 2-817)
Grania, an American actress, goes to Ireland to see her ancestral homeland and recover from exhaustion. She meets dashing Quinn Griffin and gets embroiled in mystery and intrigue on the Cliffs of Moher. Well written romantic suspense. Lots of Irish folklore.

BRAUTIGAN, Richard 1935-

In 1961, he was living in San Francisco, was married and had an infant daughter. "Like all true humorists," writes Steven

Schneck, "Richard Brautigan eschews the label. Spies and humorists can only function under cover. So rather than think of Brautigan as a comic writer, imagine a six-foot country boy, with wire-rim glasses and a homemade haircut and a shaggy Wild West moustache that doesn't quite hide a perpetual grin.... Inside this hulking innocent, this country bumpkin, is a special (very special) correspondent from a terribly literate sort of Field & Stream magazine." C.A. Vol. 53-56, p. 63.

Of several books, poetry and collections, two works seem appropriate to this bibliography.

201. The Abortion: An Historical Romance 1966. New York: Simon & Schuster, 1971. (NUC 1968-72 12-446)

202. The Hawkline Monster: A Gothic Western (B). New York: Simon & Schuster, 1974. (NUC 1974 2-835)

A naughty, satirical little venture into the Gothic elements that, I think, comes off very well. Any lover of Gothics who has a sense of humor should enjoy this Gothic farce.

BRENNAN, Alice

203. Candace (C). New York: Warner Paperback Library (75-350), 1970.

When George Haight dies and leaves Candace his home, she moves in and comes under a strange spell. A tale of possession and the supernatural.

204. Devil Take All. New York: Popular Library (00612), 1974.

205. Ghost at Stagmere. New York: Warner Paperbacks (75-076), 1973.

206. The Haunted (D). New York: Lancer, 1972.

This romantic suspense begins in an interesting manner with Jennifer off to the wilds to check on her sister-in-law who hasn't been heard from in six months. Jennifer finds her sister-in-law, apparently insane, in the care of some very suspicious relatives. From there on the story goes down hill with long and tedious rehashing and illogical behavior by the heroine.

207. House of the Fiery Cauldron. New York: Berkley Medallion, 1975.

208. Litany of Evil. New York: Lancer (74-580).

Has also written: The Brooding House (Lancer) and To Kill a Witch (Lancer).

BRENT, Madeleine

209. Moonrakers' Bride (A). New York: Doubleday, 1973.

Lucy, born in a Chinese mission and raised there until age 17, finds herself responsible for the care of 415 orphans during hard times in China. This is a fine tale of romantic suspense and adventure. Although the plot is full of fateful coincidences, the author's skill makes them acceptable, if not fully believable. An extra bonus is found in the interesting information of China and Anglo-Chinese cultural differences. A good example of a skilled author's ability to include a great deal of interesting information without detracting from the story.

210. Tregaron's Daughter. Garden City, N.Y.: Doubleday, 1971. (NUC 1968-72 12-596)

BRETONNE, Anne-Marie

211. Dark Talisman. New York: Popular Library (00240), 1975.

212. A Gallows Stands in Salem. New York: Popular Library (00276), 1975.

BRISCOE, Patty

213. Horror at Gull House. New York: Belmont-Tower, 1973.

Other works include: House of Candles (Manor) and Mist of Evil (Manor).

BRISTOWE, Anthony (Lynn)

Born in Surrey, England in 1921. Married Elizabeth Canning, 1944. Attended Eton College four years; the University of Grenoble (diploma); the University of London (diploma in agriculture). Before becoming a writer, he worked as an editorial assistant, director of a nursery, and a stockbroker. Also taught a course and wrote books on fly fishing.

214. The Tunnel (C). New York: Belmont (B60-2025), 1970.
After a promising and nicely written beginning, this sentimental Gothic dwindles to a tedious "Perils of Pauline" theme and becomes absolutely predictable and dull. Too bad.

BROCK, Rose (pseud.) see HANSEN, Joseph

BRONTE, Louisa (pseud.) see ROBERTS, Janet Louise

BROOKS, Laura Frances

215. The Old Evil House (D). New York: Ace, 1975.

The style of writing was so boring that about forty pages and the last chapter were quite sufficient. The plot seemed evident from the first. A husband and wife are tricked into buying a "haunted house." Mentally maladjusted neighbors and dull dialogue round out the scene. Phooey.

BROWN, Carter (pseud.) see YATES, Alan Geoffrey

BROWN, Morna Doris
(Elizabeth Ferrars, E. X. Ferrars)

Born 9/6/07 in Rangoon, Burma. Married Robert Brown in 1940. Home is now in East Lothian, Scotland. Brown is a professional detective story writer with more than forty mysteries to her credit so far.

216. Alibi for a Witch, by Elizabeth Ferrars. London: Collins (Crime Club), 1952. (NUC pre'56 79-265)

217. The Seven Sleepers (C), by Elizabeth Ferrars. New York: Walker, 1970; New York: Dell, 1972. (NUC 1968-72 13-358)
A fairly entertaining murder mystery about a young man burdened by the Bluebeard-type murders committed by his great grandfather. A long-lost relative now seems to want to rake up the old story. The ending could have been improved. There are Gothic elements.

BROWN, Zenith (Jones) 1898-

Uses pseudonym of Leslie Ford and has written dozens of mystery-detective-type novels featuring Mr. Pinkerton. Not considered Gothic for the purposes of this bibliography.

BUCHANAN, Marie

Began writing imaginative stories when she was five years old. She studied European languages and psychology at London University and held various jobs in several countries of Europe before returning to England in 1955. She lives there now with her husband and three children. After publishing ten crime novels under a pseudonym, she caught the attention of the growing parapsychological market with her ... novel Anima. (From the jacket of The Dark Backward).

218. Anima (B). New York: St. Martin's, 1972. (NUC 1968-72 13-581). Pub. by Gollancz in London as: Greenshards.
Certainly not a traditional Gothic but deals, in contemporary terms, with some of the same supernatural phenomena dealt with

on a more primitive level by earlier Gothic novelists. The theme deals with parapsychological matters and is handled in a moderately interesting manner.

219. The Dark Backward. New York: Coward, McCann & Geoghegan, 1975.
Apparently a more complex treatment of parapsychological phenomena and probably well worth a try by those interested in the subject.

220. An Unofficial Breath: A Novel. New York: St. Martin's, 1973. (NUC 1974 3-27)

BUCKINGHAM, Nancy

The later Nancy Buckingham books are under the joint authorship of John Sawyer and Nancy Buckingham Sawyer, both retired advertising writers.

221. Call of Glengarron (B for plot, C for narrative and D for characters). New York: Ace (09101), 1968.
Lucy delivers her dead cousin's son to his father at Glengarron Castle and suspects the father of having murdered her cousin. Attempts are made on Lucy's life. Good basic sentimental Gothic. Disappointing that the castle is just a prop and is not made more a part of the story.

222. Cloud over Malverton (B). New York: Ace, 1967.
Written, evidently, pre-husband partnership. I liked very much the heroine's good sense. The author didn't take the easy way of using the heroine's witlessness to add suspense to the plot. Dulcie inherits a vaccine factory from her long-lost father and finds intrigue and romance. A very nice little romantic suspense.

223. The Dark Summer. New York: Ace (13841), 1972.

224. The Hour before Moonrise. New York: Ace (34361), 1972.

225. The House Called Edenhythe (C). New York: Hawthorn Books, 1972; New York: Dell, 1973. (NUC 1968-72 13-612)
Rachael, pennyless, just widowed and pregnant, goes to her husband's family in London. There she finds intrigue and romance. A very routine story with a predictable plot and no characters of any depth. Standard sentimental Gothic.

226. The Legend of Baverstock Manor. New York: Ace, 1973.

227. Storm in the Mountain. New York: Ace, 1973.

228. Valley of the Ravens (D). New York: Hawthorn Books, 1973.

Sarah goes home after her father's death and finds the family still upset over her sister's elopement and suspected thievery five years before. And someone wants Sarah out of the way. A very routine story with little to commend it other than the sentimental Gothic formula.

Further works include: Quest for Alexis and Return to Vienna (Ace).

BUDLONG, Ware 1905-1967
(Lee Crosby; see also Joan Winslow)

229. Doors to Death (C), by Lee Crosby. New York: Belmont (B50-629), 1965.
Dorcas joins other kin for a meeting at Crane Mansion, called by the head of the clan. They are marooned in the spooky house by a hurricane and two family members die suddenly and violently. Who done it? Essentially a murder mystery with a Gothic setting.

230. Midsummer Night's Murder, by Lee Crosby. New York: Dutton, 1942. (NUC pre'56 82-495)

231. Night Attack, by Lee Crosby. New York: Dutton, 1943. (NUC pre'56 82-495)

232. Terror by Night, by Lee Crosby. New York: Dutton, 1938. (NUC pre'56 82-495)

233. Too Many Doors, by Lee Crosby. New York: Dutton, 1941. (NUC pre'56 82-495)

Has also written: Bridge House, by Lee Crosby (Belmont).

BURFORD, Eleanor see HIBBERT, Eleanor

BURKE, John (Frederick) 1922-
(Jonathan Burke, Joanna Jones, Sara Morris)

In spite of some paperback claims, Burke's work appears to be mystery-detective and is not included here.

BURKE, Jonathan (pseud.) see BURKE, John Frederick

BURKE, Noel (pseud.) see HITCHENS, Dolores (Birk)

BURKHARDT, Robert Ferdinand and Eve
(Rex Jardin)

234. The Devil's Mansion (C), by Rex Jardin. New York: The Fiction League, 1931. (NUC pre'56 278-156)

This in many ways could be a prototype of the Gothic stories so common in the 60's and 70's. A young girl is engaged as a companion to a recluse somewhere in the hinterlands of Canada and finds when she arrives that she is a prisoner in a most bizarre household. Fortunately for her, a young man was coincidentally stranded near the house on a stormy night and takes an interest in the girl and eventually effects her rescue ... though not until some mighty strange things happen. Not a bad story but a bit quaint by today's standards.

BURNS, Sheila (pseud.) see BLOOM, Ursula

BURT, Katharine (Newlin) 1882-

235. Fatal Gift. Philadelphia: Macrae-Smith, 1941. (NUC pre'56 86-440)

The "fatal gift" is beauty and the book is not Gothic.

236. Lady in the Tower (C). Philadelphia: Macrae-Smith, 1946. (NUC pre'56 86-441)

Jenny Thorne takes a job as nurse to invalid Felicia Grise in order to learn the truth behind the 20-year-old murder of Felicia's husband and the accusation that Jenny's mother is the murderess. Not a bad tale of romantic suspense.

237. The Red Lady (B). Boston & New York: Houghton Mifflin, 1920. (NUC pre'56 86-441)

This was fun! Janice goes to a remote Southern mansion as housekeeper and becomes involved in a dramatic intrigue surrounding a hidden treasure. This is just the type of Gothic story that became so popular in the 60's and 70's, and much better written than most.

Burt has written many other books which appear to be romances and/or sentimental Gothics. They may be found listed in the NUC pre'56 Vol. 86, pages 440-1.

BUTLER, Gwendoline Williams

Born 8/19/22 in London, England. Married Lionel Butler (professor of medieval history at the University of St. Andrews) in 1949. They have one child and their home is in Scotland. Butler has written some twelve murder mysteries. Sarsen Place was reviewed as "Gothic."

238. Sarsen Place (B). New York: Coward, McCann & Geoghegan, 1974. (NUC 1974 3-167)

A low-keyed, very nicely written tale which I would classify as sentimental Gothic. There's a lot of philosophical meat on the bones of a tale of family intrigue and murder. Very enjoyable.

BUTTERWORTH, Michael

Born 1/10/24 in England. Married second wife, Jenny Spalding (a writer) in 1957. There are six children. Butterworth's home is in Suffolk, England, and he has worked as a tutor in drawing, an editor, art director and, after 1963, became a full-time writer. States that he is "a firm believer in ghosts and owns a 16th-century house which is haunted." Contemporary Authors, Vol. 25-28, p. 123.

239. The Black Look. Garden City, N.Y.: Doubleday (Crime Club), 1972. (NUC 1968-72 14-473)

240. Flowers for a Dead Witch (C). Garden City, N.Y.: Doubleday (Crime Club), 1971. (NUC 1968-72 14-474)

Butterworth in his "Author's Note" attributes the idea for this book to the Victorian novelist Edna Lyall whose book In the Golden Days (1880's) uses "Mondisfield Hall" for a setting as does Butterworth. This book represents a switchover to an emphasis on the romantic suspense theme and a deemphasis of the Gothic. Nonetheless an entertaining tale of Canadian, Polly Lestrange (!), who visits her ancestral home in England and becomes entangled in local intrigue and murder.

241. The Soundless Scream. Garden City, N.Y.: Doubleday (Crime Club), 1967. (NUC 1968-72 14-474)

242. The Uneasy Sun. Garden City, N.Y.: Doubleday (Crime Club), 1970. (NUC 1968-72 14-474)

243. Villa on the Shore (C). Garden City, N.Y.: Doubleday (Crime Club), 1974. (NUC 1974 3-172)

Natasha becomes secretary to a famous TV star and author living in Italy and is introduced to "la dolce vita." When she learns that her predecessor died tragically, intrigue develops. A fast-paced tale, heavy on exotic characters and bizarre behavior. Romantic suspense of limited depth.

244. Walk Softly, in Fear. London: Lane, 1968.

CADELL, Elizabeth
(Harriet Ainsworth)

Has written more than forty romances, a few under the name Harriet Ainsworth. None seem to qualify as Gothic except Brimstone.

245. Brimstone in the Garden (A). New York: Morrow, 1950. (NUC pre'56 88-603)

I found this a delightful little whimsical Gothic. The setting is a tiny, remote English village, populated with a number of eccentric and thoroughly charming characters. There are love stories in three generations, going on simultaneously, two nasty demons stranded in the village for six weeks and raising Hell, and one of the most amusing ghosts it has been my pleasure to meet.

246. Canary Yellow. London: Hodder & Stoughton, 1965; New York: Morrow, 1965. (NUC 1956-67 17-536)

Elaine wins a cruise to the Canaries and in the process loses a fiancé, gains new friends and experiences and, eventually, gets involved in a murder. This is a competent story--long on romance and short on mystery. No Gothic elements. Those looking for mystery and suspense will probably be bored.

CAIRD, Janet (Kirkwood)

Born 4/24/13 in Livingstonia, Malawi of missionary parents. Married James B. Caird in 1938. They have two children. Caird received an M.A. (with honors) from Edinburgh University in 1935 and did graduate study at the University of Grenoble and the Sorbonne. Her home is in Inverness, Scotland. Her career has been teaching English, French and Latin and she has written, in addition to her Gothics, a children's book and has poetry and short stories in progress. Her avocational interests are archaeology, travel and art.

247. In a Glass Darkly. New York: Morrow, 1966. In England, pub. as Murder Reflected (London: Mill, 1966). (NUC 1956-67 18-31)

248. The Loch. London: Bles, 1968; Garden City, N.Y.: Doubleday (Crime Club), 1969. (NUC 1968-72 14-628)

249. Murder Remote. Garden City, N.Y.: Doubleday (Crime Club), 1972. (NUC 1973 3-38)

250. Murder Scholastic. London: Bles, 1967; Garden City, N.Y.: Doubleday (Crime Club), 1968. (NUC 1956-67 18-31)

251. Perturbing Spirit (B). London: Bles, 1966. (NUC 1956-67 18-31)

A slow paced, tidy little tale set in a Scots' border town and around a local annual festival that the community has been persuaded to "liven up" with a bit of authentic folklore. This is a tale very much in the tradition of Maturin's Melmoth. Low-keyed but undoubtedly Gothic.

CALDER-MARSHALL, Arthur

Born 8/19/08 in Wallington, Surrey, England. Educated at Hertford College, Oxford, B.A. 1930. His career has been that of schoolmaster, author, biographer and critic. He has several novels and biographies listed in the pre'56 NUC.

252. The Scarlet Boy (A). London: Hart-Davis, 1961; New York: Harper, 1962. (NUC 1956-67 18-72)

A middle-aged British historian runs into more than he bargains for when commissioned to find a cheap old house for an old friend. A most engaging tale of ghostly and human relations, liberally sprinkled with wit and philosophy.

CALDWELL, Celeste

253. Thirteen Towers (B). New York: Belmont-Tower, 1974.

A clever author, this, who creates a bizarre situation and environment and builds an entertaining tale thereon. What this story lacks in depth, it makes up for in imaginative wit and a well described hurricane.

CALIN, Anne

254. A Multitude of Shadows (D). New York: Lancer (72-109), 1966.

A totally tedious tale about Alexandra, newly married to rich artist Phillip, who is threatened by Phillip's dear friends and hangers-on, Tony and Allicen. Dullsville and not Gothic.

CAMERON, Eleanor Elford

255. House on the Beach. New York: Pocket Books, 1972. (NUC 1973 3-92)

A good example of a tale which bears no relation whatsoever to its "Gothic" paperback cover. This is a murder mystery and I feel would have been published as such if the main character had been male rather than female.

CAMERON, Kate

256. The Awakening Dream (Whispering Hills No. 5). New York: Nordon (Leisure Books 171NK), 1974.

257. The Curse of Whispering Hills (Whispering Hills No. 2). New York: Nordon (Leisure Books 154NK), 1974.

258. Evil at Whispering Hills (Whispering Hills No. 1). New York: Nordon (Leisure Books 141NK), 1973.

259. Legacy of Terror (Whispering Hills No. 4). New York: Nordon (Leisure Books 166NK), 1974.

260. Shadows on the Moon (Whispering Hills No. 3). New York: Nordon (Leisure Books 158NK), 1974.

261. Shadows of the Past (Holderly Hall No. 2) (B). New York: Nordon (Leisure Books 209NK), 1974.

A swell little tale of true Gothic descent. Rachel, home on vacation from Oberlin College, finds the arrival of a long-lost cousin brings both horrifying phenomena and an increase in her ability to see into the past. This book makes an interesting comparison to Arnold Bennett's The Glimpse--similar subjects but one a Gothic treatment and one not.

CAMERON, Lou

(L. J. Arnold, Steve Cartier, W. R. Marvin)

Born 6/20/24 in San Francisco, California and has been a professional writer and artist since 1957. His works are primarily mystery-detective but a few seem to qualify as Gothic.

262. Behind the Scarlet Door (C). Greenwich, Conn.: Fawcett-Crest (T2493), 1971.

Straight from "horror Gothic" with a contemporary setting and a police detective added. Lt. Detective Price, of Welsh descent, is assigned to a case that evidently involves a Welsh-based witches' coven. A clever story, though possibly a bit much for those of delicate constitution.

263. The Black Camp. Greenwich, Conn.: Fawcett (Gold Medal K1286), 1963. (NUC 1968-72 15-301)

CAMPBELL, Alice (Ormond) 1887-

Twenty-four murder mysteries listed in the NUC pre'56 Vol. 92, pp. 113-15. One example:

264. With Bated Breath (F). New York: Random House, 1946; New York: Paperback Library, 1968. (NUC pre'56 92-115)

This appears to be something the author dug out of a back cupboard and got published due to the new fad for supposed Gothic stories. An incredibly jumbled writing style made very tough reading; half-way through the book I gave up in dizzy despair. I didn't even care enough to read the last chapter. Avis joins a bunch of crazy folk bombing around in an old English manor house and it's all really too too confusing.

CAMPBELL, Hope
(Virginia Hughes, G. McDonald Vallis)

All works appear to be juvenile Gothics.

CAMPBELL, Margaret <u>see</u> LONG, Gabriella Margaret

CAMPBELL, William Edward March 1894-1954
(William March)

265. <u>The Bad Seed</u>, by William March. New York: Rinehart, 1954. (NUC pre'56 92-331)
One of the forerunners of the 1970's fad using the "possessed child" theme which I find generally abhorrent.

CANFIELD, Miriam

266. <u>The Tuscany Madonna</u>. New York: Lancer, 1965.

CARDIFF, Sara

267. Fool's Apple (C). New York: Random House, 1971. (NUC 1968-72 16-8)
With husband, Raoull, Elizabeth comes to settle the estate at her family home on the Atlantic coast near Boston. The arrival of her cousin, Kimball, precipitates several crises and by the end of the story, life is very different for Elizabeth. Competently written in many ways though the characters are cliché and the plot is, in my opinion, unduly lurid and melodramatic.

268. <u>The Inner Steps</u>. New York: Random House, 1973. (NUC 1972 3-188)

269. <u>The Severing Line</u> (C). New York: Random House, 1974. (NUC 1974 3-458)
Fashion model Andrea goes to a Vermont mansion to recuperate from hepatitis and also to see her old lover, Judd Cole. Threats occur and intrigue slowly develops. Again, competently written. Though having some charm, the plot is heavier on romance than I prefer, the characters are "types." The heroine is very human.

CAREW, Jean (pseud.) <u>see</u> CORBY, Jane Irenita

CARFAX, Catherine

270. <u>The Semper Inheritance</u>. London: Hale, 1972. (NUC 1968-72 16-32)

271. The Sleeping Salamander (C). New York: Stein & Day, 1972. (NUC 1973 3-194)

This supposed tale of romantic suspense is, instead, besotted with history and seems to add a little sub-plot of intrigue just to keep the reader's attention during the history lesson. Those who enjoy historical novels may appreciate this dip into 16th-century French history, but if you're looking for a Gothic, look elsewhere.

CARLETON, Mrs. Marjorie Chalmers

272. The Bride Regrets. New York: Morrow, 1950.

273. Cry Wolf. New York: Morrow, 1945. (NUC pre'56 95-411)

274. Dread the Sunset. New York: Morrow, 1962. (NUC 1956-67 19-343)

See also no. 277.

275. Lorinda. New York: Dodd, Mead, 1939. (NUC pre'56 95-411)

276. The Night of the Good Children. New York: Morrow, 1957. (NUC 1956-67 19-343)

277. Shadows on the Hill (C). New York: Morrow, 1947; New York: Pyramid (N2927), 1966. Also pub. as: Dread the Sunset.

An entertaining mystery. Ellen, a violinist on vacation, takes a temporary job at a posh home for the aged and discovers intrigue and murder. Romantic suspense.

278. The Swan Sang Once. New York: Morrow, 1947. (NUC pre'56 95-411)

279. The Swinging Goddess. Boston: Small, Maynard, 1926. (NUC pre'56 95-411)

280. Their Dusty Hands. Boston: B. J. Brimmer, 1924. (NUC pre'56 95-411)

281. Vanished. New York: Morrow, 1955. (NUC pre'56 95-411)

CAROL, Robin

282. The Gypsy's Curse (D). New York: Universal Pub. & Distr. (Award Books AN1182), 1972. [© Camille Bourgeois].

A silly little tale of semi-Louisiana Gothic drama. The whole story is to be found in the first and last chapters with what's between simply a retrospective filler.

CARPENTER, Margaret 1893-

283. Experiment Perilous (B). Boston: Little, Brown, 1943; New York: Pocket Books, 1945. (NUC pre'56 96-314)

Through a series of coincidences, Dr. Bailey meets a wealthy philanthropist, Nicholas Bederaux, and his gorgeous wife, Allida. Bailey senses Allida is terribly frightened and when he tries to learn more, uncovers some sinister goings on. This is romantic suspense with a male main character and makes interesting comparison with works written from the heroine's perspective. A nicely wrought tale.

CARR, John D(ickson) 1905-

From a huge output of mystery-detective fiction, Carr has several that seem to bridge the border of Gothic.

284. The Burning Court. New York: Harper, 1937. (NUC pre'56 96-415)

285. Castle Skull (C). New York: Harpers, 1931. (NUC pre'56 96-415)

This story reminded me very much of Sherlock Holmes and The Hound of the Baskervilles. An urbane super-sleuth and his writer-assistant (the narrator) are engaged to solve a murder committed at Castle Skull in Germany. There are Gothic elements but this is definitely a novel of detection and does not at all make it to the level of Conan Doyle. If one could identify a category of Gothic-detective fiction, this would qualify.

286. The Demoniacs (C). New York: Harpers, 1962; New York: Bantam (F2767), 1964. (NUC 1956-67 19-451)

Set in the mid-18th century in London, this somewhat tame horror Gothic doesn't quite make the grade. I suspect that this is because Carr seemed to get too involved with the accuracy of his historical setting and characters and forgot to pay attention to the plot. I think it is, however, definitely Gothic.

287. The Eight of Swords. New York: Harpers, 1934. (NUC pre'56 96-416)

288. House at Satan's Elbow (B). New York: Harper & Row, 1965; New York: Univ. Pub. & Distr. (Award Books AQ1353), 1974. (NUC 1956-67 19-451)

Definitely one of those tales which straddles the fence between Gothic and detective fiction. A cut above the average.

289. The Witch of the Low-Tide: An Edwardian Melodrama. New York: Harpers, 1961. (NUC 1956-67 19-452)

CARR, Philippa (pseud.) see HIBBERT, Eleanor

CARRINGTON, Glenda

290. Master of Greystone (A). New York: Berkeley Medallion, 1977. [© Karen Glenn].

This 1977 version of a more than 200-year-old plot was a perfect example of the timelessness of some themes in the hands of a skillful writer. This one has introduced some most satisfying innovations and I highly recommend it.

CARTER, Alberta Simpson

291. An Adopted Face. New York: Popular Library, n.d. [© Alfred Bercovici, 1975].

292. The Falmount Heiress (F). New York: Curtis Publications, 1973.

Bess "sells her soul" to impersonate a dead heiress. The story sounded thoroughly predictable from the first couple of chapters and the last three chapters indicate the middle was not likely worth reading.

CARTER, Angela

Born 5/7/40 in Sussex, England. Upon leaving school, worked for three years as a reporter. Many of her poems have appeared in literary magazines and a collection of children's stories was to have been published in 1967. She has traveled in Japan and the U.S.S.R. She claims "witch blood on her father's side; solid radical trade-unionists on her mother's." Contemporary Authors. Vol. 53-56, p. 91.

293. Heroes and Villains. London: Heinemann, 1969; New York: Simon & Schuster, 1969. (NUC 1968-72 16-194)

Book Review Digest (70:238) classifies this as "science fiction gothic."

294. The Infernal Desire Machines of Dr. Hoffman. London: Hart-Davis, 1972; pub. in U.S. as: The War of Dreams. New York: Harcourt Brace, 1974. (NUC 1974 3-5113).

295. The Magic Toyshop. London: Heinemann, 1967; New York: Simon & Schuster, 1968. (NUC 1968-72 16-195). John Llewllyn Rys Prize in 1968.

The publisher calls this book "almost gothic." It's a weird story, but I find little in the way of Gothic elements. Melanie's parents are killed and she and siblings go to live with toymaker uncle Philip, in a bizarre household. I found nothing to commend this story unless one is the type who enjoys looking at freaks. (Contemporary Authors calls this a "children's book"--Ho! Ho!)

296. Several Perceptions. London: Heinemann, 1968; New York: Simon & Schuster, 1968. (NUC 1968-72 16-195). Somerset Maugham Award in 1969.

297. Shadow Dance. London: Heinemann, 1966; In the U.S.: Honeybuzzard. New York: Simon & Schuster, 1967. (NUC 1956-67 19-528)

CASE, David 1937-

298. The Cell, and other Tales of Horror. New York: Hill & Wang, 1969. (NUC 1968-72 16-270)

299. Fengriffin: A Chilling Tale (A). New York: Hill & Wang, 1970; New York: Lancer (74-728), 1971. (NUC 1968-72 16-270)

An elegant and thoroughly perfect horror Gothic. No better example could be found to show the viability of Gothic literature in the twentieth century.

CAVENDISH, Peter (pseud.) see HORLER, Sydney

CECIL, Henry (pseud.) see KELLER, David H.

CHANDOS, Fay (pseud.) see SWATRIDGE, Irene

CHAPMAN, Hester W(olferstan)

Born 11/26/1899 in London, England. Privately educated. Married twice, both husbands now deceased. Worked as a mannequin in Paris in the early years, then, intermittently, as telephone operator, secretary, governess and schoolmistress. During WWII worked for the Fighting French and the American Red Cross. Chapman has a large output of what appear to be essentially sentimental and historical romances, for example:

300. Limmerston Hall (C). New York: Coward, McCann & Geoghegan, 1973. (NUC 1973 3-393)

Anne Milson goes to Pond House to be co-guardian of a nephew and niece along with Neville Quarrendon, a mysterious and enigmatic man who has a passion for a nearby manor, Limmerston Hall. The story is mainly about the relationship between Anne and Neville and largely a character study. The manor and atmosphere are Gothic. The story is engrossing and well written, with a very strange, and for this reader unsatisfying, ending.

CHARLES, Iona

301. Grenencourt. New York: Popular Library (00264), 1975.

302. When Only the Bougainvillea Blooms (C). New York: Popular Library (00296), 1975. [© Carolyn Nichols & Stanlee Coy].

A very run-of-the-mill tale of Karen who returns to the Virgin Islands after a year in N. Y. C. as a TV producer. In the process of gathering data for a documentary she uncovers a land fraud. Superficial, contrived and not Gothic.

CHARLES, Theresa (pseud.) see SWATRIDGE, Irene and Charles

CHIMENTI, Francesca

303. Night Falls Too Soon (C). New York: Pyramid (T2634), 1972.

A very routine neo-Gothic about Allegra Balmoral who goes to Greentree mansion as a governess for a retarded child and finds the usual hornet's nest of intrigue and romance.

CHIPPERFIELD, Robert Orr (pseud.) see OSTRANDER, Isabel Egenton

CHRISTOPHER, John

Has published several novels of mystery and science fiction, all listed in the NUC.

304. The Little People (C). New York: Simon & Schuster, 1967. (NUC 1956-67 23-16)

This tale seems to border the categories of horror Gothic and science fiction. The setting is Gothic and the "little people" are sci. fi. I enjoyed the author's style and most of the tale, but found the "little people" theme very unsatisfactory for my tastes. The author's skill aroused my curiosity and kept me reading but I don't think the total effort came off at all well.

CHRISTOPHER, Louise (pseud.) see HALE, Arlene

CLARK, Cecily

305. Ravensley Manor (C). New York: Pocket Books, 1976.

More a period romance than a Gothic. The heroine's father gets done in late in the tale and there is the who-done-it theme. But the primary emphasis is historical romance and not particularly interesting in my view.

CLARK, Lydia Benson

306. Yesterday's Evil (B). New York: Ace (94355), 1974.
Not a bad little tale of modern-day witchcraft and retribution. I think the author handled the subject credibly and maintained a fast-paced entertaining story throughout. A contemporary treatment of very old themes.

CLAUDIA, Susan (pseud.) see JOHNSTON, William

CLEMENTS, Abigail

307. Mistress of the Moor (C). Greenwich, Conn.: Fawcett, 1974.
This story starts off with great promise and follows closely the neo-Gothic formula. It is flawed greatly by the drippy behavior of the heroine whose bad judgement in crises and total lack of understanding of the people around her causes much more trouble than necessary.

CLIFFORD, Francis (pseud.) see THOMPSON, Arthur Leonard Bell

CLYNE, Terence (pseud.) see BLATTY, William Peter

COFFMAN, Virginia (Edith)
(Victor Cross, Virginia C. DuVaul)

Born 7/30/14 in San Francisco, California. Received an A.B. from the University of California at Berkeley in 1938. Home is in Reno, Nevada. Has been a full-time writer since 1965 before which she worked as a secretary and writer in movie and TV studios, office manager in a real estate office, free-lance editor, actress, lecturer and drama teacher. Because of her current large reading public, all known works are included here.

308. The Affair at Alkali. New York: Arcadia House, 1960; pub. in England as Nevada Gunslinger. London: Gresham, 1962. (NUC 1975 3-946)

309. The Beach House. New York: New American Library (Signet Q6479), 1970.

310. The Beckoning. New York: Ace, 1965.

311. Black Heather. New York: Lancer, 1966.

312. Blood Sport, by Victor Cross. New York: Award Books, 1967.

313. Call of the Flesh. New York: Lancer, 1968.

314. The Candidate's Wife. New York: Lancer, 1968.

315. Castle at Witches' Coven. New York: Lancer (74-506), 1966.

316. Castle Barra (F). New York: Warner Paperback, 1966.
Too much "why did he do that?" and "what does it all mean" speculation by the heroine. Catharine goes to S. France, after being acquitted in the poisoning death of her husband, to secure her husband's estate for her stepson. She nearly gets killed a dozen times before she finds out who was behind the death of her husband and the attempted murder of her stepson. A cramped style, shallow characters, an unduly melodramatic plot and a conceited prig of a heroine add up to a poor show.

317. Chalet Diabolique (Lucifer Cove Series No. 5) (C). New York: Lancer (74-773), 1971.
Kay Aronson goes to Lucifer Cove to find out the reason for her husband's precipitous departure from the place which resulted in his death. She confronts the Powers of Evil at the Cove. This book reminds me very much of the Gothic tales of the early 20th century with its naiveté of plot and philosophy. Not much substance to this mediocre tale.

318. The Chinese Door. New York: Lancer, 1967; London: Hale, 1971.

319. The Cliffs of Dread. New York: Lancer, 1973.

320. Curse of the Island Pool. New York: Lancer (74-613), 1965.

321. The Dark Gondola (B). New York: Ace, 1968.
A sequel to Moura and The Beckoning, but stands on its own as well. Anne Wicklow goes to Venice. Some interesting settings along with standard Gothic themes. Very good with the exception of a tendency to verbosity.

322. The Dark Palazzo. New York: Arbor House, 1973; Greenwich, Conn.: Fawcett-Crest, 1974. (NUC 1973 3-675)

323. The Demon Tower. New York: New American Library (Signet T4974), 1966.

324. The Devil's Mistress (Lucifer's Cove Series No. 1). New York: Lancer (74-645), 1969.

325. The Devil's Virgin (Lucifer's Cove Series No. 3). New York: Lancer (74-729), 1970.

326. The Devil Vicar (B). New York: Ace, 1966; revised and republished as Vicar of Moura, 1971.
Estelle Varney takes a temporary job in the English moorlands and learns her mysterious, cynical employer is suspected by the villagers of being the reincarnation of their infamous "devil

vicar." The heroine's wit helps this story greatly. The plot is intricate and melodramatic but keeps one guessing to the last page.

327. Evil at Queen's Priory. New York: Lancer, 1973.

328. A Fear of Heights. New York: Lancer, 1973.

329. A Few Fiends to Tea. New York: Belmont, 1967.

330. From Satan with Love (Lucifer Cove Series No. 6). New York: Lancer, 1972.

331. Garden of Shadows. New York: Lancer, 1973.

332. A Haunted Place. New York: Lancer, 1966.

333. The High Terrace. New York: New American Library (Signet Y6763), 1966; pub. in England as: To See a Dark Stranger. London: Hall, 1969.

334. Hounds of Hell. New York: Belmont, 1967. (Published with Daoma Winston's Carnaby Curse).

335. The House at Sandalwood (B). New York: Arbor House, 1974. (NUC 1974 4-94)

A well written tale of romantic suspense. Judith, just out of prison, goes to Hawaii to aid a newly wed and emotionally unstable niece. She encounters emotional entanglements, island life and murder. Coffman does a nice job with the plot, interesting characters and a vivid but unobtrusive description of Hawaii.

336. The House on the Moat. New York: Lancer, 1972.

337. Hyde Place: A Novel (D). New York: Arbor House, 1974; Greenwich, Conn.: Fawcett-Crest (P2544), 1975. (NUC 1974 4-94)

Meredith returns to San Francisco after 13 years to trace her long-lost mother and settle the family estate following the death of her father. There is a conspiracy to defraud her. Some interesting views of San Francisco at the turn of the century, but, all in all, this story never gets beyond the routine. No Gothic elements worth mention.

338. The Ice Forest. New York: Dell, 1974.

339. Isle of the Undead. New York: Lancer (74-583), 1970; pub. in England as: Voodoo Widow. London: Hale, 1970.

340. Masque of Gaslight by Virginia C. DuVaul. New York: Ace, 1970.

341. Masque of Satan (Lucifer's Cove Series No. 4). New York: Lancer, 1971.

342. The Master of Blue Mire. New York: Dell, 1971.

343. The Mist at Darkness. New York: New American Library (Signet Q6138), 1968.

344. Mistress Devon (D). New York: Arbor House, 1972; Greenwich, Conn.: Fawcett-Crest (M1879), 1973. (NUC 1968-72 19-402)

Devon, on her own and pennyless in pre-Revolutionary Boston, takes a job as seamstress for a traveling theater company and becomes deeply involved with the people therein, including Michael Dantine and Denis Varney, half-brothers and heads of the troupe. Those who prefer romantic suspense with emphasis on the romance may like this tale. I found it dull and soon tired of both Devon's personality and her love life.

345. Moura (B). New York: Crown Publications, 1959; New York: Ace Star (K175), 1959. (NUC 1956-67 24-45)

Coffman's first novel and one intimately akin to the Ann Radcliffe Gothics she mentions several times. It's all here, including the slow pace.

346. Night at Sea Abbey. New York: Lancer, 1972.

347. Of Love and Intrigue. New York: New American Library (Signet T3829), 1969.

348. One Man Too Many. New York: Lancer, 1967.

349. Priestess of the Damned (Lucifer Cove Series No. 2). New York: Lancer (74-697), 1970.

350. The Rest Is Silence. New York: Lancer, 1967. (NUC 1968-72 19-402)

351. Richest Girl in the World. New York: Lancer, 1967.

352. The Secret of Shower Tree. New York: Lancer, 1966.

353. The Shadow Box. New York: Lancer, 1967.

354. The Small Tawny Cat. New York: Lancer, 1967.

355. The Vampyre of Moura. New York: Ace, 1970.

356. The Villa Fountains. New York: Belmont, 1967.

COHEN, Susan (Handler)
(Elizabeth St. Clair)

Born 3/27/38 in Chicago, Illinois. Married Daniel E. Cohen (a writer) in 1958. They have one child. Cohen attended the University of Illinois and received a B.S. in 1962 from the New School for Social Research and an M.S.W. from Adelphi University in 1966. She was a social worker from 1962 to 1967 and now lives in Pt. Jervis, N.Y. In addition to her Gothic stories, she wrote The Liberated Couple (New York: Lancer, 1971).

357. The Singing Harp, by Elizabeth St. Clair. New York: New American Library (Signet), 1975.

358. Stonehaven (B), by Elizabeth St. Clair. New York: New American Library (Signet Q5946), 1974.

If the second half of this book had lived up to the superbly written and classic beginning, this could have been one of the top 20th-century Gothics. As it is, the author seems to have allowed her imagination to charge forth unrestrained and the result, for me at least, was a totally absurd solution to the mystery of Stonehaven and one which in great part destroyed all the effect of the craftsmanship of the earlier parts of the book. This seems a good example of the blending of horror Gothic and the occult literature of the 20th century and, with all its flaws, it's still a pretty good tale.

COLE, Lois Dwight (Taylor)
(Lynn Avery, Nancy Dudley, Alan Dwight, Anne Eliot)

Born in New York City. B.A. from Smith College. Her home is in Upper Montclair, N.J. Her career has been that of editor and author. The Lynn Avery books appear to be juveniles; the Nancy Dudley books, romances; and the Alan Dwight (written with her husband, T. A. Taylor) are adventure stories.

359. The Dark Beneath the Pines (D) by Anne Eliot. New York: Hawthorn Books, 1974. (NUC 1974 4-115)

Andrea returns to the family "camp" in the Adirondacks to help find a deceased uncle's missing fortune and some lost and valuable paintings. Although fairly skillfully written, this is a variation of the basic plot of Return to Aylforth. The inconsistencies of plot seem less forgivable the second time around.

360. Incident at Villa Rahmana, by Anne Eliot. New York: Hawthorn Books, 1972. (NUC 1973 3-691)

361. Return to Aylforth: A Novel of Suspense (C) by Ann Eliot. New York: Meredith Press, 1967. (NUC 1956-67 24-113)

Petra returns from London to Aylforth, her childhood home, to attend memorial services for a cousin and guardian only to encounter a family reunion and a conspiracy about some valuable paintings everyone thinks she can locate. This is well enough written and sufficiently entertaining to make less significant some flaws of plot. Doesn't really hang together, but gets by.

362. Shadows Waiting, by Anne Eliot. New York: Meredith Press, 1969. (NUC 1968-72 19-481)

363. Stranger at Pembroke, by Anne Eliot. New York: Hawthorn Books, 1971. (NUC 1968-72 19-481)

COLEMAN, Clara

364. Nightmare in July. Sydney, etc.: Horwitz, 1966; New York: Lancer, 1967. (NUC 1956-67 24-127)

This plot has been done ... recognized it by Chapter 2. Light suspense tale of a wife of a publisher who gets taken in by a "newly discovered" author of a supposed literary masterpiece. May have been copied from J. D. Carr.

365. The Scent of Sandalwood. New York: Lancer, 1970.

366. Timbalier (F). New York: Dell (8908), 1969. (NUC 1973 3-693)

This is a "standard southern American Gothic" in theme but so poorly written that half way through I just didn't care how it all worked out. A good example of how a standard plot either makes it or doesn't, depending on the quality of the writing.

COLTON, James (pseud.) see HANSEN, Joseph

COMER, Ralph

367. To Dream of Evil. New York: Award Books (A9055) n.d.

CONWAY, Joan Ditzel

368. Island of Fear (D). Greenwich, Conn.: Fawcett Gold Medal (T2595), 1972.

Another tale that starts out with much promise but rapidly disintegrates into a mish-mosh of disasters and melodrama. Marny returns to native Channel Island of Alderney to check up on her aunt who sent her a desperate telegram. She arrives to find her aunt missing, two old flames present, and a lot of trouble. This heroine gets top honors for all-time clod. Every ten pages the poor dear is tripping, falling, or getting injured, and generally through her own stupidity.

CONWAY, Laura (pseud.) see ANSLE, Dorothy Phoebe

COOK, Eugenia

369. The Forbidden Tower. New York: Dell, 1973.

COOKSON, Catherine (McMullen) 1906-
(Catherine Marchant)

Author of a very large number of what appear to be mostly romances, sentimental and historical, for example:

370. Evil at Roger's Cross, by Catherine Marchant. New York: Lancer, 1965.
Romance about two hurt people who find each other. Well enough written to engage one's interest in finishing the book but no Gothic or suspenseful elements.

COOPER, Jefferson (pseud.) see FOX, Gardner

COOPER, Lynna

371. Stark Island (C). New York: Avon (19463), 1974. [© Gardner F. Fox].
This book starts out with some promise as we find Inez confronting some mysterious goings on at Stark Island where she's employed as librarian for the Stark Estate. It is evidently much easier to write an entertaining first half of a story than to write a satisfactory second half and Stark Island is a very good example of an author's good beginning fizzling out to a cliché, predictable and quite uninteresting resolution.

COOPER, Parley

A native of Oregon, Cooper is an expert on the occult.... He lives in New York City, where he is currently working on a novel set in a West Coast Satanist Community (information from jacket of My Lady).

372. The Devil Child. New York: Pocket Books, 1972.
A very short and grim little tale in which the craftsmanship is insufficient to sustain a cast of very sick characters. It reminds me of a tenth-rate Shirley Jackson story.

373. My Lady Evil (C). New York: Simon & Schuster, 1974. (NUC 1974 4-374)
This book reminded me of what some scholars speak of as "Gothic fragments." It could have, for example, been one of the tales within a tale of a huge novel such as Melmoth the Wanderer. As is, it is more a short story of the occult, somewhat clever in plot but without sufficient narrative or character development to give it much depth. Not much for your money here.

CORBY, Jane Irenita 1899-
(Jean Carew, Joanne Holden)

Has written a large number of romances and nurse stories. Those included here appear to have some Gothic elements.

374. Dangerous Legacy, by Joanne Holden. New York: Arcadia House, 1966.

375. Farewell to the Castle (C). New York: Arcadia House, 1967; New York: Manor House, 1973. (NUC 1956-67 25-483)
An unpretentious and tidy little suspense and murder tale. Only Gothic element is a New England "castle" setting. Relatively unflawed but lacking in zest.

376. Girl in the Tower. New York: Arcadia House, 1966. (NUC 1956-67 25-483)

377. Nurse at the Castle, by Joanne Holden. New York: Arcadia House, 1965. (NUC 1956-67 25-483)

378. Riverwood. New York: Arcadia House, 1968. (NUC 1968-72 21-91)

CORELLI, Marie (pseud.) see MACKAY, Mary

CORREN, Grace (pseud.) see HOSKINS, Robert

COSGROVE, Rachel see PAYES, Rachel Cosgrove

COST, March (pseud.) see MORRISON, Margaret M.

COULSON, Juanita (Wellons)
(John Jay Wells)

Born 2/12/33 in Anderson, Illinois. Married R. S. Coulson (a writer) in 1954. Received a B.S. from Ball State University in 1954 and an M.A. in 1963. Her home is in Hartford City, Indiana. Career: Elementary teacher 1954-55; collator 1955-57; publisher of Yandro, a science fiction magazine 1953-70. Contributor to Fantasy and Science Fiction under the pseudonym John Jay Wells. Most work appears to be science fiction.

379. Door into Terror. New York: Berkley Medallion (S2183).

380. Stone of Blood (Birthstone Gothic No. 3) (C). New York: Ballantine, 1975.
Lyssa du Champ takes a job as singer on a riverboat at a

Wisconsin lake resort and finds mostly romance but also murder, intrigue and a rather token ghost and legend. A slick little tale with the requisite ingredients but lacking in depth and character development as well as a certain something I can only call "sincerity" that would lift if from the realm of the mediocre.

COULTON, James (pseud.) see HANSEN, Joseph

COWEN, Frances

381. Daylight Fear. New York: Ace (139154), 1973.

382. The Hounds of Carvello. New York: Ace (343558), 1973.

383. Lake of Darkness (D). London: Hale, 1971; New York: Ace (46970), 1974.

A tale with an identity crisis--or a mystery with romance and Gothic elements tossed in and not very well integrated. Agnes returns to Germany after emigrating during the War, to help trace a grandson who has disappeared. This is not a well thought out story or well written, and the flimsy crafting can not sustain some extraordinary coincidences.

384. The Nightmare Ends. New York: Ace (57725), 1972.

385. The One Between. London: Hale, 1967. (NUC 1956-67 26-244)

386. The Shadow of Polperro (D). New York: Ace (760181), 1973.

Cowen had the terrific idea of having the plot of this story revolve around an ancient ill-reputed castle, just inherited by young and lovely Esther, and leased by a film producer for a movie version of The Castle of Otranto. Sad to say, nothing comes of the great idea and the story boils down to a very tame little intrigue, lavishly fleshed out with irrelevant happenings, characters and dialogue. An unprecocious adolescent might enjoy, but I found it a dull and disappointing book.

COX, Anthony Berkeley 1893-
(Anthony Berkeley, Francis Iles)

In general, a writer of mystery-detective fiction. The following book was listed in Siemon:

387. Before the Fact: A Novel of Murder, by Francis Iles. Garden City, N.Y.: Doubleday, 1932. (NUC pre'56 125-586)

A non-pornographic Story of O. A woman lets herself become dominated by her husband to the point of cooperating with her own murder. The only relation this bears to the Gothic is that it would be a good prologue to a story of a haunting.

CRAIG, Mary Francis
(Mary Francis Shura)

Born 2/27/23 in the United States. Free-lance writer, evidently mostly of juveniles. The NUC lists "Mary Craig" as the pseudonym.

388. A Candle for the Dragon. New York: Dell, 1973.

389. The Cranes of Ibycus. New York: Hawthorn Books, 1974. (NUC 1974 15-361)

390. The Shop on Threnody Street (C), by Mary Francis Shura. New York: Grosset & Dunlap, 1972; New York: Warner Paperback (66959), 1972. (NUC 1968-72 86-650)

A fast-paced, very short tale of romantic suspense. Liza goes to visit friend Jane in Chicago and finds herself in an intrigue involving a childhood friend and dollmaker whose present circumstances seem very peculiar.

391. Ten Thousand Several Doors. New York: Hawthorn Books, 1973. (NUC 1973 12-976)

CRANDALL, Edward

392. White Violets (B). Boston: Little, Brown, 1954 (NUC pre'56 126-365)

A well told tale of romantic suspense very much the prototype of so many stories written in the 60's and 70's and very much superior to most of them.

CRAWFORD, Petrina

393. Seed of Evil (B). New York: Lancer (73-680), 2nd printing 1973.

Joanna is employed by the aged and wealthy Mr. Crask as a companion and goes to his Cornwall mansion only to discover all is not as it seemed at their London employment interview. A somewhat philosophically written tale with a believable plot and heroine--and a lousy printing job.

CRAWFORD, Rosemary

394. Image of Evil (D). New York: Dell (3996), 1971.

A very dull romance with a "Louisiana Gothic" setting but few other Gothic elements.

CREASEY, JOHN 1908-1973

Has published somewhere around 450 books including the

"Department Z" series, a flying series, "The Toff" series, "Inspector West" series, "Gideon" Series (by J. J. Marric), western series under several pseudonyms, and the "Baron" series (by Anthony Morton). Other pseudonyms include: Michael Halliday, Jeremy York, Whit Masterson, Gordon Ashe, Kyle Hunt, William K. Reilly, Norman Deane, Peter Manton and Richard Martin. The Dr. Palfrey series, written under his own name probably has Gothic elements as they generally deal with the supernatural as does the shorter series of "Dr. Cellini" books by Michael Halliday.

CRECY, Jeanne (pseud.) see WILLIAMS, Jeanne (Kreil)

CREIGHTON, Jo Anne

395. The Dark Side of Paradise (D). New York: Popular Library, 1976. [© Joseph Chadwick].

This story starts off with some promise as Virginia, in a state of amnesia, is rescued from an abandoned and sinking ship off the coast of Hawaii. Things go down hill thereafter as her rescuer takes her to his family home on a remote island and she is wooed by two brothers and hated by their girl friends and it's all too, too much. There is little suspense after the first chapter and no Gothic elements to speak of.

396. Inn of Evil. New York: Popular Library (00224), 1974.

CROMWELL, Elsie

397. The Governess (A). New York: Paperback Library (63-233), 1969. (NUC 1968-72 21-603)

Sari takes a summer job as governess to two nieces of the notorious Comte de Louvais and finds herself embroiled in a conspiracy and intrigue. Well written! The characters are solid and the heroine is truely heroic--full of beans, bright and independent. The plot is well developed and engrossing.

398. Ivorstone Manor (A). New York: Pocketbooks, 1970.

"Recovery of luck piece is crucial to the safety of Holly who is pursued by evil." A very nice little story. Good dialogue and plot. The element of the supernatural is an effectively used Gothic element.

CROSBY, Lee (pseud.) see BUDLONG, Ware

CROSS, Victor (pseud.) see COFFMAN, Virginia

CROWE, Cecily

399. Miss Spring. New York: Random House, 1953. (NUC pre'56 128-219)

400. Northwater (A). New York: Holt, Rinehart & Winston, 1968. (NUC 1968-72 22-13)

One of the very few that one reads so many to find. A beautiful story, well told. It fits the criteria for a Gothic but soars so deftly beyond that one tends not to think of it as such.

401. The Tower of Kilraven (B). New York: Holt, Rinehart & Winston, 1965; New York: New American Library (Signet D3037), 1966. (NUC 1956-67 26-471)

Recently widowed Carlotta goes to visit Ireland and stays as a paying guest at Kilraven Castle where she becomes very involved with other guests, the family and the family "ghost." Nicely written little neo-Gothic that at one time ran as a serial in Redbook magazine.

402. The Twice-Born. New York: Random House, 1972. (NUC 1968-72 22-13)

CUNNINGHAM, Cathy (pseud.) see CUNNINGHAM, Chet

CUNNINGHAM, Chet
(Cathy Cunningham)

Born 12/9/28 in Shelby, Nebraska. Earned a B.A. from Pacific University in 1950 and an M.S. from Columbia University in 1954. Married Rose Marie Wilhoit in 1953. They have three children. Under his own name has written at least eight westerns and adventure stories and two juveniles.

403. The Demons of Highpoint House (F) by Cathy Cunningham. New York: Popular Library, 1973.

A silly symphony of horror Gothic hijinks. Totally without intentional humor and therefore, I suppose, not spoof. Avoid!

CURTIN, Philip (pseud.) see LOWNDES, Marie

CURTIS, Peter (pseud.) see LOFTS, Norah

CURTISS, Ursula Reilley

Native of Yonkers, N.Y. since her birth in 1923 and writer of mystery novels which may qualify in some cases as romantic suspense, if not Gothic.

DALTON, Priscilla (pseud.) <u>see</u> AVALLONE, Michael

DANA, Rose (pseud.) <u>see</u> ROSS, William Edward Daniel

DANE, Mark (pseud.) <u>see</u> AVALLONE, Michael

DANIEL, Elna Worrell (pseud.) <u>see</u> STONE, Elna

DANIELS, Dorothy
(Works are also published under Helen Gray Weston. Which name is the pseudonym I do not know.)

404. Affair in Marrakesh. New York: Pyramid, 1968.

405. The Appollo Fountain. New York: Warner, 1974.

406. The Attic Rope (C). New York: Lancer (74663), [1970].
Nicolette goes to live with her aunt and is sent to Lakehouse to prepare for a ball to be held on the fifth anniversary of her cousin's reputed suicide. Intrigue ensues. This is "good Dorothy Daniels"--nothing fancy, but a straightforward plot, uncluttered narrative, interesting but shallow characters. Romantic suspense rather than Gothic, in my judgment.

407. The Bell. New York: Warner, 1971.

408. Blackthorn (D). New York: Pocketbook, 1975.
Carrie goes to newly purchased family home to find out why her parents are suddenly divorcing after years of happy marriage. She discovers a bleak and blighted mansion that appears to cause all who enter to hate everyone around them. Some good ideas, but a slap-dash effort, all-in-all. The plot is barely consistent, the characters have no depth and the dialogue is colorless and stilted.

409. Blue Devil Suite. New York: Belmont-Tower (B752175), 1971.

410. The Caldwell Shadow. New York: Warner, 1973.

411. The Carson Inheritance. New York: Warner, 1975.

412. Castle Morvant. New York: Warner, 1972.

413. Child of Darkness. New York: Pocket Book, 1974.

414. Conover's Folly. New York: Warner, 1971.

415. The Curse of Mallory Hall. Greenwich, Conn.: Fawcett-Crest, 1970.

416. Darkhaven. New York: Pocket Books, 1965; New York: Warner, 1974.

417. Dark Island. New York: Warner, 1972.

418. The Dark Stage. New York: Warner, 1974.

419. Dark Villa. New York: Lancer (73-682), 1967. (NUC 1968-72 22-461)

420. Diablo Manor. New York: Warner, 1971.

421. The Duncan Dynasty. New York: Warner, 1973.

422. The Eagle's Nest. New York: Lancer, 1967.

423. Emerald Hill. New York: Pocket Book, 1970.

424. The Exorcism of Jenny Slade. New York: Pocket Book, 1974.

425. Ghost Song. New York: Pocket Book, 1974.

426. Hills of Fire. New York: Warner, 1975.

427. The House of Broken Dolls. New York: Warner, 1972.

428. House of False Faces, by Helen Gray Weston. New York: Warner, 1967, repub. by Dorothy Daniels: New York: Warner, 1974.

429. The House of Many Doors. New York: Warner, 1974.

430. The House on Circus Hill. New York: Warner, 1975.

431. Illusion at Haven's Edge. New York: Pocket Book, 1975.

432. Image of a Ghost. New York: Warner, 1973.

433. Island of Bitter Memories. New York: Warner, 1974.

434. Jade Green. New York: Warner Paperbacks, 1973.

435. Lady of the Shadows. New York: Warner Paperbacks, 1970.

436. The Lanier Riddle. New York: Warner Paperbacks, 1972.

437. The Larrabee Heiress. New York: Warner Paperbacks, 1972.

438. The Leland Legacy. New York: Pyramid, [1965]. (NUC 1974 8-114)

439. The Lilly Pond. New York: Warner Paperbacks, 1965.

440. <u>The Man from Yesterday</u>. New York: Paperback Library (63-436), 1970.

441. <u>Marriott Hall</u>. New York: Warner Paperbacks, 1971.

442. <u>The Maya Temple</u>. New York: Warner Paperbacks, 1972.

443. <u>The Mistress of Falcon Hill</u>. New York: Pyramid, 1965.

444. <u>Mostly by Moonlight</u>. New York: Lancer, 1963.

445. <u>Mystic Manor</u>, by Helen Gray Weston. New York: Warner Paperbacks, 1972. Repub. as: by Dorothy Daniels, New York: Warner, 1975.

446. <u>Nightfall</u>. New York: Pocket Books, 1977.

447. <u>Poison Flower</u> (D). New York: Pocket Books, 1977.
Sweet orphaned Adeline is claimed by the wealthy reclusive Sam Briggs as his long-lost granddaughter and persuaded to move to Tophet's Realm as his heiress. The trouble is, it takes a third of the book and pages of trivial dialogue to get the story off the ground. And what follows is so grossly melodramatic and senseless that I truly regretted my patient waiting for action. Daniels consistently provides a dependable standard of mediocrity.

448. <u>Possessed</u>. New York: Pocket Books, 1975.

449. <u>The Possession of Tracy Corbin</u>. New York: Warner Paperbacks, 1973.

450. <u>The Prisoner of Malville Hall</u>. New York: Warner Paperbacks, 1975.

451. <u>Shadow Glen</u>. New York: Warner Paperbacks, 1965.

452. <u>Shadows from the Past</u>. New York: Warner Paperbacks, 1975.

453. <u>The Silent Halls of Ashenden</u>. New York: Warner Paperbacks, 1973.

454. <u>The Stone House</u>. New York: Warner Paperbacks, 1973.

455. <u>The Tormented</u> (D). New York: Paperback Library, 1969.
Most of the basics are here but the plot is not at all innovative. Sharon Aldrich returns to the old plantation to find it haunted. The characters are weak and some are ridiculous. Sharon's dialogue reveals she's a real sap. A very simple-minded tale.

456. <u>Two Worlds of Peggy Scott</u>. New York: Pocket Book (77768-8), 1974.

457. The Unearthly (C). New York: Lancer (74-723), 1970.
Hope Owen returns to the plantation following her mother's sudden death. She encounters ghosts and evil plots. A fair story but the characters are poorly drawn--except maybe Fern--and the style is juvenile. But it's a Gothic.

458. Voices on the Wind. New York: Pocket Book, 1969.

459. A Web of Peril. New York: Pyramid, 1970.

460. Witches' Castle (C). New York: Paperback Library, 1971.
Gale, a marine biologist, takes the "Witches' Castle" to live and work in. Islanders claim she is the reincarnation of a reputed witch who lived in the house a generation before. One of D. D.'s better efforts.

Some of Daniels' other works include: The Beaumont Tradition, Cliffside Castle, Cruise Ship Nurse, Dance in Darkness, Island Nurse, Strange Paradise (and sequels, Island of Evil and Raxl, Voodoo Priestess), Survivor of Darkness, The Templeton Memoirs, The Tower Room, The Unguarded and World's Fair Nurse.

DANTON, Rebecca (pseud.) see ROBERTS, Janet Louise

DARBY, Catherine

461. Falcon Rising (B). New York: Popular Library (00405), 1976.
"Peyton Place Gothic," but not too bad, by golly. A fast-paced, deft writing style and interesting characters sustain a tale teeming with dramatic people, behavior and events and make for quite a lively little tale. If others in the series are as well done, it should be lots of fun. Other books in the Falcon Saga include: No. 1 A Falcon for a Witch (00313), No. 2 The King's Falcon (00321), No. 3 Fortune for a Falcon (00329), No. 4 Season of the Falcon (00339), No. 5 Falcon Royal (00357), No. 6 Falcon Tree (00374), No. 7 The Falcon and the Moon (00391) and Falcon Sunset.

DAVENPORT, Francine (pseud.) see TATE, Velma

DAVIS, Elizabeth (pseud.) see DAVIS, Lou Ellen

DAVIS, Gordon (pseud.) see HUNT, Howard

DAVIS, Julia
(F. Draco)

Born 7/23/04 in Clarksburg, West Virginia. B.A. from

Barnard College in 1922. Home: Princeton, N.J. Her career has always been that of author. She has written several books (listed in Contemporary Authors, Vol. 1-4, p. 233) only two of which seem to qualify here.

462. Cruise with Death, by F. Draco. New York: Rinehart, 1952. (NUC pre'56 148-340)

463. The Devil's Church (D), by F. Draco. New York: Rinehart, 1951; New York: Lancer (73-479), 1966. (NUC pre'56 148-341)

American Ginger, married to titled British Robert, learns upon the advent of their child of the family curse which claims the head of the house will die before seeing his heir. This story began with some promise but a very awkward plot rapidly heads the story down hill. It turns out to be a tedious little murder mystery with Gothic elements simply thrown in and left to dangle.

DAVIS, Lou Ellen 1936-
(Elizabeth Davis)

464. My Soul to Keep (B), by Elizabeth Davis. New York: Pyramid Books (X2251), 1970.

Tracy attends a seance and is warned regarding her fiancé. The next day he is found, victim of what appears to be a ritual hanging. A well written and very satisfying tale of modern day witchcraft and spiritual phenomena.

465. There Was an Old Woman, by Elizabeth Davis. Garden City, N.Y.: Doubleday (Crime Club), 1971. (NUC 1968-72 23-108)

Suspense story of a man kidnapped by a madwoman and found with the help of his wife's ESP. Not Gothic.

DAVIS, Mildred B.

Writer of stories of mystery and detection. Although a couple of paperback editions have been promoted as "Gothic," they are not.

DAVIS, Willo *see* ROBERTS, Willo Davis

DEAL, Borden 1922-
(Lee Borden)

The works of this author also appear to be mystery rather than Gothic.

DE FORREST, Betty

466. The Snows of Yesterday (D). New York: Ace (77425), 1973.
Begins in a promising way with Julie inheriting an old house and a fabulous antique collection including relics of Marie Antoinette. When a houseful of her aunt's supposed friends descend and take over the house for antique shops, things get out of hand for both Julie and the author. Too many sub-plots, never tied together or resolved. There are ghosts and voodoo but they get lost in the tangle. And too much verbiage--in one place it takes four pages of narrative to get Julie through a door!

DE LA MARE, Walter John 1873-1956

467. The Return. London: E. Arnold, 1910; New York: Putnam, 1911. (NUC pre'56 137-373)
Books like this one make me appreciate the authors who use some economy of prose. There is here a little tale of somewhat Gothic lineage--a dip into the supernatural--but one must eke it out from amidst a lot of excess verbal baggage. All very "cute"--and very boring.

DELMONICO, Andrea (pseud.) see MORRISON, A(twood) Eula

DENNISTON, Elinore
(Dennis Allan and Rae Foley)

Denniston has written forty or more mysteries, many of them starring detective-lawyer, Mr. Potter, and many of them romantically suspenseful, for example:

468. The Last Gamble, by Rae Foley. New York: Dodd, Mead, 1956; New York: Dell (4673), 1975. (NUC 1956-67 29-52)
A polished tale of mystery and detection. The format is essentially romantic suspense with an addition of a thoroughly lovely character, Mr. Potter, who reminded me of Lord Peter Wimsey. Mr. Potter directs the beautiful Blair Masters to a job with his old friend, Glen Forbes, who is trying to start a craft colony in a community where he is suspected of murdering his two former wives. Things are coming to a crisis when Mr. Potter steps in to find the solution. Not at all Gothic, but this author, like Patricia Wentworth, bridges the gap between detective fiction and romantic suspense.

DE PRÉ, Jean-Anne
(See also Michael Avallone)

469. A Sound of Dying Roses (D). New York: Popular Library, 1971. [© Michael Avallone].

The usual less than adequate fare. Made for the market and meager indeed.

470. Warlock's Woman (D). New York: Popular Library, 1973. [© Michael Avallone].
The height of something-or-other is achieved in this book when the author uses as section headings quotes from his own work, pseudonymous and otherwise. The depth of something-or-other reveals itself in slip-shod plotting, absurd and unbelievable characters and a stifling verbosity. There was the seed of a good idea in the beginning but it dies before germination.

DERING, Joan (Rosalind Cordelia) 1917-

Works appear to be primarily mystery and detection but one may be worth mention here.

471. Not Proven. London: Hodder & Stoughton, 1966.
Barzun & Taylor in their Catalogue of Crime say of this book: "Comments on her earlier books speak of their 'strong feminine appeal.' This is doubtless true, but the present book is not to be dismissed as feminine. The women in it are intelligent, courageous, and consecutive in their actions and feelings; the writing is first-rate and the plot (in the Jane Eyre category) is admirably put together, as is the solution of the antecedent murder."

DERLETH, August (William)
(Stephen Grendon, Tally Mason)

Born in Sauk City, Wisconsin in 1909. A writer and editor who has a huge output including Sac Prairie Sagas, poetry, Wisconsin Sagas, Judge Peck mysteries, Solar Pons stories (pastiches of Sherlock Holmes), Wisconsin history, biography, junior books (more than 21), and "supernatural" fiction. He is quoted in Contemporary Authors as saying: "In the overwhelming majority of my books I am primarily an entertainer, little more than the primitive story-teller who had a place at his tribal fire. I believe in communicating as simply and directly as possible, as freshly as I can, and am not interested in various literary 'isms'--though I keep up with everything from the avant-garde to the academicians--and I am not troubled at being out of the mainstream of contemporary American writing." Contemporary Authors. Vol. 1-4, pp. 243-4.

472. Dark Mind, Dark Heart: Horror Tales. Sauk City, Wisc.: Arkham, 1962. (NUC 1956-67 29-110)

473. The House of Moonlight. Iowa City: Prairie Press, 1953. (NUC pre'56 140-71).
A very short little vignette of Sac Prairie history. Nice, but not Gothic.

474. The Lurker at the Threshold. Sauk City, Wisc.: Arkham, 1945.

475. The Mask of Cthulhu. Sauk City, Wisc.: Arkham, 1958. (NUC 1956-67 29-111)

476. Not Long for This World, with H. P. Lovecraft. Sauk City, Wisc.: Arkham, 1948. (NUC pre'56 140-72)

477. Shadow of Night. New York: Scribners', 1943. (NUC pre'56 140-72)

A rather nice novel of a wrong to be righted and the irony of revenge, but not a Gothic.

478. Someone in the Dark. Sauk City, Wisc.: Arkham, 1941. (NUC pre'56 140-73)

479. Something Near. Sauk City, Wisc.: Arkham, 1945. (NUC pre'56 140-73)

480. The Survivor and Others. Sauk City, Wisc.: Arkham, 1957.

481. The Trail of Cthulhu. Sauk City, Wisc.: Arkham, 1962.

DERN, (Erolie) Peggy (Gladdis)
(Peggy Gaddis, Roberta Courtland, Georgia Crain, Gail Jordan, Carolina Lee, Perry Lindsay, Joan Sherman and Eileen Duggan)

Her works seem to be essentially romances. For anyone interested, the NUC lists 151 books prior to 1957 and 69 between 1956 and 1967. Most of her works are also listed in Contemporary Authors, Vol. 1-4, pp. 245-6.

DEVON, Nicola

482. House of Illusion (B). New York: Ace (34426), 1969.

Jacqueline goes to the isolated and notorious Retreat to spend a week with her long-lost aunt, the widow of a famous magician. Quite a lot happens in the bizarre household before her vacation terminates abruptly. The author has some good ideas and carries them through fairly well in an entertaining sentimental Gothic.

DE WEESE, Jean

483. The Carnelian Cat. New York: Ballantine, 1975.

484. Cave of the Moaning Wind (Zodiac Gothic Series). New York: Ballantine, 1976.

485. The Moonstone Spirit. New York: Ballantine, 1975.

486. The Reimann Curse. New York: Ballantine, 1975.

487. Web of Guilt, a Zodiac Gothic-Scorpio with horoscope by Sydney Omarr (F). New York: Ballantine (25258), 1976.

Somebody got the clever merchandising idea of doing a series of books based on horoscopes. This is one of them and, if representative, I wouldn't bother with the others. It is a tediously mundane little murder mystery. A young female college prof's cousin is pitched off a balcony. Who done it? Most interesting thing about this book was some previous reader's underlining 56 instances of the word "alright" throughout the text.

DICK, R. A. (pseud.) see LESLIE, Josephine Aimee Campbell

DICKENS, Monica (Enid) 1915-

From a large number of what appear to be general novels and romances only one book seems to belong here. Dickens is the great-granddaughter of Charles Dickens.

488. The Room Upstairs (B). Garden City, N.Y.: Doubleday, 1966. (NUC 1956-67 29-474)

The tale of an old lady in an old house and her struggle for independence in her final decline. Well written and highly perceptive. Gothic in mood and some plot elements.

DIETRICK, Robert (pseud.) see HUNT, Howard

DILLON, Dora Amy (Mrs. G. F.)
(Patricia Wentworth)

Dillon's works are more of the mystery-detective genre, although some also qualify as romantic suspense. More than 70 other works are listed in the LCPC, LCAC and LCC supplement. Most of Dillon's stories star Miss Silver, a genteel, middle-aged, amateur detective.

489. The Alington Inheritance (C), by Patricia Wentworth. Philadelphia: Lippincott, 1958. (NUC 1956-67 121-453)

An interesting combination of neo-Gothic and detective formulas. Jenny Hill discovers inadvertently that she is the rightful heir to the estate where she is serving as a governess. She flees in fear of her life. Her evil cousin tracks her down, plots to kill her, killing someone else by mistake. Miss Silver gets everything sorted out.

490. Through the Wall (C), by Patricia Wentworth. Philadelphia:

Lippincott, 1950. (LCAC 1948-52 23-91)

Another romantic suspense detective. Marion inherits a house, money and a bunch of perturbing relatives and gets involved in romance and murder. Miss Silver comes to the rescue.

DINESEN, Isak (pseud.) see BLIXEN, Karen

DISNEY, Doris Miles 1907-

Writer of mysteries and detective novels. Works, in general, do not appear to be either Gothic or romantic suspense.

DOBNER, Maeva Park
(Maeva Park)

Born 2/17/18 in Elmira, New York. Attended the Elmira schools and married Charles A. Dobner in 1951. They have two children and live in Rochester, New York.

491. The Gingerbread House. New York: Dell, 1974.

492. Heather. New York: Dell, 1970.

493. The Woman in the Maze (C), by Maeva Park. New York: Dell (9656), 1970.

American, Angela goes to her half-sibling's English manor to see if their mutual father might have left her anything when he died. While probing for her legacy she also acts as a catalyst in the solution of the three-year-old murder and, of course, falls in love. Routine and rather dull sentimental Gothic.

DODGE, Langdon (pseud.) see WOLFSON, Victor

DONAHUE, Marilyn Cram

494. Sutter's Sands (C). New York: Unibook, 1971.

Gothic adventure on an estate in the Florida Keys. Characters are a bit overdone and dead carcasses hanging around without smelling are a bit unbelievable but, all-in-all, a fair effort.

DORSET, Ruth (pseud.) see ROSS, William Edward Daniel

DOUGLAS, Laura W.

495. The Mystery of Arrowhead Hill (B). New York: Bouregy, 1963; New York: Airmont, 1964.

Virginia goes to a wealthy friend's home as maid-of-honor. Things seem amiss and "Gin" soon discovers a murder and a few rattling family skeletons. This book is a cut above the average, largely due to the author's sense of humor and facility with words. The genre is murder mystery, tending toward detection.

DOWDELL, Dorothy (Florence) Karns

Born 5/5/10 in Reno, Nevada. Elementary school teacher 1948-61. Full-time writer since 1961. Writings are all juveniles and young adult books before 1973. Also has written several non-fiction works with her husband.

496. Hawk over Hollyhedge Manor. New York: Avon Books (15040), 1973.

497. The House in Munich (D). New York: Avon Books, 1975.
Sigrid goes to Germany to go through the effects of her dead physicist uncle and finds several other people are very curious about what's to be found. Her life is threatened and eventually she unravels the whole thing, of course. A mundane tale of romantic suspense.

DRACO, F. (pseud.) see DAVIS, Julia

DREW, Patricia

498. Deep in a Dark Country (B). New York: Lancer (75-444), 1973. [© Lloyd S. Kaye, 1968].
A fast-paced, well written and plotted tale of Lynn Davis, who, on a trip to Europe with her boss, becomes involved in espionage. Very satisfying story of romantic suspense.

DU BREUIL, Lorinda

499. Evil, Evil. New York: Belmont-Tower (BT50515), 1973.

500. The Legend of Molly Moor. New York: Belmont-Tower (BT50601), 1973.

DUDLEY, Nancy (pseud.) see COLE, Lois Dwight

DUERRENMATT, Friedrich 1921-

Swiss-born author, primarily a playwright.

501. The Quarry (B). (transl. by Eva H. Morreale). Greenwich,

Conn.: Graphic Society, 1962. (NUC 1956-76 31-303)

This is not really Gothic but a profoundly compelling study of Evil from, so to speak, the other side of the literary coin from Gothic. I am fascinated by the comparison of this work with David Case's Fengriffin. Both deal with the Powers of Evil, both in moving and deeply disturbing ways, but their methods are strikingly different. I believe this tale is flawed by the ending which, though comforting, seems to me less honest than Case's.

DU MAURIER, [Dame] Daphne

Born 5/13/07 in London, England. Privately educated. Married Sir Frederick Arthur Montague Browning in 1932. They have three children. She has written several well known and widely read novels tending toward historical fiction rather than Gothic. The exceptions, real or supposed, include the following:

502. The Flight of the Falcon. Garden City, N.Y.: Doubleday, 1965; New York: Pocket Book (95023) 2nd ed. 1966. (NUC 1956-67 31-376)

The Pocket Book edition calls this "a new Gothic masterpiece." I failed to find justification for anything save the "new." Suspense of a mild degree and a murder mystery are the only remotely Gothic elements. A young Italian tour guide becomes slightly involved with the murder of an old derelict who reminds him of his childhood nanny. The incident causes him to drop everything and return to his home to see if the old woman is alive. Instead he finds his supposedly long-dead brother and a lot of emotional trouble. I found little to commend this book.

503. Jamaica Inn (B). Garden City, N.Y.: Doubleday, 1936. (NUC pre'56 151-395)

Mary gets involved in a smuggler's den in 19th-century Cornwall. Characters are two-dimensional and very very bad, but all-in-all, a fair tale with a good pace.

504. My Cousin Rachel. Garden City, N.Y.: Doubleday, 1952. (NUC pre'56 151-397)

505. Rebecca. Garden City, N.Y.: Doubleday, 1938. (NUC pre'56 515-397). National Book Award for 1938.

"A classic among Gothic tales, which sold over a million copies. [The manor described in the book is] Menabilly, a 70-room manor on the coast of Cornwall.... In 1943, fulfilling a childhood dream, she [du Maurier] and her husband actually moved into the supposedly haunted mansion which had been the setting for her novel." Contemporary Authors Vols. 5-6, p. 321.

I came to du Maurier as I once came to crème brulé--with high expectations--and my reaction has been the same. It's just pudding with a fancy name. Certainly not a bad dessert, but there are many better. This book does not fit my criteria for a Gothic. I would call it romantic suspense, at most. It is nicely written, of course, but a bit in love with itself--a tendency I find typical of du Maurier's work and not appealing.

DUNLOP, Agnes M. R.
(Elizabeth Kyle, Jan Ralston)

Born in Ayr, Scotland. Educated privately. Still lives in Ayr and has pursued a career as novelist and author of books for children. She has written a huge number of what sound like juvenile Gothics.

506. The Begonia Bed, by Elizabeth Kyle. Indianapolis: Bobbs-Merrill, 1934. (NUC pre'56 152-73)

507. Broken Glass, by Elizabeth Kyle. London: Davis, 1940. (NUC pre'56 152-73)

508. Conor Sands, by Elizabeth Kyle. London: Davis, 1952. (NUC pre'56 152-73)

509. Douce, by Elizabeth Kyle. London: Davies, 1950. (NUC pre'56 152-73)

510. The Heron Tree, by Elizabeth Kyle. London: Davies, 1973. (NUC 1974 5-247)

511. Love Is for the Living (D), by Elizabeth Kyle. New York: Holt, Rinehart & Winston, 1967. (NUC 1956-67 31-436)

A tedious little romantic suspense about Anne who travels to Bruges to look up an old acquaintance. There's supposed to be some mystery surrounding their WWII romance and Anne is curious. One gets dribblets of suspense plot mixed through tons of travelog, inane conversation and irrelevant characters. Ho hum.

512. Mally Lee, by Elizabeth Kyle. Garden City, N.Y.: Doubleday (Crime Club), 1947. (NUC pre'56 152-73)

513. Mirror Dance, by Elizabeth Kyle. London: Davies, 1970; New York: Holt, Rinehart & Winston, 1970. (NUC 1968-72 26-59)

514. The Mirrors of Versaille, by Elizabeth Kyle. London: Constable, 1939.

515. Orangefield, by Elizabeth Kyle. London: Constable, 1938. (NUC pre'56 152-74)

516. The Pleasure Dome, by Elizabeth Kyle. London: Davies, 1943. (NUC pre'56 152-74)

517. Queen's Evidence, by Elizabeth Kyle. London: Davies, 1969. (NUC 1968-72 26-59)

518. The Regent's Candlestick, by Elizabeth Kyle. London: Davies, 1954. (NUC pre'56 152-74)

519. Return to Alcazar, by Elizabeth Kyle. London: Davies, 1962. (NUC 1956-67 31-436)

520. The Scent of Danger, by Elizabeth Kyle. London: Davies, 1971; New York: Holt, Rinehart, 1972. (NUC 1968-72 26-59)

521. The Silver Pineapple (B), by Elizabeth Kyle. London: Davies, 1972. (NUC 1973 4-512)

Kilmeny becomes involved in an intrigue because of her knowledge of a unique silver cup and its relation to a possible conspiracy to defraud. Somewhat better than average romantic suspense.

522. The Stilt Walkers. London: Heinemann, 1972.

523. The Tontine Belle, by Elizabeth Kyle. London: Davies, 1951. (NUC pre'56 152-74)

524. The White Lady, by Elizabeth Kyle. London: Davies, 1941. (NUC pre'56 152-74)

DUNSANY, [Lord] Edward John Moreton Drax Plunkett 1878-1957

525. The Fourth Book of Jorkens. Sauk City, Wisc.: Arkham, 1948. (NUC pre'56 152-197)

DU VAUL, Virginia C. (pseud.) see COFFMAN, Virginia

DWYER, Deanna

526. Legacy of Terror (C). New York: Lancer, 1971.

A Gothic tale set in Pittsburgh, of all places. Flawed mainly by unnursely comments by the nurse-heroine, e.g., "medical science frowns a little on psychiatry" (p. 138) and "She found that this was not unlike talking to a patient who knew he was going to die. It was merely acting, stringing together cautious lies" (p. 179). Outrageous--at least to this nurse. A story of madness, murder and possession.

Other works published by Lancer include: Children of the Storm, The Dark Summer and The Demon Child.

EATOCK, Marjorie

527. The Ivory Tower (B). New York: Curtis Books (09128), [1972].

Jan falls heir to a vast estate after severe personal tragedy. She finds herself embroiled in mystery, conspiracy and family strife. A well written and cleverly plotted tale.

EBY, Lois Christine
(John Chester Fleming, Patrick Lawson)

528. Nurse on Nightmare Island (B). New York: Lancer, 1966.
A dumb title that doesn't do justice to a well written and suspenseful tale. Helen surmised from letters that her former patient, Dr. Jenkins, was on the verge of a relapse and went to Morago Island where he was convalescing. She becomes involved in a tangled web of intrigue.

EDEN, Dorothy Enid
(Mary Paradise)

Was born in 1912 and spent her childhood on a farm in New Zealand. Education was sketchy and completed by a secretarial course which took her into a legal office, first in the small market town of Ashburton in the heart of the Plains, and then to the city of Christchurch where she spent some years, working as a law clerk until the end of the War. By that time her hobby of writing was profitable enough to make it a full-time job, which it has been ever since. She now lives in London. (Information from Ace edition of Lady of Mallow.)

529. Afternoon for Lizards. London: Hodder & Stoughton, 1961. (NUC 1956-67 32-302)

530. Afternoon Walk. London: Hodder & Stoughton, 1971. (NUC 1968-72 26-455)

531. Bella. London: Hodder & Stoughton, 1964. (NUC 1956-67 32-302)

532. The Bird in the Chimney. London: Hodder & Stoughton, 1963. (NUC 1956-67 32-302)

533. Bride by Candlelight. London: Macdonald, 1954. (NUC pre'56 155-410)

534. Bridge of Fear. New York: Ace (07974), 1972.

535. The Brooding Lake. New York: Ace, 1953. Also pub. as: Lamb to the Slaughter.

536. Cat's Prey (C). New York: Ace (09255), 1970.
Antonia travels to New Zealand to attend the wedding of a long-lost cousin Simon and check on a recent inheritance. Possible attempts on her life and other disconcerting happenings build to the

inevitable conclusion that something is wrong. A skilled author manages to make a modestly enjoyable story out of what is, for me, a very tired plot formula. Romantic suspense.

537. Crow Hollow. New York: Ace (12354), 1972.

538. Darkwater. New York: Coward-McCann, 1964. (NUC 1956-67 32-302)

539. Darling Clementine (C). London: Macdonald, 1955; in U.S. pub. as: Night of the Letter. New York: Ace, 1955. (NUC pre'56 155-410)

Evil comes into the happy lives of Bridget and Fergus with the arrival of mother's helper, Prissie. Bridget's crazy family and their antics help to liven up a tale which gets off to a slow start. Essentially a mystery-suspense.

540. The Daughters of Ardmore Hall. New York: Ace (13883), 1972.

541. The Deadly Travelers. New York: Ace (14184), 1975.

542. Death Is a Red Rose (D). London: Macdonald, 1956; New York: Ace, 1970. (NUC 1956-67 32-302)

Fate brings Cressida to Arabia's house to take the place of her dead and mourned daughter. Frightening events ensue and C's life is threatened. Outcome of the plot is evident early in the story. Inferior romantic suspense.

543. Face of an Angel, by Mary Paradise. New York: Ace (G593), n.d.

544. Lady of Mallow (B). New York: Coward-McCann, 1962; New York: Ace (K171), [1960]. (NUC 1956-67 32-302)

Sarah and Ambrose plan to expose as a fraud the recently returned heir of Mallow, who arrived just in time to prevent Ambrose from inheriting by default. Sarah becomes a governess in the Mallow household and hopes to find evidence of fraud. Things don't work out as she expects.

545. The Laughing Ghost. New York: Ace (47404), 1972.

546. Listen to Danger. New York: Ace (48476), 1957. Romantic suspense.

547. The Marriage Chest. London & N.Y.: Coward-McCann, 1966; Greenwich, Conn.: Fawcett, n.d. (NUC 1956-67 32-302)

548. Melbury Square. New York: Coward-McCann, 1970. (NUC 1968-72 26-455)

549. The Millionaire's Daughter. Greenwich, Conn.: Fawcett-

Crest, 1975.
Not Gothic.

550. Never Call It Loving. London: Hodder & Stoughton, 1966; Greenwich, Conn.: Fawcett, 1974. (NUC 1956-67 32-302)
Historical novel based on the lives of Katherine O'Shea and Charles Stewart Parnell.

551. The Pretty Ones. London: Macdonald, 1957. (NUC 1956-67 32-302)

552. Ravenscroft. New York: Coward-McCann, 1965; Greenwich, Conn.: Fawcett, 1966. (NUC 1956-67 32-302)

553. Samantha. London: Hodder & Stoughton, 1960. (NUC 1956-67 32-302)

554. Shadow of a Witch, by Mary Paradise. New York: Ace (G578), 1972.

555. The Shadow Wife. New York: Coward-McCann, 1968. (NUC 1968-72 26-455)

556. Siege in the Sun, by Mary Paradise. New York: Coward-McCann, 1967. (NUC 1956-67 32-302)

557. Sleep in the Woods. New York: Coward-McCann, 1961. (NUC 1956-67 32-302)

558. The Sleeping Bride (D). London: Macdonald, 1959; New York: Ace (77122), n.d. (NUC 1956-67 32-302)
A tedious romantic suspense.

559. Speak to Me of Love. New York: Coward-McCann, 1972. (NUC 1968-72 26-455)

560. The Vines of Yarrabee. New York: Coward-McCann, 1969. (NUC 1968-72 26-455)

561. Waiting for Willa. New York: Coward-McCann, 1970. (NUC 1968-72 26-455)

562. Whistle for the Crows (C). London: Hodder & Stoughton, 1962; New York: Ace (88555), 1962. (NUC 1956-67 32-302)
This tale starts off with promise as Cathleen travels to Ireland to work as a secretary for the aging and eccentric Matilda O'Riordan. When Cathleen begins prying into the affairs of the family, the author's only logical course would have been to have the girl fired. Instead, she is kept on and continues to pry and a dull tale of family intrigue unfolds. The two handsome O'Riordan brothers pursue Cathleen. One of them may be doing very bad things. It all winds down to a predictable conclusion.

563. Winterwood. New York: Coward-McCann, 1967. (NUC 1956-67 32-302)

564. Yellow Is for Fear. New York: Ace (94392), 1972.

EDGAR, Josephine (pseud.) see MUSSI, Mary [Edgar]

EDWARDS, Anne (Josephson)

Born 8/20/27 in Portchester, New York. Attended the University of California, Los Angeles and Southern Methodist University. Home is in New York although she lived in Europe for 16 years. Has written scripts for TV and screen plays, children's books and popular biographies.

565. Child of Night. New York: Random House, 1975.

566. Haunted Summer (B). New York: Coward-McCann, 1972; New York: Bantam (7825), n.d. (NUC 1968-72 26-530)
An unusual tale. A true historical Gothic based on the period of her life when Mary Shelley conceived the idea for Frankenstein. Although quite well written and having some very thought-provoking passages, I find myself troubled with this type of fiction on two counts: 1) I deeply felt the need for guidelines to help me know the place where fact and fiction diverged; and 2) I kept having guilty twinges of a sense of gossipy voyeurism. I am hypersensitive and know many will enjoy this book greatly.

567. The Hesitant Heart. New York: Random House, 1973.

568. Miklos Alexandrovitch Is Missing. New York: Coward-McCann, 1970. (NUC 1968-72 26-530)

569. Shadow of a Lion. New York: Coward, McCann & Geoghegan, 1971. (NUC 1968-72 26-530)
Novel about Hollywood blacklisting during the 50's. Not Gothic.

570. The Survivors. New York: Holt, Rinehart & Winston, 1968. (NUC 1968-72 26-530)

ELGIN, Mary

571. A Man from the Mist (B). New York: M. S. Mill, 1965; New York: Bantam (7548), 1966; pub. in Eng. as: Visibility Nil. (NUC 1956-67 33-114)
Except for token items of location and mood, this is not a Gothic but a fairly entertaining love story. One waits patiently for suspense which never develops. I liked this book.

572. Return to Glenshael: A Masquerade. London: Hodder &

Stoughton, 1965; in U.S. pub. as: Highland Masquerade. New York: M. S. Mill, 1966; New York: Bantam (8346), 1973. (NUC 1956-67 33-114)

573. The Woods and the Trees. New York: M. S. Mill, 1967. (NUC 1956-67 33-114)

ELIOT, Anne (pseud.) see COLE, Lois Dwight

ELLIN, Stanley (Bernard) 1916-

Works are, for the most part, mystery-detective. The Valentine Estate (New York: Random House, 1968) might be of interest to some as a romantic suspense from a male perspective and with a male main character. It makes an interesting comparison with tales of mariage de raison written from the female perspective.

ELSNA, Hebe (pseud.) see ANSLE, Dorothy Phoebe

ENGLISH, Jean

574. Dark Moonshine. New York: Ballantine, 1974.

575. The Devices of Darkness. Garden City, N.Y.: Doubleday, 1976.

576. The Scarlet Tower. New York: Ballantine, n.d.

ERSKINE, Margaret (pseud.) see WILLIAMS, Wetherby (Margaret)

ESMOND, Harriet

577. Darsham's Tower (B). New York: Delacorte Press, 1973. (NUC 1973 4-788)

Kate is hired to be a companion to Verena Darsham of the aristocratic family owning a tower home in the English village of Senwich. A skillfully written tale but the sea adds most of the excitement.

ESSEX, Mary (pseud.) see BLOOM, Ursula

EVANS, Cicely Louise

578. Nemesis Wife (A). Garden City, N.Y.: Doubleday, 1970.

(NUC 1968-72 28-260)

Well now, this is probably not a Gothic. On the other hand, it could be thought of as an all-grown-up sentimental Gothic. Whatever, it is a fine and engrossing tale, poetically written with a heroine who takes top honors for assertiveness, a heroic quality not often gracing female characters.

579. The Newel Post. Garden City, N.Y.: Doubleday, 1967. (NUC 1956-67 34-311)

EVANS, Elaine

580. Black Autumn (F). New York: Lancer, 1973.

One of the worst of the species. The bare bones of a plot are present. The rest appears to have been thrown together by the proverbial group of monkeys at typewriters. The dialogue is absurd, the characters no more than names and the story absolutely vacant.

581. A Dark and Deadly Love (D). New York: Lancer (75-403), 1972.

"In a remote valley, haunted by Indian legends, Charlotte follows the trail of family hatreds and ransomed love." Very dull plot and a dumb heroine.

582. Shadowland (F). New York: Lancer (74-705), [1970].

A trivial and poor show due to completely bizarre and unbelievable characters surrounding a nit wit heroine. Caroline is persuaded, by the most meager reasons, to drop everything and move to the Florida plantation of Shadowland to do some unspecified jobs for the fabulously wealthy Baxter Marr.

EVERETT, Gail (pseud.) see HALE, Arlene

EYRE, Katherine Wigmore

Has written several juveniles and historical novels in addition to works listed below.

583. The Chinese Box. New York: Appleton-Century, 1959. (NUC 1956-67 34-426)

584. The Lute and the Glove (C). New York: Appleton-Century, 1955; New York: Ace, [1955]. (NUC pre'56 165-42)

Anne falls heir to an English manor house that has long captivated her imagination. She moves there and becomes haunted by the neglected grave of "A.C."--evidently a 16th-century ancestor. Flawed by a maddeningly slow pace but otherwise an entertaining Gothic.

585. Monk's Court; A Novel. New York: Appleton-Century, 1966. (NUC 1956-67 34-426)

586. The Sandlewood Fan; A Novel of Suspense. New York: Meredith, 1968. (NUC 1968-72 28-369)

EYRE, Marie

587. Eyrie of the Fox. New York: Popular Library, n.d.

588. Return to Gravesend (B). New York: Popular Library (00373), 1972.

Fairly standard southern U.S. Gothic with a couple of innovative wrinkles. Molly is brought from her home in Kansas, with her Osage Indian step-brother, to take over the Louisiana plantation which has come to her by inheritance. The author's inclusion of racial issues, including prejudice against Indians, is interesting. Her phonetic spelling of the southern accents of all the characters made for hard reading.

FABIAN, Ruth

589. A Scent of Violets. New York: Popular Library (00600), 1974.

FALCON, Mary Lee

590. The Dungeon (C). New York: Belmont-Tower (BT50216), 1972; New York: Modern Promotions (A Unibook), n.d. and no copyright.

Cathy inherits a real castle on an island somewhere in the U.S. and of course goes there to take over and finds some mysterious goings on. This is certainly not the worst of its type, which is surprising in view of its publishing pedigree. Not too bad a plot and the characters have some depth.

FARMER, Patricia

591. The Legend of Piper's Hole (C). New York: Popular Library, 1973, [Maureen Lines].

There was sufficient action and the author aroused sufficient curiosity to keep me reading this tale of a young girl's adventures on the Iles of Scilly, but the book was not really very good. The plot is hypermelodramatic and the characters shallow, with several of them being introduced and left dangling. An essentially juvenile romantic suspense.

FARNSWORTH, Mona

592. The Great Stone Heart (F). New York: Pinnacle Books, 1971.

This book appears to have a plot borrowed from Dorothy Sayers' The Abominable History of the Man with Copper Fingers. I strongly suspect a hoax. The basic theme is closely allied to Sayers' story and the hero's name is even Lord Peter. The plot is absurd and full of inconsistencies. The characters are shallow and unreal. Altogether a wretched book and I can't believe a sincere one.

FARR, Caroline

593. Castle of Terror. New York: New American Library (Signet Q6653), 1965.

594. Chateau of Wolves. New York: New American Library (Signet Y6882), 1976.

595. Dark Citadel (C). New York: New American Library (Signet Y6818), 1971.

A very run-of-the-mill tale that is a murder mystery with a neo-Gothic setting. Ann goes to St. Croix to visit a handsome author. A murder is committed. Who done it?

596. Dark Mansion. New York: New American Library (Signet Q5802), 1974.

597. Granite Folly (C). New York: New American Library, 1967; Sydney: Horwitz, 1967.

The author had such a great setting in this story and, for my taste, really didn't make use of it. Gail goes to check on a castle she owns but she shows very little interest in it. A shallow tale.

598. House of Dark Illusions. New York: New American Library (Signet T5579), 1973.

599. House of Secrets. New York: New American Library (Signet T5368), 1973.

600. House of Tombs. New York: New American Library (Signet T5770), 1973.

601. The House on the Cliffs. New York: New American Library (Signet Q6157), 1974.

602. Mansion Malevolent. New York: New American Library (Signet Q6039), n.d.

603. Mansion of Evil. New York: New American Library (Signet Q6704), 1971.

604. Mansion of Menace (F). New York: New American Library (Signet Y7037), 1976.

Irene goes to a Caribbean Island to study art from Jean-Pierre Haver, a famous surrealist painter. There she finds intrigue and romance--of course. A very contrived plot and a very superficial effort in every respect.

605. Mansion of Peril. New York: New American Library (Signet Q6328), 1975.

606. The Scream in the Storm. New York: New American Library (Signet Y6762), 1975.

607. Secret of the Chateau. New York: New American Library (Signet P5334), 1973.

608. Terror on Duncan Island. New York: New American Library (Signet T5947), 1974.

609. The Towers of Fear. New York: New American Library (Signet Y7001), 1972.

610. Villa of Shadows. London, etc.: Horwitz, 1966. (NUC 1956-67 35-114)

611. Web of Horror. London, etc.: Horwitz, 1966. (NUC 1956-67 35-114)

612. Witches' Hammer (C). New York: New American Library (Signet P3135), 1967.

Samantha, an aspiring writer, is assigned to ghost a biography of Peter Castellano, a dazzling movie hero who has become a recluse in his family castle in Maine. Not a bad story at all but very short. Farr gets a lot of action in a few words.

FARRANT, Sarah

613. The Lady of Chantry Glades (C). New York: Ballantine, 1974.

A fairly entertaining tale of romantic suspense with an historical setting. Not really Gothic.

Other works published by Ballantine include: Lady of Winston Park, Lady of Monkswood Manor and Lady of Drawbridge Court.

FARRELL, David (pseud.) see SMITH, Frederick E(screet)

FAULKNER, Anne Irvin
(Nancy Faulkner)

Born 1/8/06 in Lynchburg, Virginia. Received a B.S. from Wellesley College in 1928 and an M.A. from Cornell in 1933. Her home is in New York City and her career has been that of college teacher, editor and author. She has written many children's books and "juvenile Gothics."

614. The Jade Box (D). New York: Popular Library (00610), [1974].
A very slow-paced tale about sculptress Molly who inherits a great old house and becomes involved in a conspiracy concerning an old box mentioned by her grandfather on his deathbed. It gets to the point that one doesn't really care what happens and the resolution of the plot justifies such a sentiment. A very tame tale of romantic suspense.

FAULKNER, Nancy (pseud.) see FAULKNER, Anne Irvin

FECHER, Constance see HEAVEN, Constance (Fecher)

FERM, Betty

615. Edge of Beauty. New York: Dell (3199), 1974.
Very nice quote from Virginia Woolf is the title source for this fast-paced and fairly entertaining murder mystery set in a large and prestigious N.Y.C. cosmetics firm. Not Gothic.

616. The Vengeance of Valdone (B). New York: Dell (9502), 1973.
A nicely written romantic suspense about Laura who goes to France in hopes of vindicating her father who was accused of being a traitor during WWII.

FERRAND, Georgia

617. Dangerous Inheritance. New York: Ballantine, 1974.

618. House of Glass. New York: Ballantine, 1975.

FERRARS, Elizabeth X. (pseud.) see BROWN, Morna Doris

FIEDLER, Jean (Feldman)

Born in Pittsburgh, Pennsylvania and attended the University of Pittsburgh. Married Harold Fiedler (a painter) in 1949 and has two children. She has had a varied career as social worker, high school teacher, copywriter, librarian, free-lance writer and teacher of creative writing. In addition to Atone with Evil, she has written 19 children's books. She is currently living in New York.

619. Atone with Evil (F). New York: Bantam (02216), 1976.
One of many labeled "Gothic" by the publisher but which fits none of my criteria. Shana goes to Mexico to find out the details of her husband's mysterious death. The plot is basically dull and almost smothered in extraneous occurrences. The characters are numerous and mostly irrelevant. Romantic suspense of a very poor quality.

FIELD, Medora see PERKERSON, Medora (Field)

FINLAY, Fiona (pseud.) see STUART, Vivian

FINLEY, Glenna see WITTE, Glenna Finley

FITZ, Jean De Witt

Born 2/12/12 in Oak Park, Illinois. Received an A.B. from Skidmore College in 1933. She is the wife of photographer Morgan Fitz and had a career as an English teacher, director of a college bookstore, book reviewer and editor before beginning to free-lance in 1945. Her home is in Augusta, Georgia.

620. The Devon Maze (B). Los Altos, Calif.: Geron-X, 1969; New York: Pyramid (T2493), 1971. (NUC 1968-72 30-50)
Anne marries her childhood sweetheart and neighbor, Ron Devon, heir to Devon House, one of the last Great Southern Mansions. On her wedding day she sees someone push Ron's invalid father into the lake where he is drowned and her dreams turn into a nightmare of suspicion and misunderstandings. A nicely wrought tale of romantic suspense.

621. The Viper's Bite. Los Altos, Calif.: Geron-X, 1969. (NUC 1968-72 30-50)

FITZGERALD, Arlene J. (Daily)
(Monica Heath)

Born in Orleans, Nebraska. Attended Southern Oregon College. She is married to Ralph L. Fitzgerald and has three children. Their home is in Gold Hill, Oregon. In addition to the works listed here, Fitzgerald has written seven or more nurse stories.

622. Chateau of Shadows (F), by Monica Heath. New York: New American Library, 1973.
Marva takes nine-year-old Mark for a vacation at Chateau Lodge where his mother had died three years before, an untenable plot idea to begin with. This is romantic suspense at a juvenile level, at best. The characters are shallow and the suspense is awkwardly contrived.

623. Dunleary, by Monica Heath. New York: New American Library (Signet T5614), 1967, 1973.

624. Falconlough, by Monica Heath. New York: New American Library, 1966.

625. House of Tragedy. New York: Manor Books, 1973.

626. Pamela's Palace (D). New York: Manor Books, 1975.
This author has some imaginative variations on the girl-in-quest-of-a-lost-heritage-in-an-old-mansion theme, but poor characterizations and utter predictability of the basic plot are sufficiently damaging to make this a less than average tale.

627. The Secret Citadel (D), by Monica Heath. New York: New American Library (Signet Q6266), 1975.
Chris goes to the N. W. Coast to learn more about the sudden and suspicious death of her archaeologist father. She stays with the Hunnicutt family who seem mysteriously dominated by the dead Kyle Hunnicutt and his lover, an Indian princess, also long dead. This plot had some possibilities but they were missed by the author whose main effort seemed to be hyperdramatic prose, forced and corny action and getting through with the story.

628. Secrets Can Be Fatal, by Monica Heath. New York: New American Library, 1967.

FLEMING, Jane

629. Hawthorne Wood (C). New York: Berkley, 1975. [© Steve Smith].
This story has some pleasant twists on the usual Southern American Gothic theme. Alice emigrates from Scotland to Louisiana as an indentured servant. Her year with the Perkins family involves her in drama, adventure and romance. A fairly well told tale.

FLEMING, John Chester see EBY, Lois Christine

FLETCHER, Dorothy

630. Farewell to Vienna. New York: Lancer, 1970.

631. House of Hate. New York: Lancer, 1967.

632. The Late Contessa. New York: Lancer, 1971.

633. Meeting in Madrid. New York: Lancer (74-713), n. d.

634. The Music Master (B). New York: Lancer, 1971.

This strays from the traditional Gothic themes but is a well told little tale of suspense, nonetheless. I liked Fletcher's characters, including the heroine, and the descriptions of Florence, Italy are interesting and well integrated into the story.

FLETCHER, Mary Mann

635. The House Called Whispering Winds. New York: Ballantine, 1974.

FOLEY, Rae (pseud.) see DENNISTON, Elinore

FORBES, DeLoris (Florine) Stanton
(De Forbes, Stanton Forbes; Forbes Rydell, joint pseudonym with Helen B. Rydell; Tobias Wells)

Born 7/10/23 in Kansas City, Missouri. Attended schools in Kansas. Home is in Wellesley, Massachusetts. Her career has been as assistant editor for the Wellesley Townsman, and a writer of mystery novels. With Helen B. Rydell, under a joint pseudonym of Forbes Rydell, wrote several mysteries. All in all, has written over 30 books, exemplified by:

636. The Terrors of the Earth. Garden City, N.Y.: Doubleday, 1964; in Eng. pub. as: The Long Hate (London: Hale, 1966) and reissued in U.S. as: Melody of Terror. New York: Pyramid, 1967. (NUC 1956-67 37-195)

Pyramid calls this a Gothic but to me it is a murder mystery. Recently widowed Claudia receives threatening anonymous letters leading to murder and harrowing experiences. A particularly sensitive characterization of the widow-heroine.

637. Welcome, My Dear, to Belfry House (C), by Stanton Forbes. Garden City, N.Y.: Doubleday, 1973. (NUC 1973 5-84)

Cheryl Harris comes to Belfry House, an aging Victorian manor on Cape Cod, to find out why her grandmother, a famous movie star, abandoned her as a baby. Belfry House and its bizarre inhabitants provide a "Gothic" setting for further developments. A skillfully written tale in most respects.

FORBES, Stanton see FORBES, DeLoris

FORD, Elbur (pseud.) see HIBBERT, Eleanor

FORD, Leslie (pseud.) see BROWN, Mrs. Zenith

FORREST, Wilma

638. Shadow Mansion. Greenwich, Conn.: Fawcett-Crest, 1969.
This is a weird little piece ... probably as close to a "real" Gothic as is to be found. Melodrama is intense and the characters are all mad as hatters. Madi is transferred from debtor's prison in the post Civil War South to a child care job in a former insane asylum and prisoner of war camp. The owner of the place, his family and staff populate the tale. Not a story for the squeamish or highly refined--or maybe even for the totally sane. It is a thing unto itself.

FOSTER, Iris (pseud.) see POSNER, Richard

FOX, David (pseud.) see OSTRANDER, Isabel Egenton

FOX, Gardner F.
(Jefferson Cooper; see also Lina Cooper)

Wrote numerous exotic adventures, listed in the NUC pre'56, Vol. 179 pp. 58ff.

639. Kothar-Barbarian Swordsman. New York: Nordon (Leisure Books 146SK).
"In a strange and terrifying world before--or beyond time, Kothar the Barbarian Swordsman has to fight against sorcerers, dragons, witches and incredible monsters" (paperback blurb).

640. Kothar and the Demon Queen. New York: Nordon (Leisure Books 147SK).
"The mighty barbarian swordsman sets out to destroy his most deadly adversary--a beautiful sorceress with all the Powers of Darkness at her command" (paperback blurb).

FRAME, Patricia (pseud.) see WETHERELL, June Pat

FRANKAU (Dill), (Sidney) Pamela 1908-1967
(Eliot Naylor)

Evidently a fine, and certainly a prolific, writer of stories of mystery and suspense. In general, none appear to be Gothic.

641. Road Through the Woods. Garden City, N.Y.: Doubleday, 1961. (NUC 1956-67 38-83)
Not really a Gothic or romantic suspense but it bears a fey quality that might enchant other lovers of the Gothic as it did me. A young man finds himself in Drumnair, Ireland, a victim of

amnesia and compelled by tantalizing recollections of the town and the inhabitants of its manor. A well told tale worth reading.

FREDERICKS, Harriet

642. The Dream Hunter. New York: Ballantine, 1974.

FROME, David (pseud.) see BROWN, Zenith

FURNESS, Audrey

643. House of Menace (C). New York: Paperback Library, 1966. (Orig. pub. as: Letter to a Ghost.)

Pippa Kent goes through a lot to trace a letter she finds in a secondhand desk. A fairly suspenseful tale, though coincidences abound. The original title is much more appropriate.

GADDIS, Peggy see DERN, Peggy Gaddis

GALE, Adela

644. Angel Among Witches. New York: New American Library (Signet T3989), n.d.

645. Harvest of Terror (C). New York: New American Library (Signet P4044), 1969.

Nurse Terry accompanies convalescing patient Denise to the family castle on Majorca. They encounter a strange household and murder. The promise of Gothic elements in the first couple of chapters is never fulfilled. Not bad, but not Gothic.

GALLICO, Paul (William)

Born in New York City in 1897, educated at Columbia University and married four times. Became a free-lance writer about 1936 and wrote many magazine serials, novels of great variety, screen plays and so on before his death in 1955.

646. The Hand of Mary Constable. Garden City, N.Y.: Doubleday, 1964. (NUC 1956-67 39-321)

647. Too Many Ghosts (C). Garden City, N.Y.: Doubleday, 1959. (NUC 1956-67 39-321). This is an expanded version of a serial published by the Saturday Evening Post in 1959.

"Ghost-chaser," Alexander Hero is summoned to Paradine Manor following a series of alarming manifestations. He subsequently and almost omnisciently, reveals the human sources behind the happenings. I didn't like this book. The hero, Hero, was just too too bright and wonderful. Explained ghosts are, to me, a frightful bore. The book is probably a second cousin twice removed to a Gothic.

GARRATT, Marie

648. Dangerous Enchantment. New York: Ace (K245), 1964. (Original title: And Then Look Down.)
A very routine mystery-romance. Not Gothic.

649. Festival of Darkness. New York: Ace (G583), 1975.

GELLIS, Roberta

650. Sing Witch, Sing Death (C). New York: Bantam, 1975.
A dull and predictable sentimental Gothic featuring a heroine admirable in her external individuality but crippled by her internal mediocrity.

GEORGE, Oliver (pseud.) *see* OLIVER, George

GEUMLEK, Lois

651. House in the Fog. New York: Avon (18242), 1974.

GIBBS, Mary Ann

652. The House of Ravensbourne. New York: Pyramid Books, 1965; first published in 1964 as: The Amateur Governess. (NUC 1956-67 41-370)
Historical romance. Not Gothic.

GILBERT, Anthony (pseud.) *see* MALLESON, Lucy Beatrice

GILMER, Ann (pseud.) *see* ROSS, William Edward Daniel

GOFF, Georgena

653. The Black Dog (D). New York: Belmont-Tower (50299), 1972.
A tale that reminded me of many written in the early 20th century, principally for its plot elements (the charlatan of the occult, bizarre happenings and naiveté of viewpoint). It would take a great deal more skill than this author showed to pull this one off. As it is, it seems to be an adolescent Gothic melodrama.

GOLDING, Morton (Jay)
(Stephanie Lloyd, Jay Martin, M. M. Michaeles, Patricia Morton)

Born 7/24/25 in New York City. Received a B. S. from the University of Denver 1949; M. A. 1950; graduate study at New York University. He lives in Bronx, New York and his career has been that of freelance writer since 1957. His Jay Martin books appear to be popular pornography and love stories. Also writes war and adventure books.

654. Caves of Fear, by Patricia Morton. New York: Lancer, 1968.

655. Child of Value, by Patricia Morton. New York: Lancer, 1966.

656. Destiny's Child, by Patricia Morton. New York: Belmont, 1967.

657. A Gathering of Moondust (D), by Patricia Morton. New York: Lancer, 1965.

I guess all the ingredients for a Gothic are here but this author managed to combine them in a singularly uninteresting manner. The story is packed with extraneous and dull characters and narrative and is, all-in-all, a failure.

658. Graveswood (D), by Stephanie Lloyd. New York: Paperback Library, 1966.

An indifferently written tale whose principal action takes place in the mind of the heroine. With a dull-minded heroine, the result is as expected.

659. In the Province of Darkness, by Patricia Morton. New York: Banner Books, 1967.

GORDON, Ethel Edison

Born 5/5/15 in New York. Received a B. A. (cum laude) from New York University in 1936. Married to Heyman Gordon. Her career has always been that of writer.

660. The Birdwatcher (B). New York: McKay, 1974. (NUC 1974 6-790)

Lisette, working at a top security job in N. Y. C., meets double tragedy in the death of her fiancé and the loss of top secret notes for which she was responsible. She goes to the Shetland Islands to be with a cousin and encounters romance and intrigue. A well told tale of romantic suspense.

661. The Chaperone (C). New York: Coward, McCann & Geoghegan, 1972. (NUC 1973 5-681)

Carrie, a 28-year-old art teacher at an exclusive N. Y. girls' school, accepts a summer job to accompany heiress Maria to France to visit a boy friend. Intrigue and romance ensue. Not much of a plot--another dope ring and all that--but well written.

662. The Freebody Heiress. New York: McKay, 1975.

663. Freer's Cove. New York: Coward, McCann & Geoghegan, 1972. (NUC 1968-72 35-259)

GORDON, Jane
(Pseud. for Peggy Leigh Graves and not the same as Jane Gordon, novelist, listed below.)

GORDON, Jane (novelist)

664. Mistress of Mount Fair. New York: Lancer (72-791), n.d.

665. Season of Evil (A). Sydney, etc.: Horwitz, 1966; New York: Lancer (72-784), 1965. (NUC 1956-67 43-140)
A fine and gripping story of romantic suspense grossly misrepresented by the paperback cover. A tight plot, a delightful heroine and a touch of wit ice the cake.

GRACE, Alicia

666. Hawkbill Manor (B). New York: Lancer, 1967.
A well turned tale with a setting in Antigua. Flawed by a couple of loose ends, a too rapid conclusion and a degree of carnality unusual in this type of literature. Too bad, it could have been excellent.

667. Mass for a Dead Witch. New York: Manor, 1976.

668. Wharf Sinister. New York: Lancer (74-765), n.d.

GRAHAM, Victoria

669. The Witchstone. New York: Pyramid Books, 1974. (NUC 1974 6-852)

GRAHAM, Winston (Mawdsley)

Born 6/30/10 in Victoria Park, Manchester, England. Home is in Sussex, England. Career: full-time writer. Graham's books have been translated into 15 languages and films have been made out of at least seven of them, the best known being Marnie, filmed by Alfred Hitchcock in 1964. Others might know him from the historical series Poldark set in Cornwall. His works tend toward adventure and suspense rather than Gothic.

670. Fortune Is a Woman. Garden City, N.Y.: Doubleday, 1953. (NUC pre'56 209-551)
A novel about a man who because of the war, finds himself transformed from a tramp to an insurance claims adjustor. In this position he finds romance, conspiracy and intrigue. This is a male-view romantic suspense.

671. The Tumbled House. Garden City, N.Y.: Doubleday, 1960. (NUC 1956-67 43-413)

672. Woman in the Mirror. Garden City, N.Y.: Doubleday, 1975.
A very annoying novel that is beautifully written but teases the reader by building suspense after suspense only to crash it down as another red herring. I consider that "dirty tricks." Some charming philosophical insights but all-in-all, the book left this reader wanting to toss it against the wall.

GRANT, Douglas (pseud.) see OSTRANDER, Isabel Egenton

GRAY, Alicia

673. Enchanted Circle (a trilogy). New York: Lancer, 1968.

GRAY, Angela

674. The Lattimore Arch (D). New York: Lancer, [1972].
Avis and mother move to Washington, D.C. and The Arches, inherited from her mother's long-lost love, Senator Lattimore. His family in residence is not only horrified, but murderous. If you can stand a clumsy, simplistic style, there's a mediocre story here.

675. Nightmare at Riverview. New York: Lancer, 1973.

Other works include: The Ashes of Falconwyk, The Ghost Dancers and The Golden Pocket, all published by Lancer.

GRAY, Harriet (pseud.) see PEARSON, Denise

GREEN, Anna Katharine see ROHLFS, Mrs. Anna Katharine (Green)

GREENFIELD, Irving A.

Born 2/22/28 in Brooklyn, New York. Received a B.A.

from Brooklyn College of City University of New York in 1950. Married and has two children.

676. The Ancient of Days (C). New York: Berkley Medallion, 1975.

Hard to classify but might be horror-Gothic-science-fiction. Dr. Paul Klee finds himself suddenly transferred from the 22nd century to a 17th-century Massachusetts town near Salem and into the body of the local schoolmaster. What follows is a description of a witch hunt paralleled with a filling in of 22nd-century life, and it turns out to be pretty grim all around.

677. The Carey Blood. New York: Dell, 1972.

678. Carey's Vengeance. New York: Dell, 1972.

679. Clorecrest. New York: Belmont, 1969.

680. Ichabod Rides Again. New York: Berkley, 1972.

681. The Others. New York: Lancer, 1969. (NUC 1968-72 36-278)

682. The Sexplorer. New York: Dell, 1972.

683. Succubus. New York: Dell, 1970.

684. Waters of Death. New York: Lancer (73-672), 1967. (NUC 1968-72 36-278)

GREIG, Maysie 1902-

Has written over 100 novels listed in the pre'56 NUC. They do not appear to be Gothic in spite of some paperback edition covers.

GRENDON, Stephen (pseud.) see DERLETH, August

GREY, Naidra

685. Dark Sun, Pale Shadows (D). New York: Putnam, 1973. [© Naidra Cockshut]. (NUC 1973 5-830)

Nicola travels to Portugal at the invitation of a long-lost aunt only to get embroiled in a narcotics smuggling ring. The entire plot is predictable by the end of the first few chapters. Romantic suspense at its most mediocre.

GRIERSON, Jane (pseud.) see WOODWARD, Edward

GRIFFIN, Anne J.

686. The Spirit of Brynmaster Oaks (D). New York: Avon (1973?), 1974. [© Arthur J. Griffin].

This has all the Gothic elements but nothing more. Alice goes to family estate near Long Island Sound to tend to things and runs into intrigue and a Radcliffian ghost.

GRIFFIN, Samuel Franklin

687. The Willfreud Curse. n.p.: Gold Slide Book [1972].

A strange, disjointed, but somewhat engaging tale having the seeds of a Gothic which never germinate.

Other works by this author include: Teacher of the Dead and Return of the Dark Virgin.

GRIFFITH, George (Chelwynd) 1859-1906

Several pages of this author's novels are listed in the pre'56 NUC.

688. The Mummy and Miss Nitocris; A Phantasy of the Fourth Dimension (B). London: T. W. Laurie, 1906; New York: Arno Press, 1976. (NUC pre'56 218-522)

I enjoyed this "exotic" Gothic. Although a bit quaint and dated, as is most of the "mysterious-East-type" literature, there was sufficient skill in narrative and philosophical commentary to more than sustain a slightly trite plot.

HAGGARD, [Sir] Henry Rider 1856-1925

Produced an enormous number of books during the last part of the 19th and early 20th centuries, the best known being King Solomon's Mines (London: Cassell, 1885). A large listing of works can be found in the NUC vol. 226, pp. 37 ff. A few of his 20th-century writings include:

689. Ayesha, the Return of She. New York: Doubleday, Page, 1905. (NUC pre'56 226-39)

690. Belshazzar. Garden City, N.Y.: Doubleday, Doran, 1930. (NUC pre'56 226-40)

691. The Ghost Kings (B). London: Cassell, 1908. (NUC pre'56 226-45). Also pub. as: The Lady of the Heavens.

The Gothic ancestor of this tale would probably be William Beckford's Vathek (1786) and a small group of early Gothics Bleiler calls "Oriental Gothic." This is one of the best representatives I've found of a type of Gothic which has gone out of style by the mid-20th century, due in large part, no doubt, to our more sophisticated world-view. The Romance of the Dark Continent greatly captivated the imaginations of writers well into the early 20th century. Haggard is one of them and I think this tale holds up even today. Rachel Dove, daughter of African missionaries becomes a white goddess to an African tribe and has some fabulous adventures. The whole thing is a great fantasy and, though dated, is well enough written to be quite enjoyable to this day.

692. Heu-Heu; or, The Monster. Garden City, N. Y.: Doubleday, Page, 1924. (NUC pre'56 226-45)

HALE, Arlene
(Louise Christopher, Gail Everett, Mary Anne Tate, Lynn Williams)

Born 6/16/24 in New London, Iowa. Has written a great number of romance and nurse stories--often published as "Candlelight Romances." Most appear to have few if any Gothic or suspense elements.

HALE, Jennifer

693. The House on Key Diablo. New York: Ballantine, 1974.

694. The Secret of Devil's Cave (B). New York: Lancer, 1973.
Beth returns to the Ozarks to check out her inheritance of a cave and an inn. Intrigue develops and is generally well handled except for a couple of loose ends left dangling and a rather precipitous ending.

Other works include: Ravensridge and Stormhaven, both published by Lancer.

HALL, Gimone

695. The Blue Taper (C). New York: Macfadden-Bartell, 1970.
"Louisiana Gothic" with a few new wrinkles--some of which should have been ironed out before publication.

696. The Juliet Room. New York: Manor, 1974.

697. The Silver Strand. New York: Dell, 1974.

698. Witch Suckling. New York: Manor, 1973, 1976.

HALLIDAY, Michael (pseud.) see CREASEY, John

HAMILL, Ethel (pseud.) see WEBB, Jean Francis

HAMILTON, Clare (pseud.) see LAWLESS, Bettyclare Hamilton

HANSEN, Joseph
(Rose Brock, James Colton, James Coulton)

Born 7/19/23 in Aberdeen, South Dakota. Married Jane Bancroft 1943. Education was in the public schools. Home is now in Los Angeles, California. He has had poems published under his own name in Harpers, Atlantic, Saturday Review and the New Yorker. Works under his other pseudonyms sound rather torrid.

699. Tarn House, by Rose Brock (C). New York: Avon (S450), 1971.
Lancie leaves her sick father in Kansas to check out an inheritance in Wisconsin and finds more than she bargained for. This isn't a bad story. A few innovations are made on a standard sentimental Gothic plot.

HARRIS, Larry M. (pseud.) see JANIFER, Laurence

HARRIS, Rosemary (Jeanne)

Born in London, England in 1923. Studied at Chelsea's School of Art and Courtland Institute, London. Has worked as a writer, picture restorer, and reader for M.G.M. She received the Carnegie Medal of Library Associations (England) for outstanding children's book of 1968 (The Moon in the Cloud), and has written several juveniles.

700. All My Enemies. London: Faber, 1967. (NUC 1968-72 38-626)

701. The Double Snare (B). New York: Simon & Schuster, 1975.
A young girl wakes up in an Italian hospital with amnesia following an auto accident where all identification has been lost. She is finally claimed by a wealthy Italian family and a long, involved, multiple intrigue follows. A well written, suspenseful tale, interestingly written in the first person present. The plot is complex but logical and all tied together.

702. The Nice Girl's Story (A). London: Faber, 1968; pub. in U.S. as: Nor Evil Dreams. New York: Simon & Schuster, [1973]. (NUC 1968-72 38-626)
Prudence is teaching English at a British high school and accidentally tapes a very suspicious conversation pertaining to incidents of anti-Semitism and neo-Nazism that had occurred recently. She takes the tapes to the Heathcliffian Mark Brown, an associate at the school and a refugee from a WWII concentration camp. Prue falls in love with Mark and into a heap of trouble with the conspirators.

A very well written story with a superb heroine. This book reaches beyond the standard classifications.

703. The Summer-House. London: Hamilton, 1956. (NUC 1956-67 47-357)

704. Venus with Sparrows. London: Faber, 1961. (NUC 1956-67 47-357)

705. Voyage to Cythera. London: Bodley Head, 1958.

706. A Wicked Pack of Cards (C). London: Faber, 1969; New York: Ace, 1969. (NUC 1968-72 38-626)

The only remotely Gothic element in this murder mystery is a fortune teller victim and a tarot reading which foreshadows the dire events that take place. There is a good deal of witty dialogue and some eccentric and engaging characterizations which kept me reading, but the pace is slow and the whole thing in no way comes up to the standards of Nor Evil Dreams.

HART, Carolyn

Pseudonym for Charles Garvice (1833-1920) who wrote dozens of popular sentimental romances.

HART, Carolyn Gimpel

Born 8/25/36 in Oklahoma City, Oklahoma. Received a B.A. in 1958 from the University of Oklahoma. Married P. D. Hart. They have two children and live in Oklahoma City, Oklahoma. Her writings are mostly juveniles.

707. Flee from the Past. New York: Bantam (Q8553), 1975.

The first and last chapters were sufficient to show this to be no Gothic. A college professor's wife with a past she's trying to escape is threatened and her child kidnapped and threatened with murder. The middle of the book (no doubt filled with tortured moments in the heroine's progress) I skipped and found exactly what I expected in the last chapter. Ho hum. I particularly disliked the author's idealized version of a college professor's life-style which surely bears no relation to mine--maids, M.G.'s and Mercedes indeed!

HARTE, Marjorie see McEVOY, Marjorie Harte

HARVEY, Rachel (pseud.) see BLOOM, Ursula

HAWTHORNE, Violet

708. Identical Strangers. New York: Ballantine, 1975.

709. Sweet Deadly Passion. New York: Ballantine (25071), 1976. [© Christopher Rainone].

Karen accepts an invitation to vacation with wealthy old college chum Lori at the family's Massachusetts summer mansion. She arrives to find that Lori's husband is missing and from there things get complicated with gangsters, murder and intrigue. Karen could be a budding private eye. She's a hard-drinking, tough-talking wise-guy with a heart of gold. There's not a Gothic element in sight in spite of the publisher's label.

HAYES, Leal

710. Harlequin House (B). New York: Ace, 1967.

There's a lot of story packed into the 158 pages of this standard "Louisiana Gothic." Set in post-Civil War South Carolina, and featuring a nice man and woman who marry for convenience, go through quite a number of dramatic events together and ... but you know. It's all well done and that makes the difference.

HAYWORTH, Evelyne

711. The Evil at Bayou LaForche (B). New York: Popular Library (00400), [1972]. [© Evan L. Heyman].

Claudia moves to the Louisiana plantation of her long-lost cousin Jason to become governess to Denise, Jason's autistic daughter. An intricate tale of intrigue and murder. It's about time someone made a pun about menses and "family curses," and here it is! A very neo-Gothic work with LSD playing a role, valium and librium given mention and, more seriously, some very complex and interesting characters. I liked this book.

712. Haggard's Manor (C). New York: Popular Library (00430), 1973. [© Evan L. Heyman].

"A host of friends and enemies hovered like vultures over the deathbed of J. W. Haggard. In that evil house, a ghastly fate had claimed young Jan Brainard's sister--and now it wanted her ..."--so they say! If this book hadn't been so long-winded, it might have been better. There is also an enormous amount of introspection and rambling that never does tie in with the outcome. A strange book.

HEAD, Ann (pseud.) see MORSE, Anne Christensen

HEATH, Monica (pseud.) see FITZGERALD, Arlene J.

HEATHCOTT, Mary see KEEGAN, Mary Heathcott

HEAVEN, Constance (Fecher)

Born 8/6/11 in London, England. Received a B.A. (with honors) at Kings College, University of London in 1932; London College of Music, Licentiate 1931. Career: actress 1938-64. Began writing in the 1960's. Has written several children's books as well as historical novels not included here. Her home is in Middlesex, England.

713. The Astrov Legacy. New York: Coward, McCann & Geoghegan, 1973; also pub. as: The Astrov Inheritance in England and is a sequel to The House of Kuragin. (NUC 1973 6-202)

714. Castle of Eagles (C). New York: Coward, McCann & Geoghegan, 1974; New York: Dell (4591), 1975. (NUC 1974 7-506)

The story of a pianist, Lisa, set in mid-19th century Austria. Lisa's parents die and she goes to live with an Austrian grandmother who subsequently dies. She then goes to live with her mother's first husband and gets into all kinds of trouble. This story starts out with some promise but it's never fulfilled.

715. The House of Kuragin (B). New York: Coward, McCann, 1972. (NUC 1968-72 39-431). "Best Romantic Historical Novel 1972"

Rilla Weston goes to Russia to be governess to the five-year-old child of Count Kuragin. She becomes involved in the family turmoils between the Count, his wife Natalia, the brother and so on. Essentially romance but well enough written to keep one reading.

716. The Place of Stones (D). New York: Coward, McCann & Geoghegan, 1975; New York: New American Library (Signet W7046), 1975.

Emma gets stranded in France when Napoleon declares war on England. She goes undercover as a governess and under the protection of Lucien whom she believes she loves. The story seemed a great bore and I'd had more than enough by half-way through. The heroine seemed an egotistical snob with an Oedipal fixation on her heroic and mysterious father. Dull, dull, dull.

HECHT, Ben 1893-1964

Hecht has written numerous plays, short stories, novels and movie scripts. The two books included here may be "exotic" Gothic.

717. Fantazius Mallagre; A Mysterious Oath. Chicago: Covici-McGee, 1922. (NUC pre'56 237-535)

718. The Kingdom of Evil: A Continuation of the Journal of Fantazius Mallare. Chicago: Covici, 1924. (NUC pre'56 237-537)

HERBRAND, Jan(ice M.) [McRorie]

Born 10/18/31 in Osage, Iowa. Attended the University of Puget Sound. Married Nicholas G. Herbrand in 1953. They have four children and live in Tacoma, Washington.

719. The Altheimer Inheritance. New York: Warner Paperback (75-032), 1973.

720. Lost Heritage (D). New York: Grosset & Dunlap, 1972; New York: Warner Paperback (75-003), 1973.

This is a mystery, not a Gothic. With the advent of her first pregnancy, Pat decided it's time to trace her parentage. Armed only with the knowledge that she was abandoned in a department store at age three and a few additional, very convenient memories, Pat and husband start looking for her kin. A rather boring story. The heroine is a bit of a nitwit and that doesn't help.

HERITAGE, Martin (pseud.) see HORLER, Sydney

HERSHMAN, Morris
(Evelyn Bond, Arnold English, Lionel Webb, Jess Wilcox)

Born 1/31/20. Career has been that of writer and lecturer. Has written over 40 novels under his own name and various psuedonyms. The Evelyn Bond stories appear to be the only ones possibly Gothic.

721. Bride of Terror, by Evelyn Bond. New York: Lancer, 1974.

722. The Crimson Candle (D) by Evelyn Bond. New York: Avon, 1973.

Kim goes to the home of handsome Gregory Rummel in New York after her father's death, engaged as a companion to Rummel's aunt. She becomes involved in conspiracy, murder, etc. Not especially well written. Essentially a murder mystery.

723. The Doomway, by Evelyn Bond. New York: Ballantine, 1971.

724. Evil in the House, by Evelyn Bond. New York: Lancer, 1965.

725. Heritage of Fear, by Evelyn Bond. New York: Belmont-Tower, 1974.

726. Hornet's Nest, by Evelyn Bond. New York: Avon, 1972.

727. House of Distant Voices, by Evelyn Bond. New York: Belmont-Tower, 1974.

728. House of Shadows, by Evelyn Bond. New York: Manor, 1975.

729. Lady in Darkness, by Evelyn Bond. New York: Lancer, 1965.

730. Raven's Eye, by Evelyn Bond. New York: Avon, 1972.

Other Evelyn Bond books include: Imperial Blue (Ballantine), Lady of Storm House (Lancer) and Widow in White.

HIBBERT, Eleanor Alice (Burford)
(Ellalice Tate, Eleanor Burford, Kathleen Kellow, Jean Plaidy, Elbur Ford, Philippa Carr and Victoria Holt)

Born in 1906 and still living in London, England. She was privately educated and worked as a wholesale merchant until becoming a full-time writer. She is quoted in Contemporary Authors: "I don't care about the critics. I write for the public.... I think people want a good story.... They like something which is readable and you can't beat the traditional for this."

Hibbert has published en enormous volume of works. Her Jean Plaidy books alone number over 46 and are generally historical novels, as are her Philippa Carr books. They seem to be well listed in the NUC.

731. The Bed Disturbed, by Elbur Ford. London: Laurie, 1951. (NUC pre'56 244-683)

732. Bride of Pendoric (B), by Victoria Holt. Garden City, N.Y.: Doubleday, 1963; Greenwich, Conn.: Fawcett-Crest (R778). (NUC 1956-67 49-421)

Favel Farington and Petroc Pendorric trip through all the expected clichês with just enough clever twists of plot to keep it interesting. Twins, twins, twins.

733. The Curse of the Kings (C), by Victoria Holt. Garden City, N.Y.: Doubleday, 1973; Greenwich, Conn.: Fawcett-Crest, 1974. (NUC 1973 6-320)

Judith grows through adolescence and eventually marries Tibalt, an archaeologist and her "one true love." An expedition to Egypt leads to murder and intrigue. This is basically a romance with a bit of suspense entering only toward the end of the book. I got very bored early on.

734. Dance Macabre, by Kathleen Kellow. London: Hale, 1952. (NUC pre'56 244-684)

735. Dear Delusion, by Eleanor Burford. London: Jenkins, 1952. (NUC pre'56 244-684)

736. Evil in the House, by Elbur Ford. New York: Morrow, 1954; pub. in Eng. (1953) as: Such Bitter Business. (NUC pre'56 244-684)

737. The House of a Thousand Lanterns (C), by Victoria Holt. Garden City, N.Y.: Doubleday, 1974. (NUC 1974 7-646)
The usual adequate fare set in Asia. Actually, one of H's better efforts.

738. The King of the Castle (C), by Victoria Holt. Garden City, N.Y.: Doubleday, 1967. (NUC 1956-67 49-422)
Dallas Lawson comes to France to restore the Comte de la Talles' paintings. Another typical Holt work. Competent but lacking inspiration. With the number of books she writes per year, it's a miracle her books are even readable.

739. Kirkland Revels, by Victoria Holt. Garden City, N.Y.: Doubleday, 1962. (NUC 1956-67 50-526)

740. The Legend of the Seventh Virgin, by Victoria Holt. Garden City, N.Y.: Doubleday, 1965. (NUC 1956-67 49-422)

741. Lilith, by Kathleen Kellow. London: Hale, 1954. (NUC pre'56 244-684)

742. Menfreya in the Morning, by Victoria Holt. Garden City, N.Y.: Doubleday, 1966. (NUC 1956-67 49-422)

743. The Miracle at St. Bruno's (D), by Philippa Carr. New York: Putnam, 1972; New York: Popular Library (03004), [1972]. (NUC 1973 6-320)
The paperback publisher labels this as "Gothic" but it is not. In my opinion, it is a tedious historical romance set in 16th-century England. The story is well hidden within large portions devoted to discussion of kings, their mistresses, etc., and all done through the gossiping of the characters in the story.

744. Mistress of Mellyn, by Victoria Holt. London: Collins, 1961 [pub. without pseudonym]; Garden City, N.Y.: Doubleday, 1960. (NUC 1956-67 49-422)

745. On the Night of the Seventh Moon (C), by Victoria Holt. Garden City, N.Y.: Doubleday, 1972.
Helena Trant gets messed up in a Black Forrest legend of the God of Mischief. An intricate and involved plot with the usual Holt two-dimensional characters.

746. Pride of the Peacock (C), by Victoria Holt. Greenwich, Conn.: Fawcett-Crest, 1976.
Once again, a heavy emphasis on history and romance. The story kept me reading but I was disappointed by the time I finished. Tame.

747. The Queen's Confession, by Victoria Holt. Garden City, N.Y.: Doubleday, 1968.
"Marie Antoinnette, consort of Louis XIV, King of France, fiction."

748. Rooms at Mrs. Olivers, by Kathleen Kellow. London: Hale, 1953. (NUC pre'56 244-684)

749. The Scarlet Cloak, by Ellalice Tate. London: Hodder & Stoughton, 1957. (NUC 1956-67 49-422)

750. The Secret Woman (D), by Victoria Holt. Garden City, N.Y.: Doubleday, 1970. (NUC 1968-72 40-372)

Romance, essentially without suspense, and too tepid, timid and trite for my tastes.

751. The Shadow of the Lynx (B), by Victoria Holt. Garden City, N.Y.: Doubleday, 1971. (NUC 1968-72 40-372)

Not Gothic, but an engaging story with a setting in England and Australia during the gold rush. Romantic suspense.

752. The Shivering Sands (B), by Victoria Holt. Garden City, N.Y.: Doubleday, 1969; Greenwich, Conn.: Fawcett-Crest. (NUC 1968-72 40-372)

Caroline, widow of a famous pianist, investigates the mysterious disappearance of her archeologist sister at some digs in England. Better than average.

753. Such Bitter Business, by Elbur Ford. London: Heinemann, 1953. (NUC pre'56 244-684). See also: Evil in the House, No. 736.

754. This Was a Man, by Ellalice Tate. London: Hodder & Stoughton, 1961. (NUC 1956-67 49-422)

755. To Meet a Stranger, by Eleanor Burford. London: Mills & Boon, 1957. (NUC 1956-67 49-422)

756. The Witch from the Sea (F), by Philippa Carr. New York: Putnam, 1975.

A long and tedious tale of two generations of Elizabethan women. The author gets too bogged down in historical tidbits and irrelevant conversations and reflections--at least for me. The characters are shallow and the plot gets lost in all the verbiage. It may be Gothic, but it's also a bore.

HIGGINS, Margaret

757. A Doctor for the Dead (D). New York: Ace, 1976.

A disjointed and poorly crafted attempt at combining sentimental and horror Gothic which, unfortunately, just doesn't come off. The author had no new ideas and was unable to breathe life into the old ones.

Higgins has also written The Changeling, Unholy Sanctuary and A Witch Alone, all published by Ace.

HIGHLAND, Dora

758. 153 Oakland St. (F). New York: Popular Library, 1973.
Laurette gets a summer job with a Howard Hughes-type tycoon. That's as far as I got and that was half the book. The writing was horrendously verbose and the author was clumsy and ostentatious with the plot. Essentially unreadable.

HILL, Pamela

Born 11/26/20 in Nairobi, Kenya. Education: Glasgow School of Art, D.A. 1943; Glasgow University, B.Sc. Equiv. 1952. Her home is in Scotland and she has worked variously as a pottery and biology teacher in Glasgow, Edinburgh and London and as a mink farmer in Galloway, Scotland 1965-70. She has written several historical novels not included here.

759. The Devil of Aske (C). London: Hodder & Stoughton, 1972; New York: St. Martin's Press, [1972]. (NUC 1973 6-345)
Leah, daughter of a parson in late 18th-century England, becomes orphaned and moves to the manor of Aske. She there becomes involved in the family's bizarre history. Essentially an historic romance and a bit much, really. Something of an "18th-century Peyton Place." This author seems to believe that only pathology is interesting. Competently written but poorly conceived.

760. The Malvie Inheritance. New York: St. Martin's Press, [1973]. (NUC 1974 7-681)

HILLIARD, Maurice 1931-

761. The Witchfinder: A Novel of Diabolism (D). New York: Coward, McCann & Geoghegan, 1974. (NUC 1974 7-687)
A sick story, about unbelievably sick people and, in general, a great bore. Seems fairly typical of a number of books written in the 70's which are capitalizing on a renewed interest in the occult but which it seems to me have missed the point entirely as to the reason behind that interest. I believe the lasting interest is philosophical rather than sensationalistic. What few philosophical implications this book does have are unacceptable to me.

HINES, Jeanne

762. The Slashed Portrait (C). New York: Dell, 1973. (NUC 1973 6-358)
Jody goes to the wedding of a friend and discovers ghosts and intrigue. A fairly good story, not too skillfully told. Southern U.S. Gothic.

HINKENMEYER, Michael T.

Born in St. Cloud, Minnesota and is a professor at Queens College in New York City. (Information from jacket of Summer.)

763. The Dark Below. Greenwich, Conn.: Fawcett-World, 1975.

764. Summer Solstice (D). Pub. by Berkley Pub. Corp and distr. by: New York: Putnam, 1976.

I found this an exceedingly unattractive horror Gothic. The supernatural is used to tell what boils down to an incestuous fantasy with no evident underlying philosophy. In this tale the Good does not exist. The author also saw fit to lace his tale with a good bit of what amounts to "little-boy-back-of-the-barn" sex which seems to me an insult to adult readers.

HINTZE, Naomi A(gans)

Born 7/8/09 in Camden, Illinois. Studied at Maryville College and Ball State University. Career has been that of writer.

765. Aloha Means Goodbye. New York: Random House, 1972. (NUC 1968-72 40-559)

766. Cry Witch (B). New York: Random House, 1975.

A well-crafted tale that tantalizes with Gothic possibilities which never develop but is so well done that this reader forgave. Gigi goes to Majorca to the "castle" of her grandmother following a death-bed summons.

767. Listen, Please Listen (B). New York: Random House, 1974. (NUC 1974 7-702)

Jo moves to a small New England town with her daughter to escape a haunted past. Slowly her happy relationship with her landlady begins to deteriorate and the past begins to merge with the present. This author writes well and masterfully builds suspense, steadily and maddeningly. The conclusion is straightforward and well done. Hintze is evidently not comfortable with the unexplained supernatural and I find that disappointing. This is high quality romantic suspense, nonetheless.

768. The Stone Carnation. New York: Random House, 1971. (NUC 1968-72 40-559)

769. You'll Like My Mother. New York: Putnam, 1969. (NUC 1968-72 40-559). Edgar Alan Poe Special Award for 1970.

HITCHENS, Dolores (Birk) 1908-1972
(Dolan Birkley, Noel Burke, D. B. Olsen)

Over 40 books of mystery, detection and suspense--none Gothic.

HODGE, Jane Aiken

Born 12/4/17 in Watertown, Massachusetts (daughter of poet Conrad Aiken). Received a B.S. (with honors) from Somerville College, Oxford; an A.M. from Radcliffe. She and her husband, Alan Hodge, live in Wimbledon, England. They have two children. Hodge has had a varied career of government service 1941-44, researcher for Time, Inc. 1944-47; researcher for Life 1947-48 and novelist.

770. The Adventurers. Garden City, N.Y.: Doubleday, 1965. (NUC 1956-67 50-231)

771. Greek Wedding. Garden City, N.Y.: Doubleday, 1970. (NUC 1968-72 41-103)

772. Here Comes a Candle (B). Garden City, N.Y.: Doubleday, 1967. (NUC 1956-67 50-231). Pub. by Dell, 1968 as: The Master of Penrose.

Kate, widowed and stranded in Canada in 1812, takes on the care of Jon Penrose's deeply disturbed daughter and goes with him to Massachusetts. Despised by the child's mother and caught up in war and intrigue, Kate struggles to save the child. A well written, fast-paced tale of romantic suspense.

773. Marry in Haste. Garden City, N.Y.: Doubleday, 1970. (NUC 1968-72 41-103)

774. Maulever Hall (B). Garden City, N.Y.: Doubleday, 1964; New York: Pyramid (X1177), 1965. (NUC 1956-67 50-231)

Marianne, a victim of amnesia following a carriage accident finds herself and a two-year-old child taken on at Maulever Hall where she becomes a companion and housekeeper. She falls in love with her employer's son and goes through quite a bit before recovering her memory. Some delightful characterizations and the author's ability to arouse curiosity as to the outcome kept me reading. Romantic suspense with the emphasis on the former.

775. Savannah Purchase. Garden City, N.Y.: Doubleday, 1971. (NUC 1968-72 41-103)

776. Shadow of a Lady. New York: Coward, McCann & Geoghegan, 1973. (NUC 1973 6-404)

777. Strangers in Company. New York: Coward, McCann & Geoghegan, 1973. (NUC 1973 6-404)

778. Watch the Wall, My Darling. Garden City, N.Y.: Doubleday, 1966. (NUC 1956-67 50-231)

779. The Winding Stair. Garden City, N.Y.: Doubleday, 1969. (NUC 1968-72 41-103)

HODGES, Doris Marjorie
(Charlotte Hunt)

Born 4/28/15 in Bristol, England. She has worked as a medical librarian and lecturer on writing for profit. Her home is in Blackwell, England.

780. The Cup of Thanatos, by Charlotte Hunt. New York: Ace, 1968.

781. The Gilded Sarcophagus, by Charlotte Hunt. New York: Ace, 1967.

782. Healing Stones, by Charlotte Hunt. New York: Pyramid, 1961.

783. The Lotus Vellum (C), by Charlotte Hunt. New York: Ace, 1970.
Labeled "occult fiction" and uses the word liberally throughout. Nonetheless, this book has the elements of the supernatural and intrigue that are Gothic in origin. I liked the philosophy in this book and the story was fairly entertaining. The main character, Dr. Paul Holton, a psychiatrist specializing in parapsychology, was a bit of an ass.

HODGSON, William (Hope) 1877-1918

784. Carnacki the Ghost Finder. London: Nash, 1913; Sauk City, Wisc.: Mycroft & Moran, 1947. (NUC pre'56 249-255)

HOFFE, Arthur

785. Something Evil (D). New York: Avon, 1968.
The publisher calls this "a novel of horror" but I found it little different from any run-of-the-mill romantic suspense. One major plot element--life-size statues--I found very overdone.
Laura cultivates the friendship of a new, reclusive family in town. She falls in love with Jeffrey only to learn that he has a terrible secret. The experienced reader should pretty well have figured it all out long before the end of the story.

HOFFMAN, Louise

786. Fear Among the Shadows. New York: Ace, 1974.

787. Passing Stranger. New York: St. Martin's, 1974. (NUC 1974 7-775)

788. A Quiet Passion. New York: St. Martin's, 1975. (NUC 1975 7-309)

789. To Dream of Evil (C). New York: Ace, 1975; pub. in England as: The Impossible Dream. Hale, 1973.
A perfect "C" grade story. Not badly written. Not badly plotted. But also a thoroughly predictable tale with little depth of characterization or insight.

HOLDEN, Joanne (pseud.) see CORBY, Jane Irenita

HOLLAND, Isabelle

Born 6/16/20. Educated privately and at the University of Liverpool. Received a B.A. from Tulane University in 1942. Holland has worked on various magazines including McCalls prior to 1960. Later she worked as publicity director and assistant to a publisher. Her home is in New York City.

790. Cecily. Philadelphia: Lippincott, 1967.

791. Grenelle (D). Greenwich, Conn.: Fawcett-Crest, 1976.
A jumbled story of hippie hooligans at an Episcopal seminary. Contrived and unpolished romantic suspense.

792. Kilgaren: A Novel (B). New York: Weybright & Talley, 1974; New York: Bantam (8842). (NUC 1974 7-803)
Headstrong Barbara returns to the Caribbean Isle of Kilgaren to help her brother and earn enough money to visit her boyfriend in Rome. The island is in racial-political turmoil and B. discovers an intrigue. The characters are interesting, the dialogue is peppy and the reading fun in this romantic suspense.

793. Trewlawny (B). New York: Weybright & Talley, [1974].
Kit inherits Trewlawny Fell, a massive, brooding estate on the U.S. East coast. Going there to establish an artist's colony, she becomes involved in murder and intrigue. A well written story with definite Gothic elements. The house is effectively used to develop the story.

HOLLAND, Katrin see ALBRAND, Martha

HOLMES, Mary J.

794. Chateau D'Or (C). New York: Lancer (73-542), 1966.
This author had a good plot idea and a style of simple, almost fairy tale language which I found very pleasant. I was disappointed in the resolution of the plot. A nice change from the more common formulas of romantic suspense.

HOLT, Victoria (pseud.) see HIBBERT, Eleanor Alice (Burford)

HONEYCOMBE, Gordon

795. Dragon Under the Hill (D). New York: Simon & Schuster, [1972]. (NUC 1973 6-471)

I fail to understand what pleasure one would find in either writing or reading such a grim horror-Gothic as this. A "nice British family" visiting an ancient historical site becomes possessed by some pre-historic Anglo-Saxon and Viking folk and meets with an altogether wretched fate. I find nothing to commend this tale although it was quite favorably reviewed in Book Review Digest (73-595).

796. Neither the Sea nor the Sand. New York: Weybright & Talley, [1969]. (NUC 1968-72 41-446)

HOPLEY, George see HOPLEY-WOOLRICH, Cornell George

HOPLEY-WOOLRICH, Cornell George 1903-1968
(George Hopley, William Irish, Cornell Woolrich)

Works may have some Gothic elements but probably are primarily detective and mysteries.

HORLER, Sydney 1888-1954
(Peter Cavandish, Martin Heritage)

Has written nearly fifty novels, all listed in the NUC. Examples include:

797. The Curse of Doone (D). London: Hodder & Stoughton, 1928; New York: Paperback Library, 1966. (NUC pre'56 254-678)

A curious hodge-podge of vampires, secret agents, horrid villains, romance and you name it. Made me appreciate the later separation of these themes into more specific categories with a more sophisticated outlook. Really a very naive little work in terms of what is available today and not recommended except for students of the genre. It's Gothic though.

798. The Evil Chateau (C). London: Hodder & Stoughton, 1929. (NUC pre'56 254-678)

This book was much like Monsarrat's Castle Garac. A down-and-out young fellow in Cannes gets involved with a beautiful girl and intrigue. In this case the beautiful girl is a top spy for the British secret service. As in Monsarrat's book, the castle and other Gothic elements are basically window dressing. It's a sort of pre-James Bond-type thriller and quite juvenile in both concept and execution.

799. Horror's Head. London: Hodder & Stoughton, 1932. (NUC pre'56 254-679)

800. The House of Secrets. London: Hodder & Stoughton, 1926. (NUC pre'56 254-679)

801. The Vampire. London: Hutchinson, 1935. (NUC pre'56 254-681)

HOSKINS, Robert
(Grace Corren)

Born 5/26/33. Education: Albany State College for Teachers 1951-52. Home: Richmond Hill, New York. Career: Employed in family business 1952-64; child care worker 1964-68; literary agent 1967-68. Senior editor, Lancer Books, 1969- . Avocation: numismatics. Is also an editor of science fiction.

802. The Darkest Room, by Grace Corren. New York: Lancer, 1969.

803. Evil in the Family, by Grace Corren. New York: Lancer, 1975.

804. Mansion of Deadly Dreams (C), by Grace Corren. New York: Popular Library, 1973.

Nurse Alison takes on a private case of a patient with a strange malady in a house full of trouble. She is attracted to Charles, but when her life is threatened, doesn't know who's responsible. This was a fairly entertaining although simplistic tale with underdeveloped plot elements and loose ends. There was no follow-up, for example, of the strange malady of the patient. Includes some interesting history of early nursing.

805. A Place on Dark Island, by Grace Corren. New York: Lancer, 1971.

Other Grace Corren books published by Lancer include: Country of the Blind and A Time for Terror.

HOUSTON, Margaret Bell

Houston's works generally appear to be romances and are listed in the NUC Vol. 256, p. 340. One exception seems to be:

806. Yonder (C). New York: Crown Publications, 1955; New York: Warner Paperback. (NUC pre'56 256-340)

Not a bad little sentimental Gothic set in the Florida Keys. It fits right in with hundreds like it written in the 1960's and 70's.

HOWARD, Mary (pseud.) see MUSSI, Mary

HOWARD, Vechel (pseud.) see RIGSBY, Howard

HOWATCH, Susan [Sturt]

Born 7/14/40 in Leatherhead, Surrey, England and now living in Englewood, New Jersey. She was educated at Kings College, London, where she received a bachelor of laws in 1961. Howatch was twenty when she completed Penmarric; it took her five years to write it. She worked for a year as a law clerk following graduation but was bored with practical law and decided to devote herself to writing. Within a year of coming to the U.S. her first novel was accepted for publication. While working on Penmarric she wrote six other novels, all published by Pan.

807. April's Grave. New York: Stein & Day, 1974; New York: Ace, 1969. (NUC 1974 7-917)

808. Call in the Night (C). London: Pan Books, 1973; New York: Stein & Day 1973; New York: Ace, 1967. (NUC 1974 7-917)

Claire Sullivan, a New York City English teacher, receives a desperate and uncompleted call from her sister in London and, unable to contact her sister thereafter, travels to France and England to find out what happened. Murder mystery and romantic suspense.

809. Cashelmara (A). New York: Simon & Schuster, 1974. (NUC 1974 7-917)

A delightful chronicle-type epic story of three generations of de Salises who lived in 19th-century Ireland and England. Beautifully written and engrossing from beginning to end. May be historical Gothic.

810. The Dark Shore. New York: Stein & Day, 1972; New York: Ace, 1965. (NUC 1968-72 42-98)

811. The Devil on Lammas Night (B). New York: Stein & Day, 1972; Greenwich, Conn.: Fawcett-Crest; New York: Ace, 1971. (NUC 1973 6-534)

The "heroine" Nicola, shares this tale with several other interesting characters in a well written tale of witchcraft and devil worship.

812. Penmarric. New York: Simon & Schuster, 1971. (NUC 1968-72 42-98) Literary Guild selection.

813. The Shrouded Walls (C). New York: Stein & Day, 1971; New York: Ace, 1968. (NUC 1968-72 42-98)

Fleury, orphaned and destitute, is offered marriage by Axel Brandson to enable him to claim his inheritance. They move to the family estate and become involved in murder and intrigue. Essentially a "who done it" with a Gothic setting. The plot is weak and the villain evident by mid-story.

814. The Waiting Sands. New York: Stein & Day, 1972; New York: Ace, 1966. (NUC 1968-72 42-98)

HOWE, Fanny

Many poems and short stories listed in NUC 1968-72.

815. Legacy of Lanshore (C). New York: Berkley Medallion, 1973.

Honor goes with friend Topsy to vacation at her family's summer home and finds a horrid situation. Topsy's father is a lecher, her mother an alcoholic and the family is under a curse. When a seal and a housekeeper are murdered, things, believe it or not, get worse. Melodrama's the word of the day in this mediocre neo-Gothic.

HUBBARD, Richard

816. Daughter of Despair (C). New York: Dell, 1972.

Tony falls in love with Nell and decides to meet her family. Murder and brushes with occult practices ensue at the rambling family summer mansion. Competent but routine.

HUDSON, Laura Hope

817. The Cruel Legacy (C). New York: Lancer, 1967.

Standard "Louisiana Gothic." Not bad, but nothing new.

HUFF, Tom E. (or T. E.)
(Katherine St. Clair; see also: Edwina Marlow and Beatrice Parker)

818. Meet a Dark Stranger. New York: Hawthorn Books, 1974. (NUC 1974 7-986)

819. Room Beneath the Stairs (C), by Katherine St. Clair. Indianapolis & New York: Bobbs-Merrill, 1975.

Caroline marries her childhood idol and goes to Greycliff, her childhood image of paradise. Competent management of a stock plot, stock characters and stock setting.

HUFFORD, Susan

Born in Cincinnati, Ohio in 1940. Received an M.S. from Temple University in 1961, and studied in Austria as well. As an actress and singer, she has appeared on Broadway in "Fiddler on the Roof" and "Bill," on TV and in theatrical touring companies.

"As a form I've become quite intrigued with the gothic novel ... its history and its potential for modern women. I reject the notion that the gothic revolves around a weak ineffectual female. In the past, many of these books have been written by men, using women's names but as elsewhere in our lives, women are demanding more for themselves. As a feminist, I was at first in conflict over the fact that I was writing gothic novels--a traditionally unliberated form. But now I feel quite differently." Contemporary Authors, Vols. 57-60, p. 289.

820. The Devil's Sonata (C). New York: Popular Library, 1976.
After reading the author's comments above I wished I had liked her book more. It does not, for one thing, fit my criteria for a Gothic. College professor Hilda goes to a relative's mansion, Valhalla, to visit and check up on her half-sister who is being treated in a nearby mental hospital. She arrives to find things seriously amiss and the household a hot-bed of intrigue. The pace is good and kept me reading, but I found the plot clumsy and the characters unreal.

821. Midnight Sailing. New York: Popular Library, 1975.

Also wrote: A Delicate Deceit (Popular Library).

HUNT, Charlotte (pseud.) see HODGES, Doris Marjorie

HUNT, Howard 1918-
(Gordon Davis, Robert Dietrick, David St. John)

822. The Coven, by David St. John. New York: Weybright & Talley, 1972. (NUC 1974 8-5)

823. Diabolus (D), by David St. John. New York: Weybright & Talley, 1971. (NUC 1973 6-616)
"CIA Gothic," if you can imagine. Sort of a second-rate James Bond with Gothic elements and full of male fantasy machismo. Maybe the fellas would like it, but I found it exceedingly dull.

HUNT, (Isobel) Violet 1866-1942

Writer, born in Durham, England.

824. The Governess, by Mrs. Alfred Hunt.
Listed in the New Cambridge Bibliography of English Litera-

ture, Vol. 4, p. 607.

825. The House of Many Mirrors. London: Heinemann, 1914.

826. More Tales of the Uneasy. London: Heinemann, 1925.

827. Tales of the Uneasy. London: Heinemann, 1911. (NUC pre'56 261-57)

HUNTER, Mollie see McILWRAITH, Maureen Mollie Hunter

HURD, Florence

828. Curse of the Moors. New York: Manor Books, 1975.

829. House on Trevor Street. New York: Manor Books, 1972.

830. Moorsend Manor. New York: Manor Books, n.d.

831. The Secret of Canfield House. Greenwich, Conn.: Fawcett-Crest, n.d.

832. Terror at Seacliffe Pines (B). New York: Manor Books, 1976.

Jennifer goes to the desolate and spooky Seacliff Pines to claim her inheritance following the death of Aunt Hester. A well told tale, very much in the Gothic tradition.

833. Wade House. New York: New American Library, n.d.

834. So Dark a Shadow (B). New York: Paperback Library, 1969.

I would call this pleasantly written and decently plotted little tale a romance. There is a murder and a rather tame intrigue but the emphasis is not Gothic. Short and sweet.

HUXLEY, Aldous 1894-1963

835. The Devils of Loudun. New York: Harper, 1952. (NUC pre'56 262-260)

There is a thread of a Gothic novel trailing through this otherwise rather ponderous treatise on 17th-century witchcraft, demonism and mysticism and the human condition in general. The story part has little more appeal than its 18th-century counterparts. The philosophy and commentary are not within the scope of this bibliography.

HYDE, Cynthia

836. The House of Sinister Shadows (D). New York: Avon (V2453), 1972.

A poor show all around. The plot is stilted, contrived and unbelievable. The characters are shallow and the prose is limping to unreadable. Diane has a whirlwind courtship with dashing Richard von Warning (!) and goes to his German estate to meet the family and melodrama. Romantic suspense of a less than mediocre sort.

ILES, Francis (pseud.) see COX, Anthony Berkeley

INGATE, Mary

837. The Sound of the Weir (B). New York: Dodd, Mead, 1974. (NUC 1974 8-243)

An other-worldly tale in mood and yet also a straightforward tale of love, youthful passion and murder. Very well conceived and written with a touch of the supernatural, much in the tradition of Shirley Jackson without her cynicism. Ann gives testimony that hangs her cousin for the murder of the cousin's elderly husband.

INGRAM, Eleanor M(arie) 1886-1921

838. The Thing from the Lake (A). Phila. & London: Lippincott, 1921; New York: Arno Press, 1976. (NUC pre'56 267-430)

A perfect gem of a sentimental horror Gothic.

INNES, Michael (pseud.) see STEWART, John Innes Mackintosh

IRISH, William (pseud.) see HOPLEY-WOOLRICH, Cornell George

JACKSON, O(live) T.

839. Dark Love, Dark Magic (D). New York: Magnum Books (74-739), 1969.

Nothing new here. Romantic suspense with the emphasis on romance. A tale that held promises never fulfilled.

JACKSON, Shirley 1919-1965

840. Hangsaman (D). New York: Farrar, Straus & Young, 1951; New York: Ace, 1951. (NUC pre'56 275-50)

A strange tale of adolescent fantasy during a girl's first weeks at college. Those expecting a Gothic will be disappointed. In my opinion, it is a failed attempt at "psychological horror."

841. The Haunting of Hill House (B). New York: Viking Press, 1959. (NUC 1956-67 56-301)

Probably the most disturbing ghost story I have ever read. It's a beaut!

842. The Sundial. New York: Farrar, Straus & Cudahy, 1958; New York: Popular Library, n.d. (NUC 1956-67 56-302)
The horror in this tale is certainly Gothic in origin. Jackson has too much imagination and originality to write in the clichês, however. A grim little story but thoroughly engaging as well.

843. We Have Always Lived in the Castle. New York: Viking, 1962; New York: Popular Library, n.d. (NUC 1956-67 56-302)
An essentially unclassifiable tale but Gothic in mood and atmosphere if nothing else. A quiet little horror story, delightfully told.

844. The Witchcraft of Salem Village. New York: Random House, 1956. (NUC 1956-67 56-302)

JAMES, Barbara

845. Beauty that Must Die. New York: Ace, 1973.

846. Bright Deadly Summer (C). New York: Ace (08021), 1962.
Miranda falls passionately in love with the dashing Laurie. They go to M's grandmother's and the housekeeper is robbed and murdered. Who done it? Routine romantic suspense and murder.

JAMES, Henry 1843-1916

James evidently had a brief "Gothic period" just at the turn of the century, the only 20th-century work being:

847. The Turn of the Screw. London: Secker, 1915. (NUC pre'56 276-565)
I believe this tale could be considered as much a model for the stories of the 60's and 70's as Jane Eyre is so often said to be.

JAMES, Montague Rhodes

Born in Eton, England in 1862. A British medievalist, writer of ghost stories and authority on Christian religious art. He was provost of Kings College, Cambridge (1905-18) and of Eton (1918-1936). Author of many scholarly works in addition to ghost stories. He died in 1936.

848. Best Ghost Stories of M. R. James. Cleveland & N.Y.: The World Publishing Co., 1944. (NUC pre'56 276-613)

849. The Five Jars (B). New York: Longmans, Green, 1922.

(NUC pre'56 276-615)

A short but charming adult fairy tale.

850. A Thin Ghost & Others. New York: Longmans, Green, 1919. (NUC pre'56 276-618)

JAMES, Rebecca Salsburg

851. Storm's End (B). Garden City, N.Y.: Doubleday, 1974. (NUC 1974 8-671)

Another amnesia story. The heroine awakens in the hospital and learns she is a wealthy heiress surrounded by a family she doesn't remember. She returns to her estate, Storm's End, and becomes increasingly suspicious of her real identity. Well enough written that it manages to rework a very much-used plot and still come up with an engrossing story.

JAMES, Susan

852. The Hypnotist of Hilary Mansion. New York: Pocket Books, 1977.

JANIFER, Laurence M(ark)
(Alfred Blake, Andrew Blake, Larry M. Harris, Barbara Wilson)

Born 3/17/33 in Brooklyn, New York. Has had a varied career as a pianist, arranger, editor, comedian and magazine writer. He has used about thirty-two pseudonyms in his writing which generally tends toward science fiction.

853. The Woman Without a Name. New York: New American Library (Signet D2867), 1966.

JARDIN, Rex (pseud.) see BURKHARDT, Robert Ferdinand and Eve

JENNIFER, Susan

854. The House of Counted Hatreds (C). New York: Avon, 1973.

Donna goes to help friend Ellie remodel an old house Ellie inherited. What she finds is murder and intrigue. The resolution of this story doesn't live up to the promising beginning but it is still a fair tale. The author fails to tie together the significance of the old, mysterious house with the actual events in the story.

JENSEN, Ruby Jean

855. The Girl Who Didn't Die. New York: Warner Paperback, 1975.

856. The House at River's Bend. New York: Dell, 1975.

857. The House that Samael Built (B). New York: Warner Paperback (76-496), 1974.
An engrossing horror-Gothic slightly flawed by some illogical behavior by the heroine but still quite entertaining.

858. Seventh All Hallow's Eve. New York: Warner Paperback, 1974.

JOHNSON, Martha (pseud.) see LANSING, Elisabeth Carleton

JOHNSON, William

859. House on Corbett Street; A Black Novel. New York: William Frederick Press, 1975.

JOHNSTON, Velda

860. Along a Dark Path. New York: Dell (00073), 1971.

861. The Face in the Shadows (C). New York: Dodd, Mead, 1971; New York: Dell, 1972.
Strictly a mystery. No Gothic elements. New York actress Ellen finds a drugged 12-year-old near a museum and becomes involved. Danger and suspense follow. Well written but predictable.

862. House Above Hollywood. New York: Dell, 1972.

863. A Howling in the Wood. New York: Dell, 1969.

864. I Came to a Castle. New York: Dell, 1971.

865. The Late Mrs. Fonsell. New York: Dell, 1972.

866. The Light in the Swamp (B). New York: Dodd, Mead, 1970; New York: Dell, 1971.
Catherine and daughter return to family home and mystery. An unpretentious tale, well told. A great quote from Graham Greene on page 85 won my heart for this book. Gothic elements of house and atmosphere. Setting is contemporary Long Island, N. Y.

867. Masquerade in Venice. New York: Dell, 1974.

868. The Mourning Trees. New York: Dell, 1973.

869. The People on the Hill. New York: Dell, 1972.

870. The Phantom Cottage. New York: Dodd, Mead, 1970; New York: Dell, 1971.

871. A Room with Dark Mirrors (D). New York: Dodd, Mead, [1975].

Stewardess Dottie runs into intrigue and romance on a routine trip to Paris. A very superficial story. The narrative is grossly padded, the plot is juvenile, and the characters uninteresting. No Gothic elements.

JOHNSTON, William 1924-
(Susan Claudia)

He has written several books under his own name based on TV series such as Dr. Kildare (New York: Lancer, 1963), And Loving It (New York: Grosset & Dunlap, 1967), "an original novel about NBC TV's ... Maxwell Smart, Agent 86 for Control."

872. Madness at the Castle (D), by Susan Claudia. New York: New American Library (Signet D2897), 1966.

Nurse Diane goes to vacation at a doctor friend's castle and frightening things begin to happen. Diane is led to believe she may be going crazy. A picnic for paranoiacs but little else.

873. The Other Brother, by Susan Claudia. New York: Ballantine, 1974.

874. The Searching Specter, by Susan Claudia. New York: New American Library, 1967.

875. A Silent Voice, by Susan Claudia. New York: New American Library (Signet Q6014), n.d.

JONES, Joanna (pseud.) see BURKE, John Frederick

KARK, Nina Mary (Mabey) 1925-
(Nina Bawden)

English novelist who has written several of what appear to be juvenile Gothics. Her adult works seem to be other than Gothic--for example:

876. Devil by the Sea, by Nina Bawden. London: Collins, 1957; Philadelphia: Lippincott, 1959. (NUC 1956-67 9-379)

A psychological novel about a nine-year-old girl, and her fantasies, and her miserable reality. A dreary little tale about miserable, dreary people and I wonder how the author stood writing it. Not in the least Gothic.

KAVANAUGH, Cynthia

877. Bride of Lenore (C). New York: Pyramid (R1330), 1966.
Gabrielle, returning to the U.S. via an ocean liner, meets and marries the handsome but troubled Edwin only to have him mysteriously disappear shortly after they dock in New York. Gabrielle goes to Edwin's Virginia mansion to try to trace him and uncovers a nasty plot. Could have been a better story with more meat on its bare bones.

KEEGAN, Mary Heathcott 1914-
(Mary Heathcott, Mary Raymond)

English journalist and novelist whose works appear to be more romantic than suspenseful or Gothic.

878. The Long Journey Home (C), by Mary Raymond. New York: Paperback Library, Cornet Communications 1967 (2nd printing 1971).
Cathy finds her unborn child heir to a vast estate in northern England following the tragic death of her playboy husband. She finds it awkward to take over the lives and property of her newly met kin and also finds her life threatened. A somewhat better than average treatment of a very cliché plot.

KEITH, J. Kilmeny (pseud.) see MALLESON, Lucy Beatrice

KELLER, David H(enry) 1880-?

Several novels and short stories listed in the pre'56 NUC. Some appear to be quasi-science fiction.

879. The Devil and the Doctor (B). New York: Simon & Schuster, 1940. (NUC pre'56 292-128)
This charming story could be classified as whimsical Gothic tho' I wouldn't care to undertake a rigorous defense of the decision. Some delightful characterizations, including a rather original one of the Devil.

KELLOW, Kathleen (pseud.) see HIBBERT, Eleanor

KENT, Fortune

880. The House at Canterbury (B). New York: Pocket Books, 1975.
Anne Medford moves into a big old house she inherited after her father's death. The house has some spooky qualities, as do her

reclusive neighbors. When she begins remodeling the house, threats are made on her life. Sounds routine but this is a well written, well plotted and highly suspenseful Gothic.

881. House of Masques. New York: Ballantine, 1975.

882. Opal Legacy. New York: Ballantine, 1975.

Also wrote Isle of the Seventh Sentry (Pocket Books).

KEPPEL, Charlotte

883. Loving Sands, Deadly Sands (B). New York: Delacorte Press [1974].

In 1798 an impoverished distant cousin and a paroled French officer arrive simultaneously at Adeney Cross, a wealthy but unkempt manor on the coast of England, to assume their respective duties as housekeeper and tutor. There they find a tumultuous and long-lost love and a family of a most bizarre nature.

884. Madam, You Must Die. London: Hodder & Stoughton, 1974. (NUC 1974 9-274)

KERRUISH, Jessie Douglas

885. The Girl from Kurdistan. London: Hodder & Stoughton, 1918. (NUC pre'56 294-384)

886. Miss Haroun Al-Raschid. London: Hodder & Stoughton, 1917. (NUC pre'56 294-384)

First prize in Hodder & Stoughton's "1000 guinea novel competition."

887. The Undying Monster: A Tale of the Fifth Dimension. London: Heath Cranton, 1922; New York: Macmillan, 1936. (NUC pre'56 294-384)

This book was reportedly unobtainable through interlibrary loan.

KEVERN, Barbara (pseud.) see SHEPHERD, Donald

KILLORAN, Geraldine

888. The Stones of Strendleigh (B). New York: Ace (78659), 1974.

From the cover: "it was a set of tragic circumstances that brought Rose Douglas to Strendleigh Hall--or perhaps it was fate--for she came to love the English manor and the inhabitants who treated her so kindly. Rose soon learned her ties to the manor were closer than that of a grateful houseguest. And the closer she got to the truth, the more obvious it became that one of the two handsome Stone brothers vying for her hand in marriage was really trying to rid the Hall of its guest...." A satisfying story in the best of the Gothic tradition.

KIMBRO, John M.

(Kym Allyson, Charlotte Bramwell, Milt Jaxon, Allyn Keimberg, Katheryn Kimbrough, Zoltan Lambec, Jack Milton)

Born 7/12/29, he attended three colleges in California. His home is in New York City. In addition to being a writer and novelist, he has at various times been a free-lance director, composer, teacher and masseur. Under the pseudonym Kym Allyson, has written plays and musicals.

889. The Broken Sphinx, by Katheryn Kimbrough. New York: Popular Library, 1972.

890. Brother Sinister, by Charlotte Bramwell. New York: Ballantine, 1973.

891. The Children of Houndstroth, by Katheryn Kimbrough. New York: Popular Library, 1972.

892. Cousin of Terror (D), by Charlotte Bramwell. New York: Ballantine, 1972.

Carrie is visited by a young lawyer at an institution for the criminally insane where she has been kept following the murder of her cousin. The lawyer endeavors to prove Carrie innocent and the plot goes steadily downhill thereafter. A slap-dash melodrama with few other than contrived Gothic elements.

893. The Heiress of Wolfskill, by Katheryn Kimbrough. New York: Popular Library, 1973.

894. The House on Windswept Ridge, by Katheryn Kimbrough. New York: Popular Library, 1971.

895. The Phantom Flame of Wind House, by Katheryn Kimbrough. New York: Popular Library, 1973.

896. The Shadow over Pheasant Heath, by Katheryn Kimbrough. New York: Popular Library, 1974.

897. A Shriek in the Midnight Tower (F), by Katheryn Kimbrough. New York: Popular Library, [1975].

A poorly written tale of murder at La Chat Noir, a Southern mansion where crippled, orphaned, 12-year-old Marietta narrates, very clumsily, what happens as half her household are murdered off, one by one.

898. The Specter of Dolphin Cove, by Katheryn Kimbrough. New York: Popular Library, 1973.

899. Stepmother's House, by Charlotte Bramwell. New York: Ballantine, 1972.

900. Thanesworth House, by Katheryn Kimbrough. New York: Popular Library, 1972.

901. The Three Sisters of Briarwick (C), by Katheryn Kimbrough. New York: Popular Library, 1973.

My overall impression of this book was that it was a promising rough draft for a sentimental horror Gothic. The key word, however, is rough. The plot is held together by the slenderest of threads. There are numerous characters who hold promise but who are never developed beyond two dimensions and, the heroine is, in spite of a few tantalizing paragraphs of congenial philosophy, a shallow and unsympathetic ninny. Too bad.

902. The Twisted Cameo, by Katheryn Kimbrough. New York: Popular Library, 1971.

903. Unseen Torment, by Katheryn Kimbrough. New York: Popular Library, 1974.

KIMBROUGH, Katheryn (pseud.) see KIMBRO, John M.

KING, Louise W.

904. The Day We Were Mostly Butterflies. Garden City, N. Y.: Doubleday, 1964. (NUC 1956-67 61-429)

905. The Rochemer Hag (B). Garden City, N. Y.: Doubleday (Crime Club), 1967. (NUC 1956-67 61-429)

Rich prose, a sense of humor and a marvelous hero bring this standard sentimental Gothic formula well up from the realm of mediocrity.

906. The Velocipede Handicap. Garden City, N. Y.: Doubleday, 1966. (NUC 1956-67 61-429)

KING, Stephanie

907. The Marble Virgins. New York: Ballantine, 1974.

KING, Stephen

Born 9/21/47 in Portland, Maine. Received a B. Sc. from the University of Maine, 1970. He is married and has two children.

Lives in Bridgton, Maine. Career: janitor in a mill, laundry worker, high school teacher of English.

908. Carrie: A Novel of a Girl with a Frightening Power. Garden City, N.Y.: Doubleday, 1974; New York: New American Library (Signet E6410), 1975. (NUC 1974 9-395)

A sensationalistic product of the current fad for disaster stories--this one being a psychic disaster job and obviously written with one eye to the film industry. It keeps one reading to find out what happens but its entertainment value feeds on one of our worst human qualities--fascination with disaster and madness. I found the book totally unenjoyable.

909. Salem's Lot. Garden City, N.Y.: Doubleday, 1975.

KINGSBURY, Myra

910. Island of Fog. New York: Ballantine, 1974.

KINGSLEY, Bettina

911. The House on the Drive (F). New York: Dell (5283), 1975.

Roberta's husband receives a stupid and melodramatic cable from his family in the U.S. and leaves their honeymoon to take care of it. The rest of the story is just like the telegram. The spurious device of attempting to create excitement and suspense by having a bumbling heroine confronted with a ludicrously melodramatic situation just doesn't work and I fail to understand why the formula survives. The "shilling shocker" at its worst.

KIRK, Russell (Amos)

Born 10/19/18 in Plymouth, Michigan. Education: Michigan State B.A. 1934; Duke University M.A. 1941; St. Andrews University D. Litt. 1952 (the only American to hold this earned degree). Home: Mecosta, Michigan. Career: Professor of history 1946-52; research professor of politics C. W. Post College (N.Y.) 1957- . Holds several honorary degrees. Many scholarly works including The Conservative Mind.

912. A Creature of the Twilight. New York: Fleet Publishing Corp., 1966.

913. Old House of Fear (B). New York: Fleet Publishing Corp., 1961; New York: Avon, 1962. (NUC 1956-67 61-514)

Author's note: "This Gothick tale, in unblushing line of direct descent from The Castle of Otranto, I do inscribe to Abigail Fay." Kirk's intent seems obvious and I think he carried it off very well. Written from the hero's perspective, Hugh Logan, an American lawyer travels to a remote island in the Hebrides to buy the island for his tycoon employer, MacAskival. Once on the island, Hugh falls in love with The MacAskival and finds a hotbed of conspiracy and intrigue. A very entertaining story, competently written.

914. The Surly Sullen Bell. New York: Fleet Publishing Corp., 1962. (NUC 1956-67 61-514)
Ten stories and sketches, uncanny or uncomfortable. Claimed by the author to be "unabashedly Gothick."

KISTLER, Mary

915. Night of the Tiger (B). New York: Lancer, 1972.
Kate returns to her family ranch in Western Texas to find her life threatened in an adult and deadly version of a childhood game of "Bloody Arrow." A well written and nicely paced tale of romantic suspense.

KNIGHT, Alanna

916. Legend of the Loch (B). London: Hurst & Blackett, 1969. New York: Lancer, 1970.
Beth Ryan goes to Glengarron to see the castle her mother has deeded to her. There she finds romance and intrigue. Not at all a routine tale. A well written story with three dimensional characters, a very "human" heroine and just a touch of the supernatural.

917. The October Witch (B). London: Hurst & Blackett, 1971; New York: Lancer, 1971. (NUC 1968-72 51-322)
A well crafted tale in an almost classic style.

KNIGHT, Kathleen Moore
(Alan Amos)

Has written 35 or more works of mystery and detection, none of which appear to be Gothic. For example:

918. The Robineau Look. Garden City, N.Y.: Doubleday (Crime Club), 1955. (NUC pre'56 300-257)
Cynthia Robineau decides to visit a family reunion after receiving a curiously worded invitation. She meets some interesting long-lost kin and gets involved in murder and romance. Not a bad little murder mystery but not Gothic as advertised by the publisher.

KNYE, Cassandra

919. The House that Fear Built (D). New York: Warner Paperback (64-888), 1966.
Nan goes to Mexico with fiance Hans to meet her future

in-laws. Her life is threatened the night they arrive at the huge castle built by Hans' ancestors to be the center of a new German Reich before WWI. This book was too crammed with melodramatic events and too scant on substance to come off well. The heavy characters are unbelievably bad and there are numerous gruesome and unnecessary deaths--even a matador and a bull in a bull fight. Too much.

KOSNER, Alice

920. My Sister Ophelia (D). New York: Berkley Medallion, 1975.
A very routine tale of romantic suspense. Alice goes to Carolina Island to take care of her four-year-old niece following the mysterious disappearance of her sister and the child's mother, Sara, who subsequently turns up murdered. In the process of finding "who done it" a rather sordid family history is revealed and everyone except the heroine and her cop boyfriend end up mad or dead.

KURLAND, Michael
(Jennifer Plum)

Born 3/1/38 in New York City. Attended Hiram College 1955-56; University of Maryland 1960-61; Columbia University 1962-64. Now living in Kensington, California and works as a writer. He has written several war novels under his own name.

921. The Secret of Benjamin Square, by Jennifer Plum. New York: Lancer, 1972.

KYLE, Elizabeth (pseud.) see DUNLOP, Agnes Mary Robertson

LAFORE, Laurence Davis

Born 9/15/17 in Narberth, Pennsylvania. Education: B.A. Swarthmore (highest honors) 1938; M.A. Fletcher School of Law & Diplomacy 1939, Ph.D. 1950. Home: Iowa City, Iowa. Career: college teaching, various schools. University of Iowa, professor of history 1969- . Has written widely on history and diplomacy.

922. The Devil's Chapel (B). Garden City, N.Y.: Doubleday, 1964. (NUC 1956-67 65-373)
An elegantly written tale of modern-day witchcraft and deviltry. Julian Holland comes to Llanbrynmall, Pennsylvania as the new rector of the Episcopal church. He finds a decimated congregation and a strangely behaving community. In addition to a good story, there are some interesting observations regarding attitudes toward Evil.

923. Nine Seven Juliet: A Mystery Novel. Garden City, N.Y.: Doubleday, 1969. (NUC 1968-72 54-303)

924. Stephen's Bridge. Garden City, N.Y.: Doubleday, 1968. (NUC 1968-72 54-303)

LAMB, Antonia (Blick)

Born 10/3/43 in New York City. Attended Columbia University 1962-3. Worked as a ballet dancer, off-Broadway actress, B-girl, ballet teacher, artist's and photographer's model, sales clerk, credit analyst and in a Christmas ornament company. Currently a practicing astrologer.

925. The Greenhouse (D). New York: Pyramid (T2579), 1966.
Rowan goes to visit an aunt she hasn't seen for years and gets involved in murder and intrigue. The aunt is a horticulturist, specializing in rare and exotic plants--thus the title. This is a mediocre romantic-suspense. The plot is unimaginative and the characters shallow.

926. Greystones. New York: Pyramid, 1966.

927. Lady in Shadows. New York: Lancer, 1968.

LAMBERT, Christine (pseud.) see LOEWENGARD, Heidi

LAMBOT, Isobel

928. A Taste of Murder. New York: Ace, 1966.
Ace is the only one who could call this a Gothic. It is a murder mystery, pure and simple, with the emphasis on the latter.

LAMONT, Marianne (pseud.) see RUNDLE, Anne

LANCE, Leslie [Mossop]

Born in Great Yarmouth, England. Home is in Dartmouth, Devon, England. Career: novelist and farmer. Has written numerous romances in addition to works listed here.

929. The Bride of Emersham (C). New York: Pyramid, 1967.
Verity goes in search of a missing cousin and finds romance, murder and so on. A fair tale if you can stomach the heroine's egotism, vanity and mean mouth.

930. Dark Stranger. n.p.: Lowe, 1946.

931. The House in the Woods (C). New York: Ace, 1973.
Cecil Lynton agrees to a marriage of convenience with Garnet St. Maurus to help provide for her niece and help the dying Garnet

secure his estate. Cecil goes to the House in the Woods and learns about the family and its problems. One of those stories that build slowly and go crashing to a precipitous conclusion which always seems as though the author tired suddenly of the whole thing.

LANSING, Elisabeth Carleton (Hubbard) 1911-
(Martha Johnson, Margaret Irwin Simmons)

Writer of numerous nurse stories and many juveniles, listed in the NUC pre'42, Vol. 315, pp. 529 ff.

LA SPINA, (Fanny) Greye (Bragg)

Born 7/10/1880 in Wakefield, Massachusetts. Her career was mainly that of a free-lance writer but she also worked as a commercial photographer, private secretary, office manager and tapestry weaver. Lifelong interest in the supernatural and the occult. A contributor of more than 100 serials, novelettes and short stories to various magazines.

932. Invaders from the Dark (C). Sauk City, Wisc.: Arkham House, 1960; pub. in paperback in 1960 as: Shadow of Evil.
A tale of the occult and werewolf phenomena. Pace fair. Suspense poorly developed. Characters shallow.

LATIMER, John 1937-

933. Border of Darkness (B). Garden City, N.Y.: Doubleday (Crime Club), 1972. (NUC 1973 8-232)
Horror Gothic. Be prepared for an unhappy ending. Not a bad tale, if you're tough.

934. Maria Marten; or The Murder in the Red Barn: A Victorian Melodrama. London: Heinemann, 1971. (NUC 1968-72 55-136)

LATIMER, Jonathan 1906-

935. Sinners and Shrouds (C). New York: Simon & Schuster, 1955.
Horror Gothic. A bit bizarre but an interesting story.

LA TOURRETTE, Jacqueline

Born 5/5/26 in Denver, Colorado. Education: San Jose University 1948-51; St. Margaret's Hospital, Eping, England, nurses' training 1958. Home: Santa Clara, California. Career: teletype operator; medical secretary 1961-

"All of my books have required research.... I try to make background material as accurate as possible, no matter how fantastic the plot of the novel. Would rather travel than anything else ... besides write. I spent five years in Alaska, one year in England and Ireland, and have been to Italy [where she researched The Pompeii Scroll] twice. My interest in anthropology and archaeology has never left me and I do a lot of reading in these fields, along with others." Contemporary Authors, Vol. 49-52, p. 322.

936. The Joseph Stone. New York: Leisure Books, 1971.

937. The Madonna Creek Witch. New York: Dell, 1973.

938. A Matter of Sixpense. New York: Dell, 1972.

939. The Pompeii Scroll (A). New York: Delacorte Press, 2d printing, 1975.

This is a very proud child of its 18th-century Gothic ancestors. There are very few Gothic elements, but a beautifully crafted "female" story of adventure and romantic suspense. Archaeologist Joyce Lacy becomes involved in trying to recover a stolen Italian antiquity and the story is just grand in every sense.

940. The Previous Lady. New York: Dell, 1974.

LAURIA, Frank

941. Baron Orgaz. New York: Bantam, 1974.

Maybe 200 years from now the S/M homosexuals and the smoking, drinking, pill-popping mystics of this tale will seem as quaint and harmless as do now the naughty nuns and friars of its Gothic ancestors. But for now, and for me ... de trop!

942. Lady Sativa. New York: Curtis, n.d.

943. Raga Six. New York: Bantam Books, 1972. (NUC 1973 8-245)

LAWLESS, Bettyclare Hamilton
(Clare Hamilton)

Born 11/22/15 in New York City. Attended the University of California and art and fashion art schools. Worked as a free-lance commercial and fashion artist 1936-41 and a contracts secretary since 1959. Her home is in San Leandro, California.

944. Twilight Forest (D), by Clare Hamilton. New York: Pyramid, 1973.

I gave up in utter boredom when, by the first 100 pages, the heroine had gone to San Francisco, met her niece and nephew, traipsed around town, bought new clothes, planned a party, put down her sister and had begun to think her brother-in-law a pretty nifty guy. The author had another 160 pages to turn this dull romance into an interesting Gothic but the odds seemed all against it.

Also wrote Seadrift House.

LAWRENCE, Louise

945. The Wyndcliffe: A Story of Suspense. New York: Harper, 1975.
"An archly romantic gothic tale in which a love-lorn poet, 150 years dead, roams the windswept terrain, trying to make sense of the eternal questions concerning art, love, loneliness, being, nothingness and the music of the spheres. He is a figment (is he or isn't he?--only his author knows for sure) of Anna's imagination.... Together they go in for a lot of walking and talking, until at length her brother and sister entreat her back to the world of living--but oh! She's much the wiser for all those moonlit raps. If you know a teen-age girl who's looking for an escape route through 'silver mud and lemon mist,' this one's for her" (Alex Nelson, New York Times Book Review, p. 26 My 4 '75).

LAWRENCE, Margery H.

946. Bride of Darkness (C). London: Hale, 1967; New York: Ace (07301), 1969, 1973.
Nicely written horror Gothic tale flawed mainly by a very slow pace and a predictable plot.

947. Daughter of the Nile. London: Hale, 1956. (NUC 1956-67 66-495)

948. Master of Shadows. London: Hale, 1959. (NUC 1956-67 66-495)

949. Number Seven, Queer Street. Sauk City, Wisc.: Mycroft & Moran, 1969. (NUC 1968-72 55-270)

950. Skivvy. London: Hale, 1961. (NUC 1956-67 66-495)

LAWSON, Patrick (pseud.) see EBY, Lois Christine

LEADER, Mary

951. Triad (C). New York: Coward, McCann & Geoghegan, 1973; New York: Bantam Books, 1974. (NUC 1973 8-272)
One contemporary perspective on the old themes of possession and the supernatural is, of course, the psychological. This story, somewhat effectively, attempts to blend them all. Brenwen begins to have strange and frightening experiences, blackouts, and so on and eventually gets to a psychiatrist who realizes she has a

second self. In spite of some nice tries, the author's attempt just doesn't come together. She manages to hold the reader's attention well and shock the reader with events, but there were too many promises never fulfilled.

LEE, Elsie <u>see</u> SHERIDAN, Elsie Lee

LEECH, Audrey

952. <u>The Terror of Stormcastle</u>. New York: Warner Paperback, 1973.

953. <u>The Witches of Omen</u>. New York: Pyramid (T2411), n.d.

LEIGH, Susannah

954. <u>Dark Labyrinth</u> (F). Greenwich, Conn.: Fawcett Gold Medal, 1975.

Partial reading inspired no interest in this story in which the heroine is blinded by an attempt on her life. The style and prose seemed tedious and the promise of repeated traumas leading to a solution to the mystery was insufficient to merit further reading. Romantic suspense at its weakest.

LEIGH, Veronica

955. <u>The Boris Story</u>. New York: Manor, 1976.

956. <u>The Cat of Nine Tales</u>. New York: Manor, 1976.

957. <u>Dark Seed, Dark Flower</u>. New York: Manor, 1974.

958. <u>Voodoo Drums</u>. New York: Manor, 1975.

LESLIE, Josephine Aimee Campbell 1898-
(R. A. Dick)

959. <u>The Ghost and Mrs. Muir</u> (B), by R. A. Dick. Chicago: Ziff-Davis, 1945; published under real name by: New York: Pocket Books, 1974. (NUC pre'56 328-256)

A charming whimsical Gothic that seemed enjoyable even after the movie and a TV series.

960. <u>Unpainted Portrait</u>, by R. A. Dick. London: Hodder & Stoughton, 1954. (NUC pre'56 328-257)

LESTER, Teri

961. The Ouija Board (C). Sydney: Horwitz, 1969; New York: New American Library, 1969.
The ouija board spelled out a warning when Lisa touched the planchette. A tormented spirit warned of danger. An amusing but essentially trivial tale.

LETTON, Jeannette (Dowling)

962. Allegra's Child. Philadelphia: M. Smith, 1969. (NUC 1968-72 56-322)

963. Cragsmoor (F). Philadelphia: M. Smith, 1966; New York: MacFadden, 1968. (NUC 1956-67 68-165)
Kate returns to Thanksgiving dinner at the family home with sister, newlywed niece and husband and becomes involved in a murderous plot. This is a psychological suspense tale and the suspense only develops in the last third of the book.

964. Don't Cry Little Sister. Philadelphia: M. Smith, 1971. (NUC 1968-72 56-322)

965. Incident at Hendon. Philadelphia: M. Smith, 1967. (NUC 1956-67 68-165)

966. Jenny & I: A Novel of Suspense. Philadelphia: M. Smith, 1963. (NUC 1956-67 68-165)

967. The Robsart Affair, written with Francis Letton. New York: Harper, 1956. (NUC 1956-67 68-165)
Historical novel.

LEVY, Barbara

Author of several historical novels.

968. The Shining Mischief (C). New York: Putnam, 1971. (NUC 1968-72 56-415)
Story of a French family in the champagne business and an American businessman and his sister who becomes involved with the family and a nasty little conspiracy. A bit hard to categorize this rather long-winded story. It falls somewhere between a mystery and romantic suspense. Those looking for a Gothic will be disappointed.

LILLIE, Helen

969. The Listening Silence (B). New York: Hawthorn Books, [1970].
Margaret, a successful New York public relations executive, returns to her native Scotland following the sudden death of her older

sister. She finds an inheritance, a handsome cousin and a mystery as to the cause of her sister's death. Very nicely crafted story of romantic suspense. Also includes a sensitive treatment of the problems of deafness.

LINDLEY, Erica

970. The Brackenroyd Inheritance (A). New York: New American Library (Signet W6795), 1975.

Fern goes to Brackenroyd Hall to accept her joint inheritance with Bruno de Lacie and discovers a destiny fraught with problems. Sounds like a hundred other tales, but it isn't. This is one of the best of what the neo-Gothic can be--an imaginative, skillful treatment of the classic formula.

LINDOP, Audrey Erskine 1920-

Author of mystery and suspense stories. Not Gothic.

LINSAY, Perry (pseud.) see DERN, Peggy

LITTLE, Paul H.
(Paula Little, Paula Minton, Hugo Paul)

Born 2/5/15 in Chicago, Illinois where he still lives. B.S. from Northwestern University, 1937. Before becoming a full-time writer in 1964 he worked as a radio announcer in San Francisco and an advertising manager. He has a series of rather torrid novels written under his own name: The Agony of Desire, Sins of Tonia, etc.

971. Engraved in Evil, by Paula Minton (C). New York: Lancer (73-605), 1964.

When she comes of age, Geraldine travels from Switzerland and all across the U.S. on the trail of her past and her inheritance. She rebounds from disappointed love to true romance in this tale that to me seemed adolescent both in concept and style.

972. Hand of the Imposter, by Paula Minton. New York: Lancer, 1965.

973. Orphan of the Shadows, by Paula Minton. New York: Lancer, 1965.

974. Secret Melody, by Paula Minton. New York: Lancer, 1964.

975. Thunder on the Reef. New York: Lancer, n.d.
"Hawaiian gothic."

LITTLE, Paula (pseud.) see LITTLE, Paul H.

LLOYD, Stephanie (pseud.) see GOLDING, Morton (Jay)

LOCKE, Douglas

976. Death Lives in the Mansion. New York: Lancer (74-516), n.d.

977. The Drawstring. New York: Lancer (73-493), 1966.
I found the writing style of this author so obtuse that I gave up in despair after fifty pages. Annlea, widowed actress, has gone to the American Southwest to check out her husband's family.

LOEWENGARD, Heidi Huberta (Freybe) 1911-
(Martha Albrand, Katrin Holland, Christine Lambert)
Has written over twenty books which, in general, might be called "romantic intrigue." Her works do not fit my criteria for Gothic.

LOFTS, Nora (Robinson) 1904-
(Peter Curtis)

Works are mostly romances and historical novels. Exceptions:

978. The Devil's Own, by Peter Curtis (B). Garden City, N.Y.: Doubleday (Crime Club), 1960; New York: Pyramid, 1966. Also pub. by Doubleday in 1970 as: The Little Wax Doll, by Norah Lofts. (NUC 1956-67 70-112)
"The gentle school mistress was charmed by Canon Thornby and the peaceful English village of Walwyck. But there was a sinister old woman and whispers of witchcraft. It all seemed nonsense to Deborah. Logic began to crumble when a little boy was struck down with a strange illness, a wax doll with a severed head was discovered, and a villager met with a grim death." A fine story, well told. The characterizations are 3-D and the delightful heroine is over 40--hoorah!

979. House at Sunset. Garden City, N.Y.: Doubleday, 1962; Greenwich, Conn.: Fawcett-Crest (Q2492), 1974. (NUC 1956-67 70-113)

LONG, Frank Belknap 1903-

Principally a writer of science fiction.

980. The Goblin Tower. Cassia, Fla.: Dragonfly Press, 1935. (NUC pre'56 340-69)

981. The Horror from the Hills. Sauk City, Wisc.: Arkham, 1963. (NUC 1956-67 70-226)

LONG, Gabriella Margaret Vere (Campbell) (Costanzo) 1888-1952 (Marjorie Bowen, Margaret Campbell, George R. Preedy, Joseph Shearing, John Winch, Robert Paye)

From a huge output of mystery stories, romances and historical novels, I have selected a few which tend toward the Gothic. The George Preedy books seem to be all historical novels. To add to the confusion, some works have been published under different titles and different pseudonyms. For example, Forget-Me-Not, by Marjorie Bowen, The Strange Case of Lucille Clery by Joseph Shearing and Woman of Intrigue are all the same historical romance.

982. Black Magic, by Marjorie Bowen. London: A. Rivers, 1909. (NUC pre'56 70-312)

983. The Burning Glass, by Marjorie Bowen. London: Collins, 1918. New York: Dutton, 1920. (NUC pre'56 70-312)

984. The Golden Violet, by Joseph Shearing. London: Heinemann, 1936; New York: Berkley, 1965. (LCPC pre'42 136-279)

Long has a certain style for historical-sentimental Gothic that, for me, just doesn't come off. Maybe it's her lack of sympathy with any of her characters.

985. Great Tales of Horror, by Marjorie Bowen. London: Lane, 1933. (NUC pre'56 70-314)

986. The Spectral Bride, by Joseph Shearing. New York: Smith & Durrell, 1942. Pub. in England in 1942 as: The Fetch. (LCC supp 42-47 34-60). Also pub. as: The Spectral Bride, by Margaret Campbell. New York: New American Library (Signet Y6431), n.d.

987. The Spider in the Cup, by Joseph Shearing. New York: Smith & Haas, 1934; New York: Berkley, 1965. (LCPC '42 136-280). Pub. in England as: Album Leaf; also pub. as: Spider in the Cup, by Margaret Campbell. New York: New American Library (Signet W6557), n.d.

A long, and I thought, verbose tale that is much more closely allied to historical romance than my tastes prefer and just not all that entertaining in general. I fail to understand its numerous publications.

988. A Stranger Knocked, by Joseph Shearing. New York: privately printed for the friends of the Aldus Printers, Xmas 1963. (NUC 1968-72 86-176)

LONG, Lyda Belknap

989. Crucible of Evil (D). New York: Avon (19646), 1974.
Amanda's father dies in a fall downstairs in their huge and brooding New Orleans mansion and she is distraught by horrible apparitions. A very clumsy tale both in plot and writing style. Much of the suspense seems contrived and the plot tediously simplistic.

990. The Shape of Fear. New York: Ballantine, n.d.

991. The Witch Tree. New York: Lancer (74-722), n.d.

LORAINE, Phillip (pseud.)

Numerous works of mystery and suspense, a few of which have some Gothic relationship.

992. The Break in the Circle. New York: M. S. Mill, 1951. (NUC pre'56 341-174)

993. Day of the Arrow (C). New York: M. S. Mill, 1964; New York: Lancer (72-909), 1965. (NUC 1956-67 70-328)
Not a bad little tale, told from the male perspective. The hero goes to Belloc Castle to help his old sweetheart find out what is wrong with her husband--also an old and dear friend. Although not entirely according to the Gothic formula, I think this would still qualify. The plot and characters are a bit thin in spots but, in general, this is an interesting story.

994. Voices in an Empty Room (D). New York: Random House, 1974. (NUC 1974 10-513)
In my view, a very dull tale of ghostly goings on and possession set in a wealthy section of contemporary San Francisco. The pace was so slow that I finally gave up and checked out the ending to find it as predictable as I expected.

LORDAHL, Jo Ann

995. Those Subtle Weeds (C). New York: Ace, 1974.
The title comes from a nice quote from Edna Millay. The theme is "Florida Gothic," of a very routine nature except for some interesting Florida history.

LORENZEN, Coral E.

996. Shadow of the Unknown. New York: New American Library (Signet T4427), 1972.

LORING, Ann

997. The Mark of Satan. New York: Universal Pub. & Distr. (Award Books AN1324), 1970.

LORRIMER, Claire

998. A Voice in the Dark (B). London: Souvenir Press, 1967; New York: Avon, 1968. (NUC 1968-72 58-149)

A very satisfactory and innovative treatment of a standard neo-Gothic formula: young girl goes to wealthy household and finds intrigue and romance. The heroine, Laura, an English tourist visiting Florence, through a series of believable coincidences becomes engaged as a companion in the household of Comte Domenico dell'Alba. Alba's life is threatened (one of many happy switches) and Laura becomes involved.

LOTTMAN, Eileen (Shubb)
(Maud Willis)

Born 8/15/27 in Minneapolis, Minnesota. Attended the University of Iowa. She now lives in New York City. Career: film press agent, publicity director, copy chief, editor and writer. "I write for fun and money. I wrote my first book in order to pay for a flute, which I took up when I began free-lancing and found I had time to practice. My husband's work [CPA] allows us to travel the best way--3 to 6 months in each new place. I feel extraordinarily lucky, may never try to write for arts' sake." Contemporary Authors, Vol. 57-60, p. 360.

999. The Devil's Rain. New York: Dell, 1975.

1000. Doctor's Hospital, by Maud Willis. New York: Pocket Books, 1975.

1001. The Hemlock Tree (B). New York: Popular Library, 1975.

Molly Flute buys a converted barn on Long Island and gets involved in quite a mess. Likable story but overdramatized.

1002. Summersea, by Maud Willis. New York: Coward, 1975.

LOVECRAFT, H(oward) P(hillips) 1890-1937

"Born and lived in and near Providence, Rhode Island. He was an ailing youth and never attained much health. He traveled little and bent his energies on writing and amateur printing, while also pursuing an interest in astronomy and the occult. He created mythic lands and persons and used these in his stories of the supernatural. His work is highly prized by a devoted band of readers, to those outside the circle he seems to write pretentiously and badly, and his imaginings appear to lack originality." Barzun and Taylor, p. 712.

1003. Best Supernatural Stories by..., ed. & introd. by August Derleth. Cleveland & N.Y.: World Pub. Co., 1945. (NUC pre'56 343-103)

1004. Beyond the Wall of Sleep. Sauk City, Wisc.: Arkham, 1943. (NUC pre'56 343-103). Pub. in 1955 as: The Dream Quest of Unknown Kadath.

1005. The Case of Charles Dexter Ward: A Novel of Terror. London: Gollancz, 1951. (NUC pre'56 343-103)

1006. The Dunwich Horror. New York: Bart House, 1945. (NUC pre'56 343-104)

1007. The Haunter of the Dark & Other Tales of Horror. London: Gollancz, 1951. (NUC pre'56 343-104)

1008. The Lurker on the Threshold, with August Derleth. Sauk City, Wisc.: Arkham, 1945. (NUC pre'56 343-104)

1009. The Shadow over Innsmouth. Everett, Pa.: Visionary Pub. Co., 1936. (NUC pre'56 343-104)

1010. The Shunned House. Athol, Mass.: W. P. Cook, 1928. (NUC pre'56 343-105). Preface by Frank Belknap Long. Also published in: At the Mountains of Madness and Other Tales of Terror. New York: Ballantine, 1971; 5th printing, 1974.

This was essentially a short story and much in the tradition of Poe although lacking Poe's elegance of style.

1011. Supernatural Horror in Literature. New York: Abramson, 1945. (NUC pre'56 343-105)

LOVELL, Marc (pseud.) see McSHANE, Mark

LOVESMITH, Janet

1012. Inherit the Shadows. New York: Popular Library, n.d.

1013. Legacy of Fear (D). New York: Popular Library, 1971.

A complete collection of Gothic elements assembled in an ultramelodramatic tale stretching toward the pinnacle of the absurd. Unreal characters are led through unbelievable escapades with illogical results. Ho hum!

LOW, Dorothy Mackie see LOW, Lois Dorothea

LOW, Lois Dorothea (Pilkington) 1916-
(Dorothy Mackie Low, Lois Paxton)

Writer of romances and mysteries and although a couple that I read seemed quite good, they were not Gothic.

LOWNDES, Marie Adelaide (Belloc)

Born in England in 1868. Sister of Hilaire Belloc. Author of historical works, novels, plays and especially murder and mystery tales. A huge output listed in the NUC pre'56 Vol. 343, pp. 490-98. She died in 1947.

1014. Lizzie Borden: A Study in Conjecture. New York: Longmans, Green, 1939. (NUC pre'56 343-493)

1015. The Lodger (D). New York: Scribner, 1913. (NUC pre'56 343-493)

A fictional treatment of the "Jack the Ripper" case. I found it tedious. And I do not like romanticizing real crimes.

1016. The Lonely House. New York: Doran, 1920. (NUC pre'56 343-494)

1017. The Terriford Mystery. Garden City, N.Y.: Doubleday, 1924. (NUC pre'56 343-496)

LUTRELL, Wanda

1018. House of Elnora Garland (D). New York: Belmont-Tower, 1971.

A modern-day haunted house story of less than mediocre quality. The plot is unimaginative, the heroine exceedingly mundane and the philosophy juvenile.

LYNCH, Frances

1019. Candle at Midnight. New York: Dell, 1977; also pub. as: Twice Ten Thousand Miles. New York: St. Martin's, 1974.

The first 100 pages are romance--dull, verbose romance at that. Beth leaves a domineering aunt to take a P.R. job at a stately home and the reader is assumed to be endlessly interested in the day to day life of the inhabitants thereof. Assumption wrong, for this reader, at least. No Gothic elements as far as I read.

LYNCH, Miriam
(see also Claire Vincent)

1020. Bells of Widow's Bay. New York: Pinnacle Books, 1971.

1021. The Brides of Lucifer. New York: Manor, 1976.

1022. A Crime for Christmas. New York: Arcadia House, 1959. (NUC 1956-67 71-305)

1023. An Echo of Weeping (D). New York: Lancer, [1971].
A classy title and a good quote from Melville are about all this book has to commend it. Begins rather intriguingly as Maria decides to find out why her reclusive sister hasn't returned from an unprecedented visit to "friends," but it all comes to naught.

1024. House of Yesteryear. New York: Ballantine, 1974.

1025. A Meeting with Murder. New York: Arcadia House, 1956. (NUC 1956-67 71-305)

1026. Road to Midnight. New York: Ballantine, 1974.

1027. The Secret of Lucifer's Island (D). New York: Paperback Library (52-422), 1967.
Connie agrees to go with her aunt to visit some wealthy show business folk on the fabulous Lucifer's Island off the northeast U.S. coast. They find their arrival quite unwelcome and themselves thrown into the midst of a nasty little conspiracy. Melodrama abounds, and that's about all.

1028. The Witches' Song. New York: Manor, 1976.

1029. Your Casket Awaits, Madam. New York: Arcadia House, 1957. (NUC 1956-67 71-305)

LYNN, Kay

1030. Dark Shadows. London: Hutchinson, 1935. (NUC pre'56 347-365)
Tried to get this book on interlibrary loan and nobody could find it.

1031. Laughing Mountains. New York: Dutton, 1936. (NUC pre'56 347-365)

LYNN, Margaret (pseud.) see BATTYE, Gladys (Starkey)

LYONS, Delphine C.

Has also written the Whole World Catalogue.

1032. The Depths of Yesterday. New York: Lancer, n.d.

1033. Flower of Evil (B). New York: Pyramid (T2859), 1965 & 1972.

Suzannah gets a job as horticultural assistant to Jeremy Osborne and finds a troubled household when she arrives. This is a better than average neo-Gothic. Lyons writes competently and manages to build and sustain curiosity as to the outcome of a tale which follows very traditional lines.

Other books include: House of Four Windows, Phantom at Lost Lake and Valley of Shadows, all published by Lancer.

McALLISTER, Annie

1034. House of Vengeance (C). New York: Berkley Medallion, 1976. [© Bruce Cassiday].

Film buffs should enjoy this innovative neo-Gothic set in a Hollywood movie studio during the 1920's. For me the Gothic tale seemed secondary to the film nostalgia.

MACARDLE, Dorothy 1889-

In addition to works listed here, has also written non-fiction (Irish & European history) and plays.

1035. Dark Enchantment. Garden City, N.Y.: Doubleday, 1953. (NUC pre'56 348-356)

1036. Fantastic Summer. London: Davies, 1946. (NUC pre'56 348-356)

1037. The Unforseen (B). Garden City, N.Y.: Doubleday, 1946. (NUC pre'56 348-357)

A low-keyed but carefully wrought tale of extra-sensory phenomena and how they can affect lives. Characters are well drawn and the plot is entertaining. Virgilia develops precognition after moving to a rural Irish cottage.

1038. The Uninvited. Garden City, N.Y.: Doubleday, 1942; pub. in London as: Uneasy Freehold. (NUC pre'56 348-356)

McCAFFREY, Anne

Born 4/1/26 in Cambridge, Massachusetts. Received a B.A. (cum laude) from Radcliffe in 1947 and studied voice for nine years. Lives with husband in Sea Cliff, New York. She describes her work as "speculative fiction."

1039. Decision at Doona. New York: Ballantine, 1969. (NUC 1968-72 59-47). "Ballantine Science Fiction 01576"

1040. Dragonflight. New York: Walker, 1969; New York: Ballantine, 1968. (NUC 1968-72 59-47). Hugo Award.

1041. The Mark of Merlin (C). New York: Dell (5466), 1971.
James Carlyle Murdock (Carla) and her dog Merlin travel to mid-winter Cape Cod to join her guardian for a rest following the death of her father, an army colonel during WWII. Carla learns her father did not die in battle but was murdered. Who done it? All the suspects very conveniently manage to arrive at the isolated, snow-bound Cape Cod house. The heroine's name and resulting confusion are the best part of this mediocre romantic suspense cum murder mystery.

1042. Ring of Fear. New York: Dell (7445), 1971.

McCARTHY, Cormac

Born 7/20/33 in Providence, Rhode Island. Attended the University of Tennessee four years. His first novel, The Orchard Keeper, won for him the travel award of the American Academy of Arts & Letters, the William Faulkner Foundation Award for the notable first novel of 1965, and a Rockefeller Foundation grant. He now lives in Rockford, Tennessee with his English wife whom he met and married during his travels.

1043. Child of God. New York: Random House, 1974. (NUC 1974 10-663)

1044. The Orchard Keeper. New York: Random House, 1965. (NUC 1956-67 71-427)

1045. Outer Dark. New York: Random House, 1968. (NUC 1968-72 59-62)
Book Review Digest (68:845) classifies this as Gothic but to me it would barely qualify, if at all. A grim, surrealistic tale, it reminded me most of an Ingmar Bergman movie.

McCLOY, Helen

1046. Mister Splitfoot. New York: Dodd, Mead, 1968; New York: Avon (S401), 1969.
Included here, as are many other books, because of the misleading paperback cover which calls this a "haunting novel of posession and death." Not so. This is a slightly better than average murder mystery. The supernatural is employed only indirectly and is not a part of the story--merely a device.

McCRAE, Elizabeth

1047. House of the Whispering Winds (C). New York: New American

Library (Signet D2903), 1966.

Anne goes to Switzerland as English tutor to 20-year-old Joceylyne. On the trip over she meets Ken and becomes interested in a Hungarian noblewoman he is attempting to trace. Lo and behold, the tutorial job ties in with the missing lady. This is not a bad story of romantic suspense, but it is greatly flawed by pages and pages of plot rehashing and speculation by the heroine which grinds the pace to a near halt too often.

Also wrote The Intrusion, published by the New American Library.

McEVOY, Marjorie Harte
(Marjorie Harte)

Born in York, Yorkshire, England. Privately educated. Has worked as an assistant matron at a girl's school and auxiliary nurse as well as a novelist. She has written a whole series of nurse stories and romances. The few with Gothic leanings are listed here.

1048. Eaglescliffe (D). New York: Lenox Hill, 1971.

This little tale has all the elements of the neo-Gothic genre but is just too tidy and contrived. A perfect example of a well-done-made-for-the-market book. It's all there, decently written, but also completely predictable and a complete bore.

1049. The Grenfell Legacy. London: Jenkins, 1968; New York: Pyramid, n.d.

1050. No Castle of Dreams. London: Jenkins, 1960.

1051. Softly Treads Danger. London: Jenkins, 1963.

McGERR, Patricia

Born 12/26/17 in Falls City, Nebraska. A.B. University of Nebraska, 1936; M.S. Columbia University, 1937. Lives in Washington, D.C. Before becoming a self-employed writer in 1948, worked as a publicity director and editor. She has written a large number of works that are essentially detective-mystery and are listed in the Catalogue of Crime. I call the readers' attention to three in particular.

1052. Dangerous Landing (B). New York: Dell, 1975.

A cleverly plotted, well written story about grandmother Kale, learning to fly (literally and symbolically) and getting caught up in a dangerous adventure. To say more would give too much away. It is refreshing to find a tale of romantic-suspense and adventure that doesn't pander to the cult of the youthful heroine!

1053. Pick Your Victim. Garden City, N.Y.: Doubleday (Crime

Club), 1947. (NUC pre'56 350-674)
Called in the Catalogue of Crime "a masterpiece."

1054. The Seven Deadly Sisters. Garden City, N.Y.: Doubleday (Crime Club), 1947. (NUC pre'56 350-674)
Also highly recommended though not Gothic.

McHUGH, Frances Y.

1055. Bluethorne (D). New York: Arcadia House, 1966; Tel Aviv, Israel: Sharon Pub., n.d. (NUC 1956-67 72-122)

A very trivial romantic suspense. Lynn goes to Bluethorne as governess to a five-year-old girl and gets involved in family intrigue. The only interesting thing in the book is when Charles gets stabbed in the back with a boomerang(!)

1056. The China Shepherdess. New York: Arcadia House, 1966. (NUC 1956-67 72-122)

1057. The Pale Pink House. New York: Arcadia House, 1967. (NUC 1956-67 72-122)

1058. Shadow Acres. New York: Arcadia House, 1967. (NUC 1956-67 72-122)

McILWRAITH, Maureen Mollie Hunter
(Molly Hunter)

A native of Scotland, she attended Preston Lodge School in East Lothian, Scotland. She and her husband Michael, and their two sons live in the Highlands near Inverness. Hunter is the author of a number of popular books for young people, including The Kelpies Pearls, whose fantasy and rhythmic language are derived from Celtic folklore, one of Hunter's favorite studies. (Information from the Avon edition of The Thirteenth Member.)

1059. The Thirteenth Member (C), by Mollie Hunter. New York: Harper & Row, 1971; New York: Avon (V2479), 1972.

Published by Avon as an adult Gothic, I wonder how it differs from the author's juvenile works. To me the tale, although Gothic, was definitely written for the younger set--simple prose, simple characters and simple plot.

McINTOSH, Katherin

1060. Darkness Appeas'd. London: Long, 1932.

MACK, Evalina (pseud.) see McNAMARA, Lena Brooke

MACKAY, Mary 1864-1924
(Marie Corelli)

English novelist of Italian and Scottish parentage. Adopted in infancy by Charles Mackay, the poet. Her biography has been written by Eileen Bigland, Marie Corelli (1953). A partial bibliography is listed here. Although frequently referred to as an author of "Gothics," most of Corelli's works seem to me to be romances or philosophical, social and psychological novels.

1061. Angel's Wickedness, by Marie Corelli. New York: Beers, 1900. (NUC pre'56 122-620)

1062. The Devil's Motor: A Fantasy, by Marie Corelli. London: Hodder & Stoughton, 1910. (NUC pre'56 122-622)

1063. The Secret Power (A), by Marie Corelli. Garden City, N.Y.: Doubleday, 1921. (NUC pre'56 122-626)

Wow! Corelli is NOT what I expected--at least in this lovely book. This is more of a mystical tale in the vein of Arnold Bennett than a Gothic. It is also an eloquent feminist tract. Morgana Royal, a heroine to lead all heroines, has everything--fabulous wealth, great intelligence, and not bad looks. What she does with it all is the gist of the story. A bonanza of feminist ammunition.

1064. The Strange Visitation of Josiah McNason; a Ghost Story, by Marie Corelli. London: Newnes & New York: International News Co., 1904. (NUC pre'56 122-628)

This story has a plot uncomfortably close to that of Dickens' Christmas Carol.

1065. Wormwood, by Marie Corelli. New York: Collier, n.d. (NUC pre'56 122-629)

Somewhat the Lost Weekend of the late 19th century. Wormwood is the anglicized word for absinthe and this is a story of the devastation that addiction to absinthe can cause. A powerful and dramatic tale, but, though applicable to other addictions, somewhat dated--and not Gothic.

MACOMBER, Daria

1066. A Clearing in the Fog (B). New York: World Pub. Co., 1970; New York: New American Library (Signet T4727), 1971. (NUC 1968-72 59-446)

Cory accepts a spur-of-the-moment invitation to visit the Charleston, South Carolina home of newly met Scriven. When she arrives she discovers a shocking secret. A well written story, although essentially a murder mystery.

1067. Return to Octavia. New York: New American Library,

1967. (NUC 1956-67 72-314). Orig. pub. as: Hunter, Hunter, Get Your Gun.

McSHANE, Mark
(Marc Lovell)

Born in Sydney, Australia in 1930. McShane is married and has four children. Attended Technical College, Blackpool, Lancashire, England. His home is now in Majorca, Spain, after living in twelve different countries. His special interests include criminal psychology and psychic research. The McShane novels, although primarily mystery and detection, might be of some interest to readers of Gothic fiction, for example, Seance on a Wet Afternoon, London: Cassell, 1961.

1068. The Ghost of Megan (B), by Marc Lovell. Garden City, N. Y.: Doubleday (Crime Club), 1968. (NUC 1968-72 58-256)
An entertaining mystery about an American movie star who decides to get away from it all and ends up at a mansion in Wales where some very mysterious things happen. Although several elements are used, this is not really a Gothic but a transitional work somewhere between mystery-detection and Gothic.

1069. The Imitation Thieves, by Marc Lovell. Garden City, N. Y.: Doubleday (Crime Club), 1971. (NUC 1968-72 58-256)

1070. An Inquiry into the Existence of Vampires (B), by Marc Lovell. Garden City, N. Y.: Doubleday, 1974.
A very neat, tightly written little horror Gothic about a young Canadian who travels to a remote English village to investigate a rumor of vampirism. Cleverly written and conceived.

1071. A Presence in the House, by Marc Lovell. Garden City, N. Y.: Doubleday (Crime Club), 1972. (NUC 1968-72 58-256)

MADDEN, Anne Wakefield

1072. The Amberley Diamonds. New York: Ballantine, 1973.
A love story with an incidental mystery. Not Gothic and not very good.

MALLESON, Lucy Beatrice 1899-
(Anthony Gilbert, Anne Meredith)

Malleson's books are basically detective fiction, although she often uses the character Arthur Crook, a detective lawyer, almost as an appendage to an otherwise neo-Gothic story. Another of the transitional authors between Gothic and detective fiction. She has written 100 books or more.

MALLET, Anne

1073. House on Eagle Ledge. New York: Belmont-Tower, 1974.

MALM, Dorothea

1074. On a Fated Night (D). Garden City, N.Y.: Doubleday, 1965; New York: Lancer (75-594), 1966. (NUC 1956-67 73-272)

An American artist studying in Paris meets and marries a handsome aristocrat only to discover he has used her for vengeance and is mad. I found Malm's style very difficult reading and most annoying--mainly due to the copious use of dots, dashes and partial sentences. Also most distracting was the use of phonetic spelling of the French characters' English pronunciation.

1075. To the Castle. London: Davies, 1955. (NUC pre'56 357-578)

Other works include: Claire (Putnams, 1956), Every Third Thought (Davies, 1962), Journal of the Lady Pamela Foxe (Prentice-Hall, 1947), The Paper Mistress (Coward-McCann, 1959), and The Woman Question (Appleton-Century, 1957).

MANN, Deborah (pseud.) see BLOOM, Ursula

MANN, Jack (pseud.) see VIVIAN, Evelyn Charles

MANNERS, Alexandra (pseud.) see RUNDLE, Anne

MARCH, William (pseud.) see CAMPBELL, William Edward

MARCHANT, Catherine (pseud.) see COOKSON, Catherine

MARINO, Susan

1076. Vendetta Castle (C). New York: Avon, 1971.

Andrea gets a summer job as Sicilian reader and companion to the 85-year-old matriarch of a wealthy family in an authentic Sicilian castle rebuilt in the U.S. This is a tale of romantic suspense. The castle is not used in the plot. A fairly entertaining story except I resented what seemed like the author's intrusion of personal moral judgments on social issues involved in the story.

MARKHAM, Virgil 1899-

1077. The Black Door. New York: Knopf, 1930. (NUC pre'56 362-386). Also pub. in London, 1930, as: Shock!

Subtitled: The Mystery of the Fate of Sir Anthony Veryan's Heirs in Kestril's Eyrie Castle Near the Coast of Wales. Now Set Down from Information Supplied by the Principle [sic] Surviving Actors and Witnesses (and that's just the title!).

The story, I fear, is just as verbose as the title and is a murder mystery with Gothic elements insufficient in number and relevance to qualify the work as Gothic.

1078. The Dead Are Prowling. London: Collins (Crime Club), 1934. (NUC pre'56 362-386)

1079. The Deadly Jest. London: Collins (Crime Club), 1935. (NUC pre'56 362-386)

1080. Death in the Dusk. London & N. Y.: Knopf, 1928. (NUC pre'56 362-386)

Subtitled: Being Alfred Bannerlee's Own Revision and Enlargement of His Journals from the Evening of October 2nd, 1925, to the Breaking Off, October 9th: Together with the Conclusion of the Narrative Later Supplied by Him; and the Communication of April 17th, 1926, Now First Arranged and Edited by Virgil Markham.

1081. The Devil Drives. New York: Knopf, 1932. (NUC pre'56 362-386)

1082. Red Warning. New York: Farrar & Rinehart, 1933. (NUC pre'56 362-387)

MARLETT, Melba Balmat (Grimes) 1909-

1083. Another Day Toward Dying. Garden City, N. Y.: Doubleday (Crime Club), 1943. (NUC pre'56 362-521)

1084. Death Has a Thousand Doors. Garden City, N. Y.: Doubleday (Crime Club), 1941. (NUC pre'56 362-521)

1085. The Devil Builds a Chapel. Garden City, N. Y.: Doubleday (Crime Club), 1942. (NUC pre'56 362-521)

1086. Escape While I Can (B). Garden City, N. Y.: Doubleday (Crime Club), 1944; New York: Ace, 1944. (NUC pre'56 362-521)

Long-winded but nonetheless an engrossing tale of Elizabeth

who weds Thayer and joins a rather strange household in northern Michigan. Some bizarre things happen and E., fearing for her life, leaves Thayer (would some other heroines should take such a sensible measure). Eight years later, Thayer dies and E. returns to a resolution of the mysteries.

1087. The Frightened Ones: Five Stories. Garden City, N.Y.: Doubleday, 1956. (NUC 1956-67 74-235)

MARLOW, Edwina
(see also T. E. Huff)

1088. Falconridge (D). New York: Ace, 1969 [© T. E. Huff].
This follows a Gothic formula but offers little more. Lauren goes to France to live with her aunt and uncle. She there uncovers a conspiracy, veiled in a Gothic atmosphere. Helena (the aunt) is the only non-stock character.

1089. The Master of Phoenix Hall. New York: Ace (52161), 1972.

MARLOWE, Derek

1090. Nightshade (B). New York: Viking, 1976.
A most captivating tale. A charming and subtle dip into human frailty and self delusion, subliminal Evil and the occult. Not exactly Gothic ... and yet....

MARSH, John 1907-

1091. Monk's Hollow (C). Leichester, [England]: Ulverscroft, 1971; New York: Ace (53560), 1968. (NUC 1973 9-25)
A competent and entertaining though not particularly inspired tale in the sentimental Gothic tradition.

MARSH, Richard ?-1915

More than forty works listed in the NUC, Vol. 363. Some which may be Gothic include:

1092. The Beetle, a Mystery. London: Skeffington, 1898. (NUC pre'56 363-447)

1093. Between the Dark and Daylight. London: Digby, Long, 1902. (NUC pre'56 363-447)

1094. The Garden of Mystery. London: Long, 1906. (NUC pre'56 363-448)

1095. The Goddess: A Demon. London: White, 1900. (NUC pre'56 363-448)

1096. The Seen and the Unseen. New York: New Amsterdam Books, 1900. (NUC pre'56 363-449)

1097. The Woman with One Hand. London: Literary Press, 19?? (NUC pre'56 363-449)

MARSHALL, Edison
(Hall Hunter)

Born in Rensselaer, Indiana in 1894. He was a hunter and explorer during his younger years; in the Army during WWI; and then became a writer. Marshall wrote a huge number of adventure tales (The Yankee Pasha, The Adventures of Jason Starbuck, The White Brigand, etc.) of a masculine romantic-type. Some works along the more Gothic line might include:

1098. Castle in the Swamp: A Tale of Old Carolina (B). New York: Farrar, Straus, 1948; New York: Dell, 1967. (NUC pre'56 363-520)
Sentimental Gothic with a male hero. A quest theme and quite nicely done.

1099. The Death Bell. Garden City, N.Y.: Garden City Pub. Co., 1924. (NUC pre'56 363-520)

1100. Forlorn Island. New York: H. C. Kinsey, 1932. (NUC pre'56 363-520)

1101. The Isle of Retribution. Boston: Little, Brown, 1923. (NUC pre'56 363-521)

1102. Ogden's Strange Story. New York: H. C. Kinsey, 1934. (NUC pre'56 363-522)

MARSHALL, Joanne (pseud.) see RUNDLE, Anne

MARTIN, Ethel Bowyer

Has also written juvenile Gothics.

1103. Nightmare House (C). New York: Ace, 1975.
Shelly O'Neil takes a summer job as nursemaid and travels to remote Elmwood to meet her charge. She arrives to find a strange and troubled household and some very suspicious behavior on the part of the baby's parents. The only Gothic elements are mystery and the atmosphere. The old house has no real part in the story.

MARTIN, Jay (pseud.) see GOLDING, Morton

MARVIN, Susan

1104. Chateau in the Shadows. New York: Dell, 1969.

1105. The Secret of Chateau Laval. New York: Avon, 1973.

1106. The Secret of the Villa Como (D). New York: Lancer (74-991), 1969.

Lisa goes to the Villa Como in Italy following a deathbed admonition by her mother. There she finds dull danger and indifferent intrigue. Superficial romantic suspense.

1107. Summer of Fear (D). New York: Dell (8497), 1971. [© Julie M. Ellis].

Karen goes to spend the summer in France at Lafontaine where she is to tutor 14-year-old Charles. The usual threatening things happen. The plot in this shallow tale is contrived and unbelievable and the characters inspire no interest.

1108. Where Is Holly Carleton? New York: Ballantine, 1973.

MASON, Tally (pseud.) see DERLETH, August

MATHESON, Richard 1926-

1109. Fury on Sunday. New York: Lion Books, 1954. (NUC pre'56 369-179)

1110. Hell House (A). New York: Viking, 1971; New York: Bantam (7277). (NUC 1968-72 62-22)

Holy Cow! This was a bit of horror Gothic to end all horror Gothics. Well written and quite a tale--but don't essay if you have delicate sensibilities. Things get rough.

1111. I Am Legend. New York: Fawcett Gold Medal (417), 1954. (NUC pre'56 369-179)

MAURIER, Daphne du see DU MAURIER, Daphne

MAXWELL, Helen K.

1112. The Girl in the Mask. Boston: Little, Brown, 1971. (NUC 1968-72 61-226)

1113. Leave It to Amanda (B). Boston: Little, Brown, 1972. (NUC 1968-72 61-226)

A fine novel of romantic suspense, well written.

1114. The Livingston Heirs (B). Boston: Little, Brown, 1973.

(NUC 1974 11-181)

Another very nice romantic suspense. A bit tame for my tastes.

MAXWELL, Patricia (Ponder)

Born 3/9/42 in Winn Parish, Louisiana. Lives with husband and four children in Quitman, Louisiana.

1115. The Court of the Thorn Tree. New York: Popular Library (00592), 1974.

1116. Dark Masquerade (C). Greenwich, Conn.: Fawcett-Crest, 1974.

Elizabeth poses as her dead sister and returns with her nephew to claim his inheritance and heritage at a Louisiana plantation. Routine "Southern U.S. Gothic."

1117. The Secret of Mirror House. Greenwich, Conn.: Fawcett (R2235), 1970. (NUC 1973 9-174)

1118. Stranger at Plantation Inn (C). Greenwich, Conn.: Fawcett (R2371), 1971. (NUC 1973 9-174)

On her way to a job in N. Louisiana, Lillian gets stranded at Plantation Inn due to a flood. One of the guests may be a ruthless bandit. The story covers three days at the Inn and the discovery of the bandit. Based on some historical events.

MAYBURY, Anne (pseud. ?)

"Anne Maybury, the well-known Gothic writer ... works in a London flat overlooking the trees of Kensington Gardens--a far cry from the 1640 house in which she once lived and which sparked off, she thinks, her desire to write atmosphere [sic] novels." (Information from "About the Author" in Bantam ed. of Paradise Gardens.)

1119. The Brides of Bellenmore (C). New York: Ace, 1964. (NUC 1968-72 62-248)

This tale does manage to keep moving, but just barely. Elizabeth Bellenmore returns to her family home and suspects murder in the death of her step-brother's wife. The culprit seemed evident to me early in the story. A mediocre effort.

1120. Falcon's Shadow. New York: Ace, 1964.

1121. Green Fire. New York: Ace (30282), 1972.

1122. The House of Fand. New York: Ace, 1972.

1123. I Am Gabriella! London: Collins, 1962. (NUC 1956-67 75-443)

1124. Jessamy Court (C). New York: Random House, 1974 [© Anne Buxton]. (NUC 1974 11-188)

Rachael goes to Jessamy Court posing as friend of Stephanie to try to discover why Stephanie--hospitalized in a state of acute shock--whispers only "Jessamy." A fairly good story, flawed mainly by the heroine's continual speculation. Let the reader do the speculation. The writer should get on with the story!

1125. Journey into Morning. New York: Arcadia House, 1945. (NUC pre'56 371-470)

1126. The Midnight Dancers (F). New York: Random House, 1973; Literary Guild, 1974; New York: Bantam, 1974. (NUC 1973 9-180)

Oh dear! The first third of this book reads like an article in "True Romance" and I just couldn't hack it. Interesting travelog but the prose and the tale were so odiously boring it just didn't seem worth reading to find out what happened.

1127. The Minerva Stone. Chicago: Holt, Rinehart & Winston, 1968. (NUC 1968-72 62-248)

1128. The Moonlit Door. New York: Holt, Rinehart & Winston, 1967. (NUC 1956-67 75-443)

1129. The Night My Enemy. New York: Ace, 1972 & 1976.

1130. The Pavillion at Monkshood (B). New York: Ace, 1965.

Jessica goes to Dorset and Monkshood to visit relatives when her mother gets a job with a coutourier in the U.S. Jessica finds herself caught up in a complicated intrigue of love and high finance. An entertaining romantic suspense.

1131. Ride a White Dolphin. New York: Random House, 1971. (NUC 1968-72 62-249)

1132. The Secret of the Rose. London: Collins, 1941. (NUC pre'56 371-470)

1133. Shadow of a Stranger. New York: Ace, n.d.

1134. Someone Waiting (B). New York: Ace, 1961.

Leone Sarat, a young actress, returns to her ancestral home near London at her grandmother's request just a year after her guardian's unsolved murder there. Her return looses forces leading to the solution of the murder. Hardly Gothic, but good.

1135. Stay Until Tomorrow. New York: Ace (78551), 1973.

1136. The Terracotta Palace. New York: Random House, 1971; New York: Bantam (Q6306), 1971. (NUC 1968-72 62-249)

1137. Walk in the Paradise Garden (B). New York: Random House, 1972; New York: Bantam (Q7658), 1973. (NUC 1968-72 62-249)

Justine goes to a remote Greek island to spend seven weeks with the handsome Louis prior to their formal engagement. There she meets Louis' sister Kate, their neighbors, author Matt Braddon and his retarded niece, Elaine, and a few other assorted local folk. Justine becomes more and more interested in the fey Elaine and less and less interested in Louis. Then troubles begin. A well written story of romantic suspense that manages to sustain interest through a relatively undramatic plot. The characters seem to make all the difference. One soon gets to care about what happens to them all.

1138. Whisper in the Dark. New York: Ace (88427), 1972.

1139. The Winds of Night. New York: Ace, 1963. (NUC 1973 9-180). Orig. title: Enchanter's Nightshade.

MAYFIELD, Serena

1140. Stranger in the House (D). New York: Pocket Books (77596), 1972.

A dull little tale of actress Letty who lets her agent talk her into posing as his fiancée to improve public relations with his dying rich grandmother.

MELVILLE, Jennie

1141. Burning Is a Substitute for Loving. New York: London House & Maxwell, 1964. (NUC 1956-67 76-253)

1142. Come Home and Be Killed. New York: London House & Maxwell, 1964. (NUC 1956-67 76-253)

1143. The Hunter in the Shadows. London: Hodder & Stoughton, 1969. (NUC 1968-72 62-596)

1144. Ironwood. New York: McKay, 1972. (NUC 1968-72 62-596)

1145. Murderer's Houses. London: Joseph, 1964. (NUC 1956-67 76-253)

1146. Nell Alone. London: Joseph, 1966. (NUC 1956-67 76-253)

1147. A New Kind of Killer, an Old Kind of Death. New York: McKay, 1971. (NUC 1968-72 62-576)

1148. Nun's Castle (D). New York: McKay, 1973. (NUC 1974 11-283)

This has all the ingredients of a Gothic but Melville was not able to pull them together into a coherent or satisfying tale. Selina goes for a rest to her recently co-inherited home of Nun's Castle. Some strange things happen. The details of this story include glaring inconsistencies. Poorly crafted.

1149. There Lies Your Love. London: Joseph, 1965. (NUC 1956-67 76-253)

MEREDITH, Anne (pseud.) see MALLESON, Lucy Beatrice

MERTZ, Barbara (Gross)
(Barbara Michaels, Elizabeth Peters)

Born 9/29/27 in Canton, Illinois. Education: University of Chicago Ph.B. 1947; M.A. 1950 and Ph.D. 1952. Married Richard R. Mertz in 1950. They have two children. Her career has been that of historian and writer. She has written books on Egyptology and Roman history. Now living in Potomac, Maryland.

1150. Ammie, Come Home (A), by Barbara Michaels. New York: Meredith, 1968; Greenwich, Conn.: Fawcett-Crest, 1969. (NUC 1968-72 63-144)

A beautiful example of "contemporary American Gothic." Set in Georgetown, it employs all the elements of dwelling, atmosphere, the supernatural and so on, in a contemporary setting. Tops in every respect. Also a nice double romance in mid-age and youth, with some interesting views on the "generation gap."

1151. Borrower of the Night, by Elizabeth Peters. New York: Dodd, Mead, 1973. (NUC 1973 11-46)

1152. The Camelot Caper, by Elizabeth Peters. New York: Meredith, 1969. (NUC 1968-72 75-154)

1153. The Crying Child (A), by Barbara Michaels. New York: Dodd, Mead, 1971; Greenwich, Conn.: Fawcett-Crest, 1972. (NUC 1968-72 63-144)

Terrific! Full Gothic treatment set on an island in Maine.

1154. The Dark on the Other Side (B), by Barbara Michaels. New York: Dodd, Mead, 1970; Greenwich, Conn.: Fawcett-Crest, 1970. (NUC 1968-72 63-144)

Michael plans to do a biography of the illustrious Gordon Randall and visits for a weekend--long enough to become involved in a tangled web of mystery and the supernatural. Another gem of a story. The philosophy and a terrific cat made the book for me.

1155. The Dead Sea Cipher, by Elizabeth Peters. New York: Dodd, Mead, 1970. (NUC 1968-72 75-154)

1156. Greygallows (A), by Barbara Michaels. New York: Dodd,

Mead, 1972; Greenwich, Conn.: Fawcett-Crest, n.d. (NUC 1968-72 63-144)

In the mid-19th century, an orphaned and sickly heiress is married to Baron Clare whose behavior becomes increasingly sinister as Lucy becomes increasingly wise and well. Michaels' treatment of a well-used plot demonstrates great skill.

1157. Her Cousin John, by Elizabeth Peters. New York: Dell, 1969.

1158. House of Many Shadows (A), by Barbara Michaels. New York: Dodd, Mead, 1974; Greenwich, Conn.: Fawcett-Crest, 1974. (NUC 1974 11-332)

This tidy little tale has something for everyone including real ghosts, good, solid characters and a plot that doesn't let the reader down. Meg goes to refurbish a house in Pennsylvania and to recuperate from a head injury. She meets Andy and, together, they meet the supernatural.

1159. The Jackal's Head, by Elizabeth Peters. New York: Meredith, 1968. (NUC 1968-72 63-144)

1160. The Master of Blacktower (C), by Barbara Michaels. New York: Appleton-Century, 1966. (NUC 1956-67 76-458)

I found this one a bit dull. Damaris is a second-rate Jane Eyre, in the same predicament but without the depth of character. The plot seems contrived and unduly melodramatic.

1161. The Night of Four Hundred Rabbits, by Elizabeth Peters. New York: Dodd, Mead, 1971. (NUC 1968-72 72-154)

1162. Prince of Darkness (B), by Barbara Michaels. New York: Meredith, 1969; Greenwich, Conn.: Fawcett-Crest, n.d. (NUC 1968-72 63-144)

A suspicious young Englishman comes to Middlebury, Maryland, posing as a writer and cons his way into upper crust society in order to meet a wealthy heiress. More said would reveal too much of this clever and rather complex plot. Michaels manages to create great variety in her stories and the quality is there.

1163. The Sea-King's Daughter (C), by Barbara Michaels. New York: Dodd, Mead, 1975; Greenwich, Conn.: Fawcett-Crest, 1975.

Sandy (Ariadne) goes to a Greek island for the summer to assist her estranged archaeologist father in an illegal underwater search. There are a few good characterizations and a good deal of mythology interwoven through this otherwise disappointing tale of romantic suspense. Not up to Michaels' usual quality.

1164. The Seventh Sinner, by Elizabeth Peters. New York: Dodd, Mead, 1972. (NUC 1968-72 75-154)

1165. Sons of the Wolf (A), by Barbara Michaels. New York:

Meredith, 1967; New York: Warner Paperback (64-997), 1972. (NUC 1956-67 76-458). Also pub. as: Mystery on the Moors (Warner Paperback).

Harriet and Ada come under the guardianship of a distant cousin, John Wolfson, after the death of their grandmother. A sinister plot develops. A fine tale, well written, in diary form. Gothic elements are all there and delightfully employed.

1166. Witch (A), by Barbara Michaels. New York: Dodd, Mead, 1973. (NUC 1974 11-332)

Ellen moves to an old house in the wilds of western Virginia and finds superstition, hate and a ghost. She befriends Tim, ward of a rich, attractive neighbor and stumbles upon a sinister plot. Another great cat in this story.

METCALFE, John

1167. The Feasting Dead. Sauk City, Wisc.: Arkham, 1954.

MICHAELES, M. M. (pseud.) see GOLDING, Morton

MICHAELS, Barbara (pseud.) see MERTZ, Barbara

MIDWOOD, Barton 1938-

1168. Bodkin. New York: Random House, 1968. (NUC 1968-72 63-563)

Listed in Book Review Digest as Gothic. I disagree.

1169. Phantoms: A Collection of Stories. New York: Dutton, 1970. (NUC 1968-72 63-563)

MILLAR, Margaret (Sturm) 1915-

Many of this author's works published in paperback are called "Gothic." After reading and enjoying several I believe they are more correctly classified as mystery, suspense and detection. Millar is married to Kenneth Millar (the "Ross Macdonald" of detective fiction).

MILLER, Lanora (Welzenback)

1170. The House on Wolf Trail (C). New York: Ace (34415), 1976.

A fairly entertaining tale which is essentially a murder mystery with Gothic trappings.

Other works published by Ace include: The Devil's Due and Quickthorne.

MILLHISER, Marlys (Joy)

Born in Charles City, Iowa in 1938. Now lives with husband and two children in Boulder, Colorado.

1171. Michael's Wife. New York: Putnam, 1972. (NUC 1968-72 64-168)

1172. Nella Waits: A Novel of the Supernatural (A). New York: Putnam, 1974. (NUC 1974 11-493)

A most engrossing tale of ghostly goings on in a rural Iowa community; brought to an acceptable and satisfying conclusion.

MINTON, Paula (pseud.) see LITTLE, Paul H.

MOCKLER, Gretchen

1173. Roanleigh (B). New York: New American Library (Signet D2986), 1966.

A better than average tale of amnesia and conspiracy with a neo-Gothic setting.

MONSARRAT, Nicholas (John Turney)

Born 3/22/10 in Liverpool, England. B.A. in Law (honors) from Trinity College, Cambridge University in 1931. Career: spent two years in a solicitor's office in Nottingham before giving up law to begin a career in writing in 1934. May be best known for The Cruel Sea (Knopf, 1951). Has also written numerous adventure stories.

1174. Castle Garac (C). New York: Knopf, 1955. (NUC pre'56 391-304)

It's hard to fault this little tale which does have a sufficient number of elements to be Gothic and is certainly written skillfully. Yet, somehow it lacks the zest that, for me, makes a satisfying story. The main character is a male and does all the correct things but he comes out a bit of a bore as does the entire story. Seems to me one must be a bit naive to get much of a bang out of this story.

MOOR, Emily

1175. The Shadowed Porch (C). New York: Ballantine, 1972. [© Richard Deming].

A fair tale of Gothic romance starring Jane who takes a head librarian's job in a small Missouri town and becomes deeply involved in a leading family's tragedies, past and present.

MOORE, Dorine

1176. The Legend of Monk's Court. New York: Ballantine, 1974.

1177. Masquerade at Monfalcone. New York: Berkley Medallion, 1974.

MOORE, Isabel

1178. Chateau Sinister (C). New York: Lancer, 1971.
Nurse Abigail rushes to France at the urgent summons of her brother-in-law to be with her sister during a difficult confinement. Abigail arrives to find her sister ill and her brother-in-law mad and the whole thing is unbelievable and contrived.

1179. I'll Never Let You Go. New York: Farrar & Rinehart, 1942. (NUC pre'56 393-299)

1180. It's Time to Say Goodbye. New York: Farrar & Rinehart, 1944. (NUC pre'56 393-299)

1181. The Other Woman. New York: Farrar & Rinehart, 1942. (NUC pre'56 393-299)

MORGAN, Clarinda

1182. Devil's Cavern (C). New York: Lancer (73-551), 1967.
Letitia ("Tish") goes to Ireland to claim the inheritance of her son after her husband's death. This is a strangely written book with large gaps in the plot that would make one feel that chunks of the manuscript got lost on the way to press. Awkward word usage further detracts from this, in some ways, entertaining story.

MORRIS, Sara (pseud.) see BURKE, John (Frederick)

MORRISON, A(twood) Eula
(Drucy Atwood, Andrea Delmonico)

Born 1/6/11 in Hagerman, New Mexico. Education: nursing and part-time library arts studies. Married in 1933 and has three children. Her home is in Kirkland, Washington. She has worked as a radio technician and a publicity writer.

1183. Chateau Chaumond (C), by Andrea Delmonico. New York: Ace (G747), 1968.

Romantic suspense set at an elegant Wisconsin resort where Geraldine comes with her new husband and part-owner of the resort to take up a new life. Competent but predictable.

1184. Eyrie of an Eagle, by Andrea Delmonico. New York: Ace, 1969.

MORRISON, Roberta (pseud.) see WEBB, Jean Francis

MORTON, Anthony (pseud.) see CREASEY, John

MORTON, Patricia (pseud.) see GOLDING, Morton

MOTTRAM, Ralph Hale 1883-1971

English writer who produced a large amount of history, historical fiction, romances, a couple of which may be Gothic. Castle Island (Chatto & Windus, 1931) is not.

1185. The Ghost and the Maiden. London: Hutchinson, 1940. (NUC pre'56 398-96)

1186. The Headless Hound and Other Stories. London: Chatto & Windus, 1931. (NUC pre'56 398-96)

MUIR, Jean

Born 3/4/06 in Portland, Oregon. Home is in San Francisco. Has worked as a feature writer, and free-lance writer. "Miss Muir has lived in various countries of Europe for a total of about five years. She is wholly involved at the moment in romantic suspense fiction, possibly because of 'a reaction from having so much in the magazine article line, often slanted toward a male audience.'" Contemporary Authors, Vol. 29-32, p. 431.

Author of The Adventures of Grizzly Adams (Putnam, 1970).

1187. The Smiling Medusa. New York: Dodd, Mead, 1969. (NUC 1968-72 66-493)

1188. Stranger, Tread Light (C). Boston: G. K. Hall, 1971. (NUC 1968-72 66-493)

The heroine, visiting friends in Mexico, allows her host to pick her up a date in a bar since it would evidently be unthinkable for her to go unescorted to a fancy ball she craves to attend. I had the feeling that whatever she got after that, she deserved, and I couldn't care less what it might turn out to be.

1189. The Woods Were Full of Men, written with Irma Lee Emerson. New York: McKay, 1963.

MURDOCH, (Jean) Iris 1919-

I include Murdoch here because her publishers keep calling her works "Gothic." I don't think they are. Some examples include:

1190. The Black Prince. New York: Viking, 1973; New York: Warner Paperback, 1974. (NUC 1973 9-829)

The publisher describes this book as "a thriller" and a "neo-gothic mystery." I find nothing to justify either description. I was with Murdoch for the first 175 pages but things deteriorated rapidly thereafter. The book is supposedly a posthumous publication of an autobiographical treatise by a very neurotic writer. Lots of philosophizing, at first charming, but soon becoming tiresome when nothing develops to go with it. The whole effort just doesn't come off. No Gothic elements.

1191. The Flight from the Enchanter. New York: Viking, 1956. (NUC 1956-67 81-100)

A partial reading seems to indicate a psychological-social novel. Gothic connection must be remote, if indeed present.

1192. The Severed Head. New York: Viking, 1961. (NUC 1956-67 81-101)

A social, psychological drama and, to me, a bore.

1193. The Unicorn. New York: Viking, 1963; New York: Avon, 1965. (NUC 1956-67 81-101)

A long and pretentious tale attempting to make a "fantasy of the spiritual life" out of an alcoholic's machinations.

MURFI, Lidie

1194. The Magnolia Curse (A Ravenswood Gothic) (D). New York: Pocket Books, 1973.

A poorly crafted work of Southern Plantation Gothic in which the plot is all but lost in excess and awkward verbiage.

MURRAY, Beatrice (pseud.) see POSNER, Richard

MUSE, Patricia

1195. Eight Candles Glowing (D). New York: Ballantine, 1976.

A pointless tale, indifferently told, set in Key West, Florida, with a few Gothic props. Variations on the theme of Jane Eyre and just doesn't cut the mustard.

Other works include: Sound of Rain and Belle Claudine.

MUSSI, Mary (Edgar)
(Josephine Edgar, Mary Howard)

Born 12/27/07 in London, England. Her education was "private and brief." Under pseudonym Mary Howard ("Howard" was her mother's maiden name) has written a large number of sentimental romances.

1196. The Dancer's Daughter (D), by Josephine Edgar. London: Collins, 1969; New York: Dell, 1970.
After living her first 13 years as the adopted daughter of village peasants, Isobel finds she is the legitimate daughter and heir of the lord of the local manor. She moves there to live with her new aunt and cousins--one dashing and irresponsible and the other not so dashing but enormously responsible. All that follows is completely predictable and although well written, quite a bore. Gothic elements are token.

1197. The Dark Tower, by Josephine Edgar. London: Collins, 1966; New York: Dell, 1969.
Not a bad little love story but not Gothic by my definition. A tale of two girls and their two different loves--one "good" and one "bad." The bad affair, of course, causes all the drama.

1198. The Devil's Innocents, by Josephine Edgar. London: Collins, 1972.

1199. The Lady of Wildersley, by Josephine Edgar. London: McDonald & James, n.d.

1200. The Stranger at the Gate, by Josephine Edgar. London: Collins, 1973.

Other Josephine Edgar books include: My Sister Sophie (Pocket Books, 1974), and Time of Dreaming (Pocket Books, 1974).

MYERS, Barrie

1201. Evil Ever After. New York: Popular Library, 1972.
This appears to be an outright plagiarism of Genevieve St. John's The Shadow on Spanish Swamp (New York: Belmont, 1970). The story is set in Arizona instead of Louisiana, the maid is an Indian instead of a Negro and, of course, the names of the characters are different. Otherwise the plot is identical to the finest detail. Tisk, tisk!

1202. Nightfall (B). New York: Popular Library, [© 1971, International Book Assoc.].

A long, intricately plotted tale about Claudine who makes a spur-of-the-moment decision to tutor a mulatto youth in a wealthy household on Guadaloupe. She soon finds herself embroiled in family intrigue, voodoo and all kinds of excitement. Hope it's original!

1203. The Oblivious Host (D). New York: Popular Library [© 1973, Rights & Writers, Inc.].
Sentimental Gothic--dull, contrived and verbose.

MYERS, Robert J(ohn)

Publisher of The New Republic. Holds a Ph. D. from the University of Chicago and currently lives in Washington, D. C.

1204. The Cross of Frankenstein (A). Philadelphia & N. Y.: Lippincott, 1975.
In his introduction to this book, Myers explains his fascination with the Frankenstein legend and his reasons for wanting to write a new tale. I think his work comes off very well and is unquestionably in the spirit and tradition of horror Gothic. Myers' use of the language is a pure pleasure to read. His characters are complex and his story melodramatic and gripping.

1205. The Slave of Frankenstein (B). Philadelphia & N. Y.: Lippincott, 1976.
The Victor Frankenstein, Jr. vs. The Monster saga is taken up again thirty years later in this somewhat disappointing sequel. I was hoping for some dialogue between the two and for some growth on the part of Victor. Instead one gets a good deal of history of John Brown and the Abolition Movement and the same old reactionary Victor who seems not to have learned very much in thirty years.

NAPIER, Melissa

1206. The Haunted Woman (C). New York: Pyramid (00284), 1971.
Run-of-the-mill romantic suspense.

1207. House in White Mist (D). New York: Avon (V2448), 1972.
Nurse Dorothea accepts a job at Castlewarren as nurse and companion to the ill and aging Mr. Foxkill and arrives to find a houseful of really nasty people who treat her abominably and even scare her and threaten her life. She saves her patient from a vicious plot etc., etc., etc. Napier adds nothing but tedium to an already tedious formula.

Other writings include: House by the Bridge (Avon) and Mermaid of Dark Mountain (Avon).

NAYLOR, Eliot (pseud.) see FRANKAU, Pamela

NEILL, Robert

1208. Black William. Garden City, N.Y.: Doubleday, 1955. (NUC pre'56 409-667)

1209. The Elegant Witch. Garden City, N.Y.: Doubleday, 1952; also pub. as: Mist over Pendle. London: Hutchinson, 1951. (NUC pre'56 409-667)

1210. Rebel Heiress. Garden City, N.Y.: Doubleday, 1954. (NUC pre'56 409-667)

1211. So Fair a House (B). Garden City, N.Y.: Doubleday, 1961. (NUC 1956-67 82-550)

A very nice ghost and love story but seriously flawed by verbosity. Pages and pages can be skimmed losing nothing of importance to the tale.

NEILSON, Marguerite

1212. The Dark Path (C). New York: Manor, 1976.

This tale has all the elements of sentimental Gothic but the only action comes in the last three chapters and by then I was nearly asphyxiated with boredom by the dull romance occupying the bulk of the book.

NEWMAN, Robert (Howard)

A native of New York City since his birth in 1909, and a free-lance writer for his entire career. In addition to listed works he has also written juveniles, verse, short stories, scripts for TV, radio and movies, and so forth.

1213. The Enchanter (B). Boston: Houghton, Mifflin, 1962; New York: Warner Paperback, 1967. (NUC 1956-67 83-631)

"Aching balls," (page 7) is a rather singular expression in contemporary Gothic literature! This book is, actually, misrepresented as a "Gothic" by the paperback publisher. I found it very entertaining. It is a mystery-suspense written and narrated by a man and it does make for interesting comparisons with similar material written by and about females. The book is more philosophical than the average. The male perspectives are refreshing and the depth of the plot was rewarding to this reader.

1214. Identity Unknown. Chicago & N.Y.: Ziff-Davis, 1945. (NUC pre'56 417-304)

NICOLE, Claudette

1215. Bloodroots Manor (C). Greenwich, Conn.: Fawcett-Crest, 1970.

A hypermelodramatic and clumsy plot (for example, the heroine's nakedness occurs and is discussed ridiculously often and coincidence is relied upon unduly). Nonetheless, I liked the idea of using remote Kentucky hill life as "American medieval" and the troubador, Jed, is a most charming character.

1216. Circle of Secrets (D). Greenwich, Conn.: Fawcett-Crest, 1972.

A series of mysterious phone calls and a deed to a mansion on the Sea Islands bring Ann to her friend's rescue only to find her friend had died three years previously. This story had possibilities but was flawed by a clumsy plot, trite characters and Perils of Pauline-type events.

1217. The Haunted Heart (B). New York: Pyramid, 1972.

Cathy is either a paranoid schizophrenic or an extra-sensitive receptive woman. Things come to a crisis when her husband dies in a car crash but seems to return to her home. A well written "neo-Gothic" with an Oregon setting.

1218. The Haunting of Drumroe (C). Greenwich, Conn.: Fawcett-Crest, 1971.

Eileen goes to Ireland at the urgent request of a long-lost aunt and is nearly killed upon arrival. Discovers aunt is missing and so it goes. Lacks in depth and suffers from plot flaws.

1219. The House at Hawk's End (B). Greenwich, Conn.: Fawcett-Crest, 1971.

Jean travels to Newfoundland to recuperate following a friend's death. Natural and supernatural team up to provide mystery and suspense. Very close to the Gothic tradition and an enjoyable tale.

1220. The Mistress of Orion Hall (D). Greenwich, Conn.: Fawcett-Gold Medal, 1970.

Lisa goes to Cyprus with Aunt Maggie as companion and interpreter at the family mansion, Orion Hall. Lisa soon becomes involved in the legend of the first mistress whom she resembles closely. A disappointing book. The plot had so many possibilities but the work was poorly crafted. The suspense is created by the technique of a scrape with death in every chapter and I find that a dumb device.

NICHOLS, Sarah

1221. Grave's Company. New York: Popular Library (00252), 1975.

1222. House of Rancour. New York: Popular Library (00566), 1974.

1223. The Moon Dancers (C). New York: Curtis Books, 1973. [© Lee Hayes].

A rather curious story about a Quaker girl, who upon the death of her mother, goes to live at Greystone Hall with her estranged relatives. A standard neo-Gothic plot in most respects and, if one can forgive a chapter dealing with a stallion's view of the story, the rest isn't too bad.

Also wrote: Widow's Walk.

NICOLSON, John Urban 1885-

1224. Fingers of Fear. New York: Covici Friede, 1937. (NUC pre'56 418-561)

NIGHTINGALE, Ursula

1225. Bitters Wood (F). New York: Popular Library, 1973. [© Frank Litchman].

If you can wade through the awkward narrative, the constant rehashing of what's happened so far, and the heroine's endless speculations over what's going on, you might find an entertaining story. I couldn't.

1226. Moonhaunt (F). New York: Popular Library, 1972. [© Script Associates].

Criticism of Bitters Wood (see above) holds for this story as well. The plot gets lost in verbiage.

NILE, Dorothea (pseud.) see AVALLONE, Michael

NOONE, Edwina (pseud.) see AVALLONE, Michael

NORMAN, Ames 1920-
(Norma Ames)

Lives in Santa Fe, New Mexico and has had a great variety of careers including time study engineer, advertising copywriter and artist, bookkeeper, chicken farmer. Most recently has been a wildlife management officer for the New Mexico Department of Game and Fish. He is a member of wildlife and conservation organizations and has written books on the subject.

1227. Whisper in the Forest (B), by Norma Ames. New York: Avon, 1971.

Sandra goes to New Mexico to vacation at the AOK chalet and meets some very strange neighbors indeed--members of a hippie commune, an ancient Mexican reputed to be a witch, and Panteles Theotakes, a reclusive Greek who bears an uncanny resemblance to the God Pan. Sounds a bit much, but this was a very entertaining tale, smoothly written and full of folk lore and fancy.

Also by Norma Ames: The Path Belated.

NORRIS, Kathleen (Thompson) 1880-1966

Author of a large number of romances, a very few of which are or may be "somewhat Gothic."

1228. Beauty and the Beast. Garden City, N.Y.: Doubleday, 1928. (NUC pre'56 421-610)

1229. Mystery House (B). Garden City, N.Y.: Doubleday, Doran, 1939. (NUC pre'56 421-615)

Page is engaged by a lawyer to go to Mystery House (based I'm sure on the Winchester Mansion in California) and act as a nurse-companion to the aged and invalid Mrs. Pendergast and to try to find out if there is among the various other household members a conspiracy to defraud the old lady. This is a much better Gothic than many written in the 60's and 70's. Verbose, but a few surprises make it worth reading.

1230. The Secret of Marshbanks. Garden City, N.Y.: Doubleday, Doran, 1940. (NUC pre'56 421-616)

1231. The Secrets of Hillyard House. Garden City, N.Y.: Doubleday, 1947. (NUC pre'56 421-617)

1232. Storm House. Garden City, N.Y.: Doubleday, 1929. (NUC pre'56 421-617)

1233. Through a Glass Darkly. Garden City, N.Y.: Doubleday, 1957. (NUC 1956-67 84-510)

Futurism and social idealism seem to be the themes. Not Gothic.

1234. Treehaven. Garden City, N.Y.: Doubleday, 1932. (NUC pre'56 421-618)

NORTON, Alice Mary
(André Norton)

1235. Witch World, by André Norton. New York: Ace, 1963. (NUC 1968-72 70-589)

Ace classifies Norton's work as science fiction and that may well be. But, if nothing else, this tale of witchcraft and other worlds reminds me very much of such works as Peake's Gormenghast (sans humor) or fairy tales such as Beagle's The Last Unicorn and certainly reflects the Gothic origins of the form if not itself being Gothic. Norton has written some forty other similar works, listings to be found in NUC pre'56 Vol. 423, p. 70 and NUC 1956-67, Vol. 85, p. 32.

NORTON, Patricia

1236. Daughter of Evil (C). New York: Lancer, 1973.
A fair Gothic tale is all but lost in clumsy narrative and rambling prose. Only readers with modest expectations would enjoy.

NOTTINGHAM, Poppy

1237. Hatred's Web (D). New York: Ace (31760), 1974.
Paula goes to a Louisiana plantation as companion and reader to the blind Claudine and falls in love with Claudine's husband, Evan. The author gives Paula a neurotic fear of spiders to liven up this routine plot and it doesn't help much. One of those husband-swiping fantasies that annoy me greatly.

NUELLE, Helen

1238. Evil Lives Here (C). New York: (Avalon Books) Bouregy, 1973; New York: Manor, 1974.
This book has a run-of-the-mill competency that becomes a crashing bore to those who read much at all. Juvenile melodrama and overly sentimental Gothic.

1239. The Haunting of Bally Moran. New York: Manor, 1976.

OATES, Joyce Carol

1240. Expensive People. New York: Vanguard, 1960; New York: Fawcett-Crest, 1970.
The Fawcett edition is supratitled "A Tale of Gothic Horror" and I haven't the faintest idea why they said that except to sell the book. It is not Gothic by any criteria I know of and, with due apologies to Oates and admirers, it is in my opinion, not much of anything. I would call it a slick little job of psychopathological voyeurism. If you like looking at and listening to the deeply emotionally ill, you'll get a bang out of this book.

OBOLER, Arch 1907-

Peabody Award winner and author of many plays for radio

and motion pictures, most of which he directed and produced. House on Fire is his first novel.

1241. House on Fire. New York: Bartholomew House Ltd., 1969; New York: Dell, 1970. (NUC 1968-72 71-274)

Horror Gothic. So nicely written. Such deft characterizations. And such a horrid ending. Recommended for masochists only.

O'BRIEN, Sallie

1242. Heiress to Evil (D). New York: Ballantine, 1974.

Evelyn is invited to the home of a long-lost and fabulously wealthy relative as the last surviving member of her family. She arrives to find herself unwelcome by the household and threats are made on her life. A standard production using most of the usual clichés.

O'DONNELL, Elliott 1872-1965

English writer and lecturer about unusual phenomena and the supernatural. Numerous short stories and books about ghosts and the supernatural listed in the NUC pre'56 Vol. 426, pp. 601-03.

1243. The Sorcery Club (D). London: W. Rider, 1912. (NUC pre'56 426-603)

Dated and dull horror Gothic. Three young men dabble in sorcery and come to a wretched end. Don't bother.

OGILVIE, Elisabeth 1917-

1244. Bellwood (C). New York: McGraw-Hill, 1969; New York: Dell (0670), 1970. A condensed version of this story appeared in Goodhousekeeping, June 1968. (NUC 1968-72 71-488)

Caroline, following a very trying romance, flees to a job at secluded Bellwood as companion to Tim, the five-year-old retarded son of the mysterious and handsome Rees Morgan. Caroline finds love and trouble. The author manages to sustain this standard neo-Gothic plot fairly well in spite of a very naive heroine.

1245. The Face of Innocence. New York: McGraw-Hill, 1970. (NUC 1968-72 71-488)

1246. No Evil Angel. New York: McGraw-Hill, 1956. (NUC 1956-67 85-521)

1247. The Witch Door. New York: McGraw-Hill, 1959. (NUC 1956-67 85-521)

Several other works appearing to be juveniles or romances are listed in the NUC pre'56 Vol. 427, pp. 609-10.

O'GRADY, Rohan (pseud.) <u>see</u> SKINNER, June (O'Grady)

OLECK, Jack

1248. <u>House of Mystery</u>. New York: Warner Paperback, 1973. Short stories. Horror Gothic.

OLIVER, George
(Oliver Onions)

Born in Bradford, Yorkshire, England in 1893. Trained as an artist but devoted himself to literature after working as a book and poster designer and magazine illustrator.

1249. <u>The Collected Ghost Stories of Oliver Onions</u>. London: Nicholson & Watson, 1935. (NUC pre'56 430-653)

1250. <u>The Drakestone</u>, by Oliver Onions. London: Hurst & Blackett, 1906. (NUC pre'56 430-653)

1251. <u>The Exception</u>, by Oliver Onions. London: Methuen, 1911; New York: Lane, 1911. (NUC pre'56 430-653)

1252. <u>Ghosts in Daylight</u>, by Oliver Onions. London: Chapman & Hall, 1924. (NUC pre'56 430-653)

1253. <u>The Painted Face</u>, by Oliver Onions. London: Heinemann, 1929. (NUC pre'56 430-655)

1254. <u>The Tower of Oblivion</u>, by Oliver Onions. New York: Macmillan, 1921. (NUC pre'56 430-655)

1255. <u>Widdershins</u>, by Oliver Onions. London: Secker, 1911. (NUC pre'56 430-657)

OLSEN, D. B. (pseud.) <u>see</u> HITCHENS, Dolores

ONIONS, Oliver (pseud.) <u>see</u> OLIVER, George

ORFORD, Ellen

1256. <u>The Maze</u> (D). New York: Curtis, 1973. [© William Delligan].

Allison becomes a companion to old Mrs. Hudson at a remote mansion in Maine. I gave up in frustrated boredom when, halfway through the book nothing had yet happened except the heroine's overdramatization of a series of trivial, annoying events. For her to conclude that her life was cursed because her purse was stolen, for example, catapulted me into a lack of sympathy with the heroine that was never restored.

ORGAN, Perry

Born in California, spent part of her childhood in the Orient and finished her education in Boston and London. She now lives in Toronto with her husband and three children. Her poetry has appeared in The London Magazine and The Paris Review. The House on Cheyne Walk is her first novel.

1257. The House on Cheyne Walk (D). New York: Coward, McCann & Geoghegan, 1975.

The ingredients of a Gothic are here: heiress and teacher Sarah is called by her brother-in-law to his English household to care for her five-year-old nephew following the tragic death of her younger sister. If you can wade through interminable boring dialogues, diary entries and semi-irrelevant narrative, you will find an intrigue. I couldn't.

ORR, Helen

1258. Web of Days. New York: Ace, 1975.

Ace calls this a "Gothic," but it's not. "Office melodrama" is about it. Thoroughly uninteresting to me.

OSBORNE, Dorothy

1259. Whispering Willows (B). New York: Popular Library, 1973.

Marcia came to W. W. to seek her real family following the death of her adoptive parents. She discovers a strange crew and a fantastic old house full of secret passages, mystery and romance. Osborne does a good job of developing her cast of interesting characters.

1260. My Enemy's Friend. New York: Coward, McCann & Geoghegan, 1972. (NUC 1968-72 72-639)

1261. The Yellow Gold of Tiryns. New York: Coward, McCann & Geoghegan, 1969. (NUC 1968-72 72-639)

OSTRANDER, Isabel Egenton 1883-1924
(Robert Orr Chipperfield, Douglas Grant, David Fox)

Barzun and Taylor credit Ostrander with the original label

"suspense story" and as the originator of the HIBK (Had I But Known) cliché. I believe it goes back much farther. Most of Ostrander's work seems to be crime stories. A few which may have Gothic elements predominating are as follows:

1262. The Black Joker. New York: McBride, 1925. (NUC pre'56 434-447)

1263. Ethel Opens the Door, by David Fox. New York: McBride, 1922. (NUC pre'56 434-447)

1264. Island of Intrigue (D). New York: McBride, 1918. (NUC pre'56 434-448)

A silly little romantic suspense in which the plot became evident within the first fifty pages. Would today, I believe, be classified as a "juvenile" and is suitable for none but the most timid of tastes.

1265. Unseen Hands (D), by Robert Orr Chipperfield. New York: McBride, 1920. (NUC pre'56 434-449)

The villain is plainly pointed out in this murder mystery and family intrigue before page 16 and a quick check of the last chapter proves it. Why bother with the in-between?

OSTRANDER, Kate

1266. Dance with a Ghost (D). New York: Berkley Medallion, 1976.

A very annoying story of romantic suspense which teases the reader with unfulfilled promises of the supernatural. For example, the title refers to a Halloween costume party. The plot is often obscured by irrelevant characters, dialogue and speculation. The heroine's behavior is less than heroic and, all-in-all, it's a poor show.

1267. Foxfire Cove. New York: Berkley Medallion, 1975.

1268. The Ghosts of Ballyduff (D). New York: Popular Library, 1972.

Ostrander is unable to sustain the promising beginning where Moira goes to Ireland to visit a long-lost aunt at her ancient castle. An example of how disastrously dull a formula plot can be when the tale is not well crafted.

1269. Ring of Darkness. New York: Berkley Medallion, 1974.

PACKER, [Lady] Joy (Peterson) 1905-

Born in Cape Town, South Africa. Worked as a free-lance

writer and in broadcasting and traveled with her husband, an Admiral in the Royal Navy, over several continents. Her books have been translated into nine languages. Has written travel books and memoirs as well as several novels, none of which appear to be Gothic but at least one of which has been published and advertised as such:

1270. The Man in the Mews. London: Eyre & Spottiswoode, 1964; New York: Ace, [1964]. (NUC 1956-67 87-270)

Gothic only to Ace. A domestic melodrama and, in my view, not one of much interest.

PADGET, Meg

1271. House of Strangers (C). New York: Lancer, 1965.

Sara goes to her fiancé's home to meet his family and finds threats to her life and a mystery in the huge old mansion filled with mirrors. Fair story, but awkwardly crafted.

PAIGE, Leslie

1272. House Possessed. New York: Belmont-Tower, 1974.

PARADISE, Mary (pseud.) see EDEN, Dorothy

PARGETER, Edith Mary 1913-
(Ellis Peters)

English novelist and translator. Her book The Assize of the Dying has been filmed under the title "The Spaniard's Curse," and Death and the Joyful Woman was filmed for "The Alfred Hitchcock Hour" on television. Her work includes romances, mysteries, historical novels and possibly an occasional romantic suspense. The Catalogue of Crime reviews the Ellis Peters books which appear to be mystery-detection.

PARK, Maeva see DOBNER, Maeva Park

PARKER, Beatrice

1273. Betrayal at Blackcrest. New York: Dell (00751), 1971.

1274. Come to Castlemoor (C). New York: Dell, 1970. [© Tom E. Huff].

This sentimental horror-Gothic aroused my curiosity and kept me reading but was, all-in-all, disappointing in that the action never arrived until the last couple of chapters and had all the impact of a dud firecracker. Readers who prefer the emphasis on the sentimental rather than the Gothic may enjoy this story more than I did.

1275. Stranger by the Lake. New York: Dell (08255), 1971.

PAUL, Phyllis

1276. Echo of Guilt (D). New York: Lancer, 1966; originally pub. as: Pulled Down. W. W. Norton, 1964.

There are echoes of Shirley Jackson here in the large cast of weird characters but they are bent on so boring a course that one feels no inclination to seek further for the echoes of guilt. If this tale be Gothic, it is so in the most distant of kinships. Don't bother.

Other works include: Twice Lost (Lancer).

PAULEY, Barbara Anne

Born in Nashville, Tennessee but spent most of her childhood in the Connecticut-New York area where her father published movie magazines. She started writing while her husband attended Harvard Business School. She now lives in Wenham, Massachusetts with the same husband, three sons, three horses, two German Shepherds and an occasional in-residence granddaughter. (Information from jacket of Voices.)

1277. Blood Kin. New York: Dell, 1973.

1278. Voices Long Hushed (B). Garden City, N.Y.: Doubleday (Crime Club), 1976.

A very polished "Mississippi Gothic." Evidence that there is life in the old formula even yet.

PAXTON, Lois (pseud.) see LOW, Lois Dorothea

PAYES, Rachel C(osgrove)
(E. L. Arch, Rachel Cosgrove)

Born 12/11/22 in Westernport, Maryland. B.Sc. from West Virginia Wesleyan College in 1943. Payes is married, has two children, and lives in Shrub Oak, New York. In addition to the works listed here, Payes has written numerous romances and nurse stories under the name Rachel Cosgrove; science fiction under the name E. L. Arch and several other mysteries.

1279. Devil's Court. New York: Berkley Medallion, 1974.

1280. Forbidden Island. New York: Berkley Medallion, 1973.

1281. House of Tarot. New York: Berkley, 1975.

1282. Malverne Hall. New York: Ace, 1970.

1283. O Charitable Death. Garden City, N.Y.: Doubleday (Crime Club), 1968. (NUC 1968-72 74-358)

1284. The Silent Place (C). New York: Ace, 1969.
Ace calls this "Gothic." I call it a mystery--romantic suspense only because it has a "female orientation." Whatever, it is competently written and dull, dull, dull.

PEAKE, Mervyn (Laurence)

Born 7/9/11 in Kuling, Central China; moved to England in 1923. Attended grammar schools in Tientsin and Eltham College and Royal Academy schools in England. Peake was an author, poet and painter and did some book illustrations for collector's editions of poetry until his death in 1968.

In a different time, place and mood I might have really taken to Gormenghast and become a "Peake Freak." It has many qualities that I enjoy--a mythology, a horridly cynical wit, a quest theme and a world of other-worldly characters. This is the sort of literature from which cults have sprung. Evidently Peake wasn't at the right place and time for the mood of the readership. As it is, I just couldn't get involved with the tale and kept going under as I waded through what seemed tons of clever verbiage. It seems Gothic with its quest theme, pseudo-medieval setting, and its imaginative ghastliness.

1285. Gormenghast. London: Eyre & Spottiswoode, 1950. (NUC pre'56 446-428)

1286. Titus Alone. London: Eyre & Spottiswoode, 1959. (NUC 1956-67 88-613)

1287. Titus Groan: A Gothic Novel. London: Eyre & Spottiswoode, 1946; New York: Reynal & Hitchcock, 1946. (NUC pre'56 446-428)

These books were later published as a trilogy:

1288. The Gormenghast Trilogy. New York: Weybright & Talley, 1967. (NUC 1956-67 88-612)

PEARSON, Denise Naomi O'Neill 1897-
(Harriet Gray)

1289. Bride of Doom, by Harriet Gray. London: Rich & Cowan,

1956. (NUC 1956-67 89-5)

PEARSON, Diane

1290. Csardas. Philadelphia & N.Y.: Lippincott, 1975.
"Hungarian hist.-20th century-fiction." Not Gothic, but got rave reviews from our local librarians.

1291. Bride of Tancred (B). New York: Bantam (N7482), 1967.
A most satisfyingly conceived and written Gothic tale of Miriam, a Quaker, who takes a job at the remote and desolate Tancred Hall only to find a deeply troubled household. A very good story can still be made from a very much used basic plot.

1292. The Marigold Field. Philadelphia: Lippincott, 1969. (NUC 1968-72 74-399)

1293. Sarah. Philadelphia: Lippincott, 1971. Pub. in England as: Sarah Whitman. London: Macmillan. (NUC 1968-72 74-339)

PERKERSON, Medora (Field) 1892-1960
(Medora Field)

1294. Blood on Her Shoe, by Medora Field. New York: Macmillan, 1942. (NUC pre'56 450-631)
"Unfit for rational consumption. The style is HIBK [Had I But Known] compounded with Southern femininity." Barzun and Taylor, Catalogue of Crime.

PETERS, Elizabeth (pseud.) see MERTZ, Barbara

PETERS, Ellis (pseud.) see PARGETER, Edith

PETERS, Maureen 1935-
(Veronica Black)

English novelist who has also written several historical novels under her own name.

1295. Dangerous Inheritance, by Veronica Black. London: Hale, 1969; New York: Paperback Library, 1970.

1296. The Enchanted Grotto, by Veronica Black. London: Hale, 1972.

1297. Fair Kilmeny, by Veronica Black. London: Hale, 1972; New York: Berkley Medallion (S2245). (NUC 1973 2-513)

1298. A Footfall in the Mist (C), by Veronica Black. New York: Lenox Hill, [1971]; New York: Berkley Medallion (S2260), 1972.

Tarn Chester, heiress to her recently deceased father's fortune, meets and marries the handsome Robert Hunter in a whirlwind romance. She soon discovers when they move to Hunter's former wife's home, that all is not as it seemed. Not a bad little neo-Gothic tale. The denouement is a bit precipitous, but that's typical.

1299. Master of Malcarew, by Veronica Black. New York: Lenox Hill, 1971.

1300. Moonflete, by Veronica Black. London: Hale, 1972. (NUC 1973 2-513)

1301. Portrait of Sarah (D), by Veronica Black. London: Hale, 1969; New York: Berkley Medallion, 1973.

Standard Gothic formula of a young girl going to an English manor as secretary to the aged Lord. The plot in this tale is so poorly thought out that it is barely intelligible. The characters are shallow and unbelievable.

1302. The Wayward Madonna, by Veronica Black. New York: Lenox Hill, 1970; New York: Berkley Medallion (S2272).

Other works published by R. Hale are: Minstrel's Leap, Tansy, and The Willow Maid, all by Veronica Black.

PHILLIPS, Jean

1303. Day of Dark Memory. New York: Lancer, 1970.

1304. Greenwood. New York: Lancer, n.d.

1305. House of Darkness (C). New York: Avon (V2400), 1971.

Helen and her father travel to remote Mexico in search of a legendary painting. They visit a great and ancient fortress and become embroiled in an ancient family's turmoil. Not too bad a tale but nowhere near the delightful experience of H. R. Haggard's The Ghost Kings which uses similar themes with far greater skill and imagination.

PLAGEMANN, Bentz

Born 7/27/13 in Springfield, Ohio. Graduated from Cathedral Latin High School in Cleveland, Ohio. Worked in book stores in Cleveland, Chicago and Detroit and after being in the U.S. Navy from

1942-45, became a full-time writer. He is quoted in Contemporary Authors (Vol. 1-4, p. 76) as follows:

"I suffered an attack of polio in N. Africa during the war, and I walk with a long leg brace on my right leg, and with a cane. This somewhat limits my physical activities, but I have always enjoyed sketching and cooking. As for my work, I have felt for most of my writing career that I stand aside from much of the main current of thought. I am affirmative by nature and in my work, I have a deep religious commitment to a personal God; and I believe in the existence of good, and in the possibility that it may sometimes triumph over evil."

1306. The Boxwood Maze (B). New York: Saturday Review Press, 1972. (NUC 1968-72 76-80)

Lee goes to spend her usual summer with her aunt in the family mansion on the Hudson. Her aunt hopes for a marriage between Lee and a distant cousin, Brad, who is to be in the neighborhood for the summer too. All goes well until Lee becomes suspicious of certain happenings around the "castle." Then a devious and sinister plot is uncovered.

1307. Into the Labyrinth. New York: Farrar, Straus, 1948. (LCAC 1948-52 16-452)

1308. Wolfe's Cloister (B). New York: Saturday Review Press, 1974. (NUC 1974 13-512)

After growing up in Italy under the guardianship of her now dead grandmother, Amy returns to the U.S. to find her mother whom she feels to be in peril. She travels to Pennsylvania and Wolfe's Cloister where her adventuress mother is supposed to be staying with her first of many husbands, Ben Wolfe. Amy uncovers intrigue, a couple of bad surprises and a couple of good ones. The reader is treated to some charming pictures of Amish life and a little Pennsylvania history.

PLAIDY, Jean (pseud.) see HIBBERT, Eleanor

PLUM, Jennifer (pseud.) see KURLAND, Michael

POLLAND, Madeleine A(ngela) Cahill

Born 5/31/18 in Kinsale, County Cork, Ireland. Married in 1946, had two children and now lives in Hertfordshire, England. Has worked as a librarian and has written a large number of children's books.

1309. The Little Spot of Bother. London: Hutchinson, 1967. (NUC 1968-72 76-394)

1310. Thicker than Water (C). New York: Holt, Rinehart & Winston,

1965; New York: Pyramid, 1966. (NUC 1956-67 91-267)

Forty-year-old Veronica takes a sentimental journey to the deathbed of her grandmother in Ireland, not visited for over twenty-five years. Meets up with a cousin, Denny, and a conspiracy emerges. This is a frightfully slow-paced tale and quite dreary.

POSNER, Richard
(Iris Foster, Beatrice Murray, Paul Todd, Dick Wine)

Born 10/7/44 in Manhattan, New York. Education: B.A. Hofstra University, 1965; graduate study at Queens College, City University of New York. He is married, has one child and lives in Selden, New York. Posner was editor of Literary Agency 1967-72 and has been a full time writer since then.

1311. The Crimson Moon, by Iris Foster. New York: Lancer, 1973.

1312. The Dark Sonata, by Beatrice Murray. New York: Dell, 1971.

1313. Deadly Sea, Deadly Sand (B), by Iris Foster. New York: Lancer, 1972.

An action-packed romantic suspense in which a far-fetched plot gets by thanks to the author's skill. Sandy goes to spend her summer vacation on Jonquil Island and runs into quite a mess.

1314. The Moorwood Legacy, by Iris Foster. New York: Lancer, 1972.

1315. Nightshade, by Iris Foster. New York: Lancer, 1973.

1316. The Sabath Quest, by Iris Foster. New York: Lancer, 1973.

POWER, Patricia

1317. The Face of the Foe. Garden City, N.Y.: Doubleday (Crime Club), 1973. (NUC 1973 11-330)

1318. This Deadly Grief (D). Garden City, N.Y.: Doubleday (Crime Club), 1972; New York: Avon (V2477), 1972. (NUC 1968-72 77-62)

A mundane romantic murder-mystery with little to recommend it but its brevity. Not Gothic.

POWYS, John Cowper 1892-1963

1319. Maiden Castle. Hamilton, N. Y.: Colgate University Press, 1966. (NUC 1956-67 92-64)

I found a good bit of wit but soon lost the thread of plot in a teeming jungle of verbiage. I don't think this is Gothic, but after 100 pages, neither did I care.

1320. Morwyn: or, The Vengeance of God. London: Cassell, 1937. (NUC pre'56 468-539)

1321. Porius, a Romance of the Dark Ages. London: Macdonald, n.d.; New York: Philosophical Library, 1952. (NUC pre'56 468-540)

1322. Wolf Solent. New York: Simon & Schuster, 1929. (NUC pre'56 468-541)

A long chronicle of the intimate life of a young English fellow. The author keeps dropping hints of possible Gothic-type developments but they never materialize.

PREEDY, George (pseud.) see LONG, Gabriella Margaret

PRITCHETT, Ariadne

1323. Karamour (B). Greenwich, Conn.: Fawcett Gold Medal (T2812), 1968.

Unpretentious and engaging and much in the vein of Jamaica Inn and other tales of piracy along the coast of Cornwall. A good example of the art of "unadorned storytelling."

1324. Mill Reef Hall. Greenwich, Conn.: Fawcett-Crest, 1968.

PROLE, Lozania (pseud.) see BLOOM, Ursula

PURDY, Anne

1325. Dark Boundary. New York: Vantage Press, 1954. (NUC pre'56 475-520)

PURDY, Jennie Bouton (Shubael)

1326. The Dark Strain, by Shubael. New York & London: The Abbey Press, 1903. (NUC pre'56 475-525)

Might be worth investigating. I haven't found a copy.

QUENTIN, Dorothy
(Linda Beverly)

Author of romances and nurse stories, none of which seem to be Gothic.

RADCLIFFE, Janette (pseud.) see ROBERTS, Janet Louise

RAGOSTA, Millie J.

1327. Lorena Veiled. New York: Ballantine, 1974.

1328. Taverna in Terrazzo (C). New York: Ballantine, 1975.
A perfect "C" effort in romantic suspense. For the reader with moderate expectations, this book should be entertaining. The author does a nice job setting up the story of Italian-American Virginia who goes to visit her Italian kin following the tragic death of her parents. The intrigue that develops is weak and not very suspenseful.

RALSTON, Jan (pseud.) see DUNLOP, Agnes

RANDALL, Florence Engel

Born 10/18/17 in Brooklyn, New York. Now living in Great Neck, New York. Her short stories have been published in several well known women's magazines.

1329. Haldane Station (B). New York: Harcourt Brace, 1973. (NUC 1973 11-620)
Seventeen-year-old Rachael goes with her family to an old house in the tiny town of Haldane Station to check on the mysterious disappearance of Aunt Emily. An innovative and gripping story of ghostly and other-worldly phenomena.

1330. Hedgerow. New York: Harcourt Brace & World, 1967. (NUC 1956-67 93-605)

1331. The Place of Sapphires (B). New York: Harcourt Brace, 1969; Greenwich, Conn.: Fawcett-Crest, 1969. (NUC 1973 11-620)
A good tale of haunting and possession. Two sisters rent a house on an island near Martha's Vineyard following an accident fatal to their parents. Strange things begin to occur in the house.

RANDALL, Rona (pseud.) 1911-

1332. The Arrogant Duke. New York: Ace (02940), 1972.

1333. Broken Tapestry. London: Hurst & Blackett, 1969. (NUC 1968-72 78-575)

1334. Dragonmede (B). New York: Simon & Schuster, 1974; New York: Ballantine, 1975. (NUC 1974 13-987)

Eustasia, daughter of the notorious Luella, grows up sheltered from the coarser sides of her mother's life and eventually marries the dashing Julian--heir to Dragonmede and great wealth. Things take a decided turn for the worse when the happy couple return to Dragonmede and Eustasia finds herself surrounded by conspiracy and mystery.

1335. A Girl Called Ann. New York: Ace (28865), 1973.

1336. Hotel De Luxe. New York: Ace (34301), 1972.

1337. Knight's Keep (C). New York: Ace, 1967.

Jane Bewleigh, daughter of a poor London preacher, comes into a fortune upon the death of Uncle Silas. She's invited to the family estate of Knight's Keep and the story follows rather predictable lines thereafter. The character of the heroine emerges as a vain and haughty soul and is not what I think the author intended. An example of a specific type heroine-fantasy that emulates those qualities least admirable in females.

1338. Midnight Walker. New York: Ace (52995), 1973.

1339. Mountain of Fear. New York: Ace, 1975.

1340. Shadows on the Sand. New York: Ace (76076), 1973.

1341. The Silver Cord. New York: Ace (76551), 1972.

1342. Time Remembered, Time Lost. New York: Ace (80250), 1973.

1343. Walk into My Parlor. New York: Ace (87101), 1972.

1344. The Witching Hour. New York: Ace (89901), 1974.

Other works which may be Gothic include: Seven Days from Midnight and The Willow Herb, both published by Ace.

RANDELL, Christine

1345. Black Candle (C). New York: Paperback Library, 1968.

Lorna returns to her estranged father's Irish farm to find mystery and treachery. Some delightful Irish dialogue.

1346. Curse of Deepwater. New York: Warner Paperback (75-409), 1974.

Additional works include: Mallory Grange, The Secret of Tarn-End House, The Weeping Tower, Whisper of Fear and A Woman Possessed.

RANDOLPH, Ellen (pseud.) see ROSS, William Edward Daniel

RATCLIFFE, Susan

1347. The Castle Captive (D). New York: Avon (S373), 1968.

Begins interestingly with medieval scholar, Marge, going to visit a long-lost cousin in his 800-year-old castle in Northern England. Sad to say, the plot immediately collapses into a Perils of Pauline melodrama, the heroine spending her time in vividly described screams and ridiculously contrived dangers, all winding down to a dumb "Commie plot" denouement that seems to be the second-rate theme of the 60's (as is drug traffic for the 70's). A disappointing book.

RAYMOND, Mary (pseud.) see KEEGAN, Mary Heathcott

READ, Piers Paul 1941-

English writer whose 1973 novel The Upstart (Lippincott) was listed by Book Review Digest as Gothic. It does not fit my criteria, nor does Monk Dawson (Lippincott, 1970). Three other of his works might be Gothic:

1348. The Enchanted Egg. London: Hutchinson, 1963; pub. in U.S. as: The Magical Egg. Philadelphia: Lippincott, 1965.

1349. The Magic Light. London: Hutchinson, 1959.

1350. The Spell of Chuchuchan. London: Hutchinson, 1966; New York: World Pub., 1967.

REDDOCK, Jennifer

1351. A Chair for Death. New York: Popular Library, n.d. [© George McNeill].

1352. The Legacy of Mendoubia (D). New York: Popular Library, 1973. [© George McNeill].

A routine little romance about Leonie, widowed during the Civil War and accused of complicity in husband's supposed crimes. She flees to Tangier and her unknown in-laws. So poorly written that the first 100 pages inspired no interest to continue.

REISNER, Mary

1353. Bride of Death (C). New York: Belmont (B50-807), 1968.
Murder-mystery about an author who rents a house near a remote coastal village and becomes involved in the investigation of a murder committed in a neighboring house. Not bad for type but certainly not Gothic as advertised by the publisher.

1354. Death Hall. New York: Belmont (B75-2089), n.d.

1355. The Four Witnesses. New York: Dodd, Mead, 1947; pub. as: Web of Fear. New York: Belmont, 1967. (LCC supp. 1942-47 31-120)

1356. The House of Cobwebs (F). New York: Dodd, Mead, 1944; New York: Belmont, 1965. (LCC supp. 1942-47 31-120)
I found the jumbled style of this book almost unreadable. The first part involves the murder of a twin's horrid wife. Characters are poorly drawn. I had no desire to finish the book and there were no Gothic elements as far as I read.

1357. Katherine and the Dark Angel. New York: Dodd, Mead, 1948. (LCAC 1948-52 17-315)

1358. Mirror of Delusion. New York: Dodd, Mead, 1946. (LCC supp. 1942-47 31-120)

1359. Shadows on the Wall. New York: Dodd, Mead, 1943. (LCC supp. 1942-47 31-120)

RENIER, Elizabeth (pseud.) see BAKER, Betty D.

REYNOLDS, Bonnie Jones

"Bonnie Jones Reynolds grew up on a dairy farm near Utica, N.Y. Aspiring to a career as a ballerina, Bonnie moved to New York City, but became instead a magician's assistant, one-half of a ballroom dancing team, a successful model, and finally an actress with a Broadway show to her credit. She traveled around the world, then moved to Hollywood, where she met and married television producer Gene Reynolds. She still does an occasional TV role, but her passions nowadays run to home, husband, her pets--and, of course, writing." (Information from Bantam ed. of The Truth About Unicorns.)

1360. The Truth About Unicorns (A). New York: Stein & Day, 1972; New York: Bantam (T7780), 1973. (NUC 1973 11-806)
This was a super book! Marvelously sensitive handling of witchcraft and so-called "occult phenomena." A fine family saga

as well ... and a love story. Original, imaginative and enormously entertaining.

RICE, Anne (O'Brien)

1361. Interview with a Vampire (C). New York: Knopf, 1976.
Seems indicative of this generation when psycho-socio-philosophy creep even into the literature of horror-Gothic. The absurd lengths to which introspection may go are at last met in this study into the inner life of a vampire. Some of the details of vampire life elaborated upon I found repulsive and without redeeming social value. The whole thing just doesn't come off, in my view--as seems to be true, now that I think of it, with most vampire stories.

RICH, Kathleen

1362. The Lucifer Mask (C). New York: Tower, 1967.
Somebody's trying to kill Juliette and one must plod through a good bit of dull stuff to find out who. Run-of-the-mill romantic suspense.

RICHARD, Susan

1363. Ashley Hall. New York: Warner Paperback, 1967.

1364. Terror at Nelson Woods (C). New York: Warner Paperback, 1973.
Michelle marries Tim and goes with him to the family estate in Quebec where Tim's stepmother lives and manages the family mill. Michelle's life is threatened soon after their arrival. A worn out plot and this treatment does little to add anything new. Some interesting information about Quebec, but that's about all.

Other works include: Intruder at Maison Benedict and The Secret of Chateau Kendell.

RICHARDSON, Mozelle Groner

Mystery writer born 1/26/14 and now living in Oklahoma City, Oklahoma. Quoted in Contemporary Authors (Vol. 33-36, p. 714) as follows: "I have never been ambitious to write, and never expected to--but Foster-Harris, director of the Professional Writer's School at Oklahoma University, got hold of me and unleashed a torrent of imaginative violence that, while surprising to me, has been a source of no little concern to my family! All this happened when I was 53 and now ... I have four books behind me and a whole new world has opened up before me."

1365. A Candle in the Wind (C). New York: Morrow, 1973.

(NUC 1974 14-182)

Journalist Jenifer is summoned to Ireland as heir to Castle Kilrain and becomes embroiled in mystery and intrigue. Not a bad little neo-Gothic. It kept me reading in spite of tending toward the juvenile.

1366. The Curse of Kalispoint. New York: Warner Paperback, 1971.

1367. The Masks of Thespis. New York: Warner Paperback, 1973.

1368. Portrait of Fear. New York: Warner Paperback, 1971.

RICO, Don

1369. Lorelei (C). New York: Belmont, 1966.

A sad and dreary little horror-Gothic. Not badly written but recommended only for those who enjoy becoming depressed.

RIDDELL, Charlotte Eliza Lawson (Cowan) ("Mrs. J. H. Riddell")

Wrote a large number of mysteries, romances and some Gothics during her lifetime, 1832-1906. For further works see LCPC pre'42 Vol. 125, pp. 630 ff.

1370. Uninhabited House (in Five Victorian Ghost Novels). New York: Dover, 1971.

1371. Weird Stories. London: Home & Van Thal, 1946. (LCAC 1948-52 17-430).

RIEFE, Alan (Barbara Riefe)

Free-lance writer (has written for at least 27 network TV programs), born in Waterbury, Connecticut in 1925 and now living in Greenwich. He has also written mystery-detective fiction.

1372. Auldearn House, by Barbara Riefe. New York: Popular Library, 1976.

1373. Barringer House, by Barbara Riefe. New York: Popular Library, (00348), 1976.

1374. Rowleston, by Barbara Riefe. New York: Popular Library, 1976.

RIEFE, Barbara (pseud.) see RIEFE, Alan

RIGSBY, Howard
(Vechel Howard)

Born 11/12/09 in Denver, Colorado. Career has been that of professional writer and he has written plays, scripts and verse as well as the "Vechel Howard" books that seem to be westerns.

1375. The Avenger. New York: Crowell, 1957. (NUC 1956-67 95-492)

1376. Calliope Reef. Garden City, N.Y.: Doubleday, 1967. (NUC 1956-67 95-492)

1377. Clash of Shadows. Philadelphia: Lippincott, 1959. (NUC 1956-67 95-492)

1378. The Tulip Tree (B). Garden City, N.Y.: Doubleday, 1963; New York: Paperback Library, 1963. (NUC 1956-67 95-492)

A gentleman's point of view and interesting in several respects. Competently written with probably the most "real" ghosts I've encountered. Somewhat philosophical and those not so inclined may find it slow-paced. One glaring loose end.

RINEHART, Mrs. Mary (Roberts) 1876-1958

A writer of prodigious output whose work, in general, could be classified as murder mystery romantic suspense. Some of her books are quite entertaining but none that I know of include sufficient elements to be considered Gothic. For the most part, they seem to emphasize the murder mystery formula.

ROBERTS, Dan (pseud.) see ROSS, William Edward Daniel

ROBERTS, Janet Louise
(Louisa Bronte, Rebecca Danton, Janette Radcliffe)

Born 1/20/25 in New Britain, Connecticut. Education: B.A. Otterbein College, 1946; Columbia University M.S.L.S., 1966. Home: Dayton, Ohio. Career: Reference librarian. "In early years I worked at clerk-typist positions, taking long vacations to live and write in Florence, Rome and London. After receiving my library degree, I was able to do better historical research as well as work in a public library.... The two careers compliment each other beautifully. I now travel on vacations to various places to use as backgrounds for my novels...." The Louisa Bronte books include Lord Satan, Her Demon Lover and the "Greystone" series. The Janette Radcliffe books, all published by Dell 1974-76, seem to be romances and include The Blue-Eyed Gypsy, Gentleman Pirate, White Jasmine.

1379. Black Horse Tavern, by Rebecca Danton. New York: Popular Library, 1972.

1380. The Cardross Luck. New York: Dell, 1974.

1381. Castlereagh. New York: Pocket Books, 1975.

1382. The Curse of Kenton (C). New York: Avon, 1972.

Sixteen-year-old Barbara marries Gilbert, Duke of Kenton, believing him to be dying of a heart ailment and in need of a companion and an heir. They go to Kenton Castle and Barbara begins to suspect skullduggery. This was an unpretentious tale, using all the beloved ingredients, minus ghosts, plus a little sex.

1383. The Dancing Doll. New York: Dell, 1973.

1384. Dark Rose. New York: Lancer, 1971.

1385. The Devil's Own (F). New York: Avon, 1972.

A perfectly dreadful book in every respect!

1386. The Dorstein Icon. New York: Avon, 1973.

1387. The First Waltz. New York: Dell, 1974.

1388. The Golden Thistle. New York: Dell, 1973.

Not Gothic. A "candlelight regency"--I guess that means a period love story.

1389. Isle of the Dolphins. New York: Avon, 1973.

1390. Jewels of Terror. New York: Lancer (74-702), 1970.

1391. La Casa Dorada. New York: Dell, 1973.

1392. Marriage of Inconvenience. New York: Dell, 1972.

1393. My Lady Mischief. New York: Dell, 1973.

1394. Ravenswood. New York: Avon, 1971.

1395. Rivertown. New York: Avon, 1972.

1396. Sign of the Golden Goose, by Rebecca Danton. New York: Popular Library, 1972.

1397. The Weeping Lady. New York: Lancer, 1971.

1398. Wilderness Inn. New York: Pocket Books, n.d.

ROBERTS, Willo Davis
(Willo Davis)

Born 5/29/28 in Grand Rapids, Michigan. Has always worked as a writer and currently lives in Eureka, California.

1399. Dangerous Legacy. New York: Lancer, 1972.

1400. Devil Boy. New York: New American Library, 1970.

1401. The Ghosts of Harrell. New York: Lancer, 1971.

1402. The House at Fern Canyon. New York: Lancer, 1970.

1403. Inherit the Darkness. New York: Lancer, 1972.

1404. Invitation to Evil (B). New York: Lancer, 1973.
An unpretentious mystery with a setting in Maine. Vonna Bracy checks on dead husband's family only to find an inheritance squabble, threats to her life and love. American neo-Gothic.

1405. King's Pawn. New York: Lancer (74-734), 1971.

1406. Return to Darkness. New York: Lancer, 1969.

1407. Shroud of Fog (B). New York: Ace, 1970.
Nice, tidy little murder mystery and romance. The return of Amy's former husband, Steve, after eleven years of separation brings in its wake a murder. Who done it? Steve is the chief suspect. No Gothic elements other than a mystery, but recommended.

1408. Sinister Gardens. New York: Lancer, 1972.

1409. The Tarot Spell. New York: Lancer, 1970.

1410. The Terror Trap. New York: Lancer, 1971.

1411. The Waiting Darkness. New York: Lancer, 1970.

ROBY, Mary Linn

Teacher of high school history and English. Born in Bangor, Maine in 1930 and now living in Sudbury, Massachusetts.

1412. Afraid of the Dark. New York: Dodd, Mead, 1965. (NUC 1956-67 96-206)

1413. All Your Lovely Words Are Spoken. New York: Ace, 1970.

1414. And Die Remembering. New York: New American Library, 1972.

1415. Before I Die. London: Hale, 1966.

1416. The Broken Key (C). New York: Hawthorn, 1973; New York: New American Library (Signet Q5916). (NUC 1973 11-935)

Artist Sara inherits a cottage on the Cornish estate of Penarth and goes there planning to live a secluded artist's life. Instead she becomes involved with the turbulent lives of the family at the manor. The tale develops into a "who done it" when the head of the family is murdered. Began with more promise than was fulfilled.

1417. Cat and Mouse. London: Hale, 1967.

1418. Dig a Narrow Grave. New York: New American Library, 1971.

1419. The House at Kilgallen. New York: New American Library (Signet T5671), 1973.

1420. If She Should Die. New York: New American Library, 1970.

1421. In the Dead of the Night. New York: New American Library (Signet T3948), 1969.

1422. Lie Quiet in Your Grave. New York: New American Library, 1970.

1423. Marsh House. New York: Hawthorn, 1974. (NUC 1974 14-280)

1424. Pennies on Her Eyes. New York: New American Library, 1969.

1425. Reap the Whirlwind. New York: New American Library, 1972.

1426. Shadow over Grove House. New York: New American Library, 1973.

1427. The Silent Walls. New York: New American Library (Signet Q6108), 1974.

1428. Some Die in the Beds. New York: New American Library, 1970.

1429. Speak No Evil of the Dead. New York: New American Library, 1973.

1430. Still as the Grave. New York: Dodd, Mead, 1964. (NUC 1956-67 96-206)

1431. That Fatal Touch. New York: New American Library, 1970.

1432. This Land Turns Evil Slowly. New York: New American Library (Signet T4803), 1971.

1433. The Tower Room. New York: Hawthorn, 1974. (NUC 1974 14-280)

1434. When the Witch Is Dead (D). New York: New American Library, 1972.

I don't think this story of witchcraft came off well at all. Roby kept me reading to find out what happened but I was not pleased with what I discovered. The "heroine" was a middle-aged woman who exemplified all the worst cliché characteristics of our sex and it seemed unclear how the author felt about her. Roby's handling of the witchcraft theme seemed unthought-out and disappointing. Her villain seemed to me much more sympathetic than her heroine.

1435. The White Peacock (C). New York: Hawthorn, 1972. (NUC 1973 11-935)

Murder mystery--and a mediocre one--with Gothic props. What the white peacock has to do with the tale we'll never know.

ROFFMAN, Jan (pseud.) see SUMMERTON, Margaret

ROGERS, Samuel, 1894-

1436. The Birthday. New York: Cape & Smith, 1932. (LCPC pre'42 127-454)

1437. Don't Look Behind You! (D). New York: London: Harpers, 1944; New York: Lancer, 1966. (LCC supp. 1942-47 31-587)

"A Lancer Gilt-Edge Gothic," whatever that means. This is a suspense story on the Jack the Ripper theme. The pace is terribly slow, the drama and suspense minimal and the whole thing just not worth the bother--and not really Gothic.

1438. Dusk at the Grove. Boston: Little, Brown, 1934. (LCPC pre'42 127-454)

1439. Lucifer in Pine Lake. Boston: Little, Brown, 1937. (LCPC pre'42 127-455)

1440. The Sombre Flame. New York: Payson & Clarke, [1927]. (LCPC pre'42 127-455)

1441. You'll Be Sorry! New York & London: Harpers, 1945. (LCC supp. 1942-47 31-587)

ROHLFS, Mrs. Anna Katharine (Green) 1846-1935
(Anna Katharine Green)

Wrote a very large number of books, most of which do not appear to qualify here. For further titles see LCPC pre'42, Vol. 127.

1442. The Amethyst Box, by Anna Katharine Green. Indianapolis: Bobbs-Merrill, [1905]. (LCPC pre'42 127-489)

1443. The Chief Legatee, by Anna Katharine Green. New York & London: Authors & Newspapers Assoc., 1906. (LCPC pre'42 127-489)

1444. The Circular Study. New York: McClure, Phillips, 1900. (LCPC pre'42 127-489)

1445. Dark Hollow, by Anna Katharine Green. New York: Dodd, Mead, 1914. (LCPC pre'42 127-489)

1446. The Golden Slipper, Other Problems for Violet Strange, by A. K. Green. New York: Putnam, 1915. (LCPC pre'42 127-490)

1447. The House in the Mist, by A. K. Green. Indianapolis: Bobbs-Merrill, 1905. (LCPC pre'42 127-490)

1448. The House of the Whispering Pines, by Anna Katharine Green. New York & London: Putnam, 1910. (LCPC pre'42 127-490)

1449. The Woman in the Alcove, by A. K. Green. Indianapolis: Bobbs-Merrill, 1906. (LCPC pre'42 127-492)

A naive murder mystery and in no way Gothic. Some kinship with romantic suspense due to the female main character.

ROHMER, Sax (pseud.) see WARD, Arthur S.

ROOT, Pat

1450. The Devil of the Stairs (B). New York: Simon & Schuster, 1959; New York: Lancer, 1967. (NUC 1956-67 96-614)

I would classify as "horror Gothic" this well-wrought tale of musicians and madness. Engrossing.

1451. Evil Became Them. New York: Simon & Schuster, 1952. (LCAC 1948-52 17-602)

ROSS, Clarissa (pseud.) see ROSS, William Edward Daniel

ROSS, Dan or Dana see ROSS, William Edward Daniel

ROSS, Katherine (pseud.) see WALTER, Dorothy Blake

ROSS, William Edward Daniel
(Leslie Ames, Rose Dana, Ruth Dorset, Ann Gilmer, Ellen Randolph, Dan Roberts, Dan Ross, Dana Ross, Clarissa Ross, Marilyn Ross, W. E. D. Ross, Jane Rossiter and Rose Williams)

Has written more than 130 published novels and 600 short stories under his own name and various pseudonyms. He has been most successful in the Gothic novel field and over 6 million of his Marilyn Ross series (written under the name of his wife) have sold in this country and abroad....

Born in Saint John, N.B., Canada, in 1912, Mr. Ross attended public schools there and later studied acting in New York City. He appeared at the Provincetown Playhouse and on stages throughout the U.S. and Canada. Later he formed his own company, presenting plays written by himself. In middle-age he studied journalism at the University of Oklahoma and turned to full-time writing. His wife Marilyn assists him in his busy schedule. Boston University has honored him by making a collection of his published stories, his letters and notes. (Information from cover of Lenox Hill edition of Whispering Gallery.)

The Dan Roberts books appear to be westerns; Jane Rossiter, Rose Williams, Rose Dana, Ruth Dorset and Ann Gilmer books appear to be "nursie" stories and love stories, none of which are included here.

1452. The Amethyst Tears, by Marilyn Ross. New York: Ballantine, 1974.

1453. Behind Locked Shutters. New York: Arcadia House, [1968]. (NUC 1968-72 81-282)

1454. Behind the Purple Veil, by Marilyn Ross. New York: Warner, 1973.

1455. Beware My Love, by Marilyn Ross. New York: Paperback Library, 1965. (NUC 1968-72 81-282)

1456. Beware of the Kindly Stranger, by Clarissa Ross. New York: Lancer (75-353), [1970]. (NUC 1973 12-22)

1457. Bride of Donnybrook, by Leslie Ames. New York: Arcadia House, 1966. (NUC 1968-72 81-282)

1458. Cameron Castle, by Marilyn Ross. New York: Warner, 1975.

1459. The Castle on the Cliff, by Dan Ross. New York: Bouregy, [1967]. (NUC 1968-72 81-282)

1460. The Castle on the Hill, by Ellen Randolph. New York: Avalon, 1964. (NUC 1968-72 81-282)

1461. Cavanaugh Keep, by Clarissa Ross. New York: Lancer (74-637), n. d.

1462. China Shadow, by Clarissa Ross. New York: Avon (21005), 1974.

1463. Christopher's Mansion. New York: Bouregy, [1969]. (NUC 1968-72 81-282)

1464. Dark Harbor Haunting, by Clarissa Ross. New York: Avon, 1975.

1465. Dark Legend, by Marilyn Ross. New York: Warner, n. d.

1466. Dark of the Moon. New York: Arcadia House, [1968]. (NUC 1968-72 81-283)

1467. The Dark Shadows Series, by Marilyn Ross. Includes at least thirty-one books, mostly starring Barnabas Collins, his wild family and quite an assortment of acquaintances.

1468. Dark Stars over Seacrest, by Marilyn Ross. New York: Paperback Library, 1972. (NUC 1968-72 81-283)

1469. Dark Towers of Fog Island, by Marilyn Ross. New York: Popular Library, 1975.

1470. Dark Villa of Capri (D), by Dan Ross. ? Macfadden, 1969. Also pub. as: by W. E. D. Ross. New York: Arcadia House, 1968. (NUC 1968-72 81-283)

Secretary Jill goes to Capri to trace her half-sister who married Chris Wood, moved to his villa, and reportedly died under mysterious circumstances. A slap-dash effort. Lots of action but no substance.

1471. Don't Look Behind You, by Marilyn Ross. New York: Warner, 1973.

1472. Drifthaven, by Clarissa Ross. New York: Avon, 1974.

1473. Durrell Towers, by Clarissa Ross. New York: Pyramid, 1965.

1474. Evil of Dark Harbor, by Clarissa Ross. New York: Avon (25486), n. d.

1475. Face in the Pond, by Clarissa Ross. New York: Avon, 1968.

1476. Face in the Shadows, by Marilyn Ross. New York: Warner, 1973.

1477. The Fog and the Stars, by Ann Gilmer. New York: Avalon, 1963. (NUC 1968-72 81-283)

1478. Fogbound, by Clarissa Ross. New York: Arcadia House, 1967. (NUC 1956-67 97-128)

1479. Fog Island Secret, by Marilyn Ross. New York: Popular Library, 1975.

1480. A Garden of Ghosts, by Marilyn Ross. New York: Popular Library, 1974.

1481. The Ghost and the Garnet, by Marilyn Ross. New York: Ballantine, 1975.

1482. The Ghost of Oaklands, by W. E. D. Ross. New York: Arcadia House, 1967. (NUC 1956-67 97-150)

1483. Ghost Ship of Fog Island, by Marilyn Ross. New York: Popular Library, 1975.

1484. The Ghosts of Grantmeer, by Clarissa Ross. New York: Avon, 1972.

1485. The Haunting of Clifton Court (D), by W. E. D. or "Dana" Ross. New York: Popular Library, 1972.

"Boston Gothic." Antiquarian Ann takes a job as assistant to Merridith Clifton in the antique shop on his estate. Merridith's family seem to unite in a conspiracy with the ghost of Vanessa Clifton to frighten Ann away. Greatly flawed by the contrived solution of the mystery which makes a complete dope out of the heroine.

1486. The Haunting of Villa Bagriel, by Clarissa Ross. New York: Lancer (74-770), n.d.

1487. Hearse for Dark Harbor, by Clarissa Ross. New York: Avon (20461), n.d.

1488. The Hidden Chapel, by Leslie Ames. New York: Arcadia House, 1967. (NUC 1968-72 81-283)

1489. House of Ghosts, by Marilyn Ross. New York: Warner, 1973.

1490. House on Mount Vernon Street, by W. E. D. Ross. New York: Avon, 1974.

1491. Loch Sinister, by Marilyn Ross. New York: Popular Library, 1974.

1492. The Locked Corridor, by Marilyn Ross. New York: Paperback Library, [1965]. (NUC 1975 13-825)

1493. Magic Valley, by W. E. D. Ross. London: Hale, [1970]. (NUC 1973 12-22)

1494. Marta, by Marilyn Ross. New York: Warner, 1973.

1495. Mistress of Moorwood Manor, by Marilyn Ross. New York: Warner, 1972.

1496. Mistress of Ravenswood (D), by Clarissa Ross. New York: Arcadia House, 1966; also pub. as: by Marilyn Ross. (NUC 1968-72 81-283)

Pamela, a young governess, is courted by the master of Ravenswood. Suddenly she's almost killed. Then ghosts appear. She wonders if she's going mad when she discovers a tombstone with her name on it. Shallow and juvenile.

1497. Mists of Dark Harbor, by Clarissa Ross. New York: Avon (23358), 1974.

1498. The Music Room, by W. E. D. Ross. New York: Dell, 1971.

1499. The Mystery of Collinwood (D), by Marilyn Ross. New York: Warner, 1968.

Victoria Winter is staying at Collinwood as companion to Elizabeth. The advent of the mysterious Mark Collins, alias Dr. Veno, brings dozens of attempts on Victoria's life. A superficial tale with Gothic elements but little else. This is one of the eminently dispensable "Dark Shadows" series.

1500. The Mystery of Fury Castle (D), by Marilyn Ross. New York: Warner, 1967.

Ellen goes to fiancé's Maine castle to prepare for their wedding and meets his spiritualist step-mother and doting step-sister. Threats to E.'s life are made by what seems to be the ghost of Ashley's former girlfriend. A fair plot but so superficially written that it's disappointing.

1501. Night of the Phantom. New York: Warner, 1972.

1502. Out of the Fog (D). New York: Lancer (75-352), 1970.

Vera moves to Maine to live with her elderly, rheumatoid and spiritualistic aunt. The new tenants in her aunt's adjoining house behave suspiciously and threats are made to Vera's life. The plot is weak in this shallow tale of romantic suspense. The Gothic elements are spurious.

1503. Phantom of Fog Island, by Marilyn Ross. New York: Warner, 1971.

1504. The Phantom of Glencourt, by Clarissa Ross. New York: Lancer (75-349), n.d.

1505. Phantom of the Swamp, by Marilyn Ross. New York: Paperback Library, 1972. (NUC 1968-72 81-283)

1506. Phantom of the 13th Floor (D), by Marilyn Ross. New York: Popular Library (08363), 1975.
Broadway star, Joan, begins to have spooky experiences while doing a revival of a show her murdered grandmother made famous. Essentially a murder mystery. Nothing new and no depth of anything.

1507. Ravenhurst, by Marilyn Ross. New York: Popular Library, 1975.

1508. Room Without a Key. New York: Lenox Hill, 1971. (NUC 1975 13-825)

1509. Rothhaven. New York: Manor, 1974.

1510. Sable in the Rain. New York: Lenox Hill, [1970]. (NUC 1973 12-22)

1511. Satan's Island, by Marilyn Ross. New York: Warner, 1975.

1512. Secret of Mallet Castle, by Clarissa Ross. New York: Arcadia House, 1966. (NUC 1956-67 97-128)

1513. Secret of the Pale Lover, by Clarissa Ross. New York: Lancer (75-350), n.d.

1514. Shadow over Emerald Castle, by Marilyn Ross. New York: Ballantine, 1975.

1515. Shadow over the Garden, by Clarissa Ross. New York: Lancer (75-236), n.d.

1516. The Sinister Garden, by Marilyn Ross. New York: Warner, 1972.

1517. The Spectral Mist, by Clarissa Ross. New York: Lancer (75-384)

1518. Step into Terror, by Marilyn Ross. New York: Warner, 1973.

1519. Terror at Dark Harbor (F). New York: Avon (26500), 1975.
Actress Kim agrees to portray playboy actor Johnny's fiancée when he goes to his family's summer estate on an island off Maine. There she finds suspected murder, jealousy and madness. Awkward writing makes this hard reading. The characters are "comic strip" and the whole thing is stilted, repetitive and boring.

1520. The Third Spectre, by W. E. D. Ross. New York: Arcadia

House, 1967; also pub. as: by Dan Ross. New York: Macfadden-Bartel, 1969. (NUC 1956-67 97-150)

1521. The Twilight Web (D), by W. E. D. Ross. New York: Arcadia House, 1968. (NUC 1968-72 81-283)

This is probably Ross at his best--which isn't saying much. There are the bare bones of a fairly good neo-Gothic plot here but nothing more. The characters are one dimensional, the writing is newscopy style and the events are melodramatic without atmosphere or depth. One gets the feeling that Ross could write a "good Gothic" if he ever bothered to take the time.

1522. The Vampire Contessa, by Marilyn Ross. New York: Pinnacle, 1974.

1523. Voice from the Grave, by Clarissa Ross. New York: Lancer (74-754), n.d.

1524. The Web of Love, by W. E. D. Ross. London: Hale, 1970. (NUC 1968-72 81-283)

1525. The Whispering Gallery (C), by W. E. D. Ross. New York: Lenox Hill, [1970]. (NUC 1973 12-22)

Barbara goes to the funeral of her old school chum, killed in a barn-burning a few years after she eloped with Barbara's fiancé. Barbara gets involved and uncovers skullduggery and love. Routine, formula stuff.

1526. Wind over the Citadel. New York: Lenox Hill, 1971. (NUC 1973 12-22)

1527. Winds of Change, by Ann Gilmer. New York: Bouregy, 1965. (NUC 1968-72 81-283)

1528. The Witch of Bralhaven, by Marilyn Ross. New York: Warner, 1972.

1529. Witches' Cove, by Marilyn Ross. New York: Warner, 1974.

1530. The Yesteryear Phantom, by W. E. D. Ross. New York: Lenox Hill, 1971. (NUC 1974 14-392)

Other works include: (by Marilyn Ross) The Aquarius Curse, Desperate Heiress, Face in the Fog, Fog Island, A Gathering of Evil, Haunting of Fog Island, The Locked Corridor, The Long Night of Fear, Memory of Evil, Message from a Ghost, Phantom Manor, The Phantom of Belle Acres, Satan's Rock, Secrets of Sedbury Manor, Shorecliff; (by Clarissa Ross) The Corridors of Fear, Ghost of Dark Harbor; and (by Dana Ross) Night of the Dead.

ROSSITER, Jane (pseud.) see ROSS, William Edward Daniel

RUEGG, [Judge] Alfred Henry 1854-

1531. Flash: A Moorland Mystery. London: Daniel, 1928.

1532. A Staffordshire Knot; or The Two Houses. London: Daniel, 1926. (LCPC pre'42 129-221)

RUNDLE, Anne (Lamb)
(Marianne Lamont, Alexandra Manners, Joanne Marshall, Jeanne Sanders)

Born in Berwick-on-Tweed, England and educated in the public schools. Married in 1949 and has three children. Worked as a British civil servant 1942-50 and after that became a full-time writer. Now lives in Glasgow, Scotland. Has written juvenile fiction in addition to the works listed here.

1533. Babylon Was Dust, by Joanne Marshall. London: Mills & Boon, 1970; New York: Avon, 1974.

1534. Bitter Bride Bed, by Marianne Lamont. London: Hutchinson, 1971.

1535. Candles in the Wood (B), by Alexandra Manners. New York: Putnam, 1974. (NUC 1974 10-950)
The story of Helen Comyn, child of servants from a large estate in mid-19th-century Scotland. Fate deals a strange hand and continues Helen's involvement with the family and its ghosts. A very Gothic tale written in a simple and direct manner. The author gets a lot of story with relatively few words. Some nice observations regarding human relationships in spite of the melodramatic characters and plot.

1536. Cat on a Broomstick, by Joanne Marshall. London: Jenkins, 1969.

1537. Cuckoo at Candlemas, by Joanne Marshall. London: Jenkins, 1968.

1538. Dark Changeling, by Marianne Lamont. London: Hutchinson, 1970; New York: Avon, 1973.
Strictly a romance. Not bad, but not a Gothic.

1539. The Dreaming Tower, by Joanne Marshall. London: Jenkins, 1969.

1540. Flower of Silence, by Joanne Marshall. London: Mills & Boon, 1970; New York: Avon, 1974.

1541. Follow a Shadow (C), by Joanne Marshall. New York: Putnam, 1974.

Harriet inherits some property in Spain from her godfather and goes to investigate. A very tedious tale, in my estimation. The pace is unduly slow, there are long and pointless dialogues and narrative. I finally went to the last chapter--and even that was boring.

1542. Green Glass Moon, by Marianne Lamont. London: Hutchinson, 1970.

1543. Heronbrook. London: Hale, 1974; New York: Bantam (8526), 1974.

1544. Sea Song, by Joanne Marshall. London: Mills & Boon, 1973.

1545. The Singing Swans, by Alexandra Manners. New York: Putnam, 1975.

1546. Spindrift, by Jeanne Sanders. London: Hale, 1974.

1547. The Stone Maiden (C), by Alexandra Manners. New York: Putnam, 1973. (NUC 1973 8-962)
Margaret goes to Maidenstone, the home of her disinherited and dead father's family to seek a home following her guardian's betrothal. Threats to her life complicate the otherwise happily reunited family and evidence points to Buck, the man she has come to love. A good deal of Scottish folklore helps this book. Makes an interesting comparison with M. McEvoy's Eaglescliffe which uses the same formula to much poorer advantage.

1548. The Trellised Walk, by Joanne Marshall. London: Mills & Boon, 1973.

1549. Valley of Tall Chimneys, by Joanne Marshall. London: Collins, 1975.

1550. Wild Boar Wood, by Joanne Marshall. London: Mills & Boon, 1972; New York: Avon, 1973.

RUSSELL, Charlotte Murray 1899-

Has written some twenty works that appear to be murder mysteries.

RUUTH, Marianne

1551. Game of Shadows (D). New York: Ace (27305), 1974.
Rich, innocent Eleanora is wooed and plotted against by the compelling Max Selander, research psychiatrist. An uninspired and dull tale of paranoid romantic suspense.

RYDELL, Forbes (pseud.) see FORBES, De Loris

ST. CLAIR, Elizabeth (pseud.) see COHEN, Susan

ST. CLAIR, Katherine (pseud.) see HUFF, Tom E.

ST. JOHN, David (pseud.) see HUNT, Howard

ST. JOHN, Gail

1552. Dunsan House (C). New York: Dell, 1969. [© Anita Grace].
Another "governess story" with some innovations that manage to sustain clumsiness of plot and characterization--but just barely.

ST. JOHN, Genevieve

1553. Night of Evil. New York: Belmont, 1967. Pub. with Daoma Winston's Castle of Closing Doors.

1554. The Secret of Dresden Farm (D). New York: Belmont (B75-2088), 1971.
Myra Breckenridge (!) Linden goes to defend her contested deed to Dresden Farm, once part of the fabulous Gregory estate. She becomes involved in intrigue, murder and daily attempts on her life. A weak tale of the Perils of Pauline ilk and becomes pretty boring by mid-book.

1555. The Shadow on Spanish Swamp (C). New York: Belmont, 1970.
Newlyweds June and Gregory go to G.'s family estate of Spanish Swamp Louisiana and find murder, mystery and intrigue. The author's solution to problems by killing off her characters systematically is a serious flaw in an otherwise entertaining story. The heroine is spared a lot of tough decisions by the timely demise of her foes. Note: see Barrie Myers, no. 1201, regarding use of this plot.

1556. The Sinister Voice (B). New York: Belmont, 1967.
Twins, Lola and Nola inherit a "castle" on the Hudson from a grandfather they have never seen. Strange and sinister things begin to happen upon their arrival and Lola uncovers a satanic conspiracy. I liked this author's style which made for pleasant reading, i.e., "God could have planned high noon by the straightness of Job Beaker's back." Also a good castle, and one that plays an integral part in the story.

Other works by this author include: The Dark Watch, Death in the

Desert, The Secret of Kensington Manor and Strangers in the Night, all published by Belmont.

ST. JOHN, Nicole

1557. The Medici Ring (B). New York: Random House, 1975; New York: Pocket Books (80444), 1976.

Lavinia, alone after the deaths of her mother and then her adoptive uncle decides to accept a school friend's invitation to stay in Boston in hopes of tracing her own background which seems to lead there. She finds her friend, Damaris, in a state of severe emotional turmoil and the household under a shadow. A well written story with standard neo-Gothic themes.

SALISBURY, Carola

1558. Dark Inheritance (B). New York: Doubleday, 1975.

Susannah Button's adventures and loves start out a bit like Daphne du Maurier's Jamaica Inn, but develop a far more complex and interesting plot. A fine tale of romantic suspense, well told.

SALVATO, Sharon Anne

"Salvato's roots in Ohio go back a long time. There is a store on the outskirts of German Village, established in 1843, that bears her maiden name. Her uncle, William Bush, 102, taught Indians and was called Bicycle Bill after the means he used to get into areas no wagon could reach. Salvato, a diving champion of great skill, is the mother of four sons." (Information from jacket of Briarcliff.)

1559. Briarcliff Manor: A Novel (D). New York: Stein & Day, 1974. (NUC 1974 14-659)

The first 100 pages are strictly drawing room drama and period romance and all of a mediocrity of style and idea that made it thoroughly tedious and inspired no interest to read further.

SANDERS, Jeanne (pseud.) see RUNDLE, Anne

SANDERS, Joan

Born in Three Forks, Montana and grew up in Star Valley, Wyoming and Ogden, Utah. Attended Stanford University and holds a B.A. from the University of Utah. Now lives in Logan, Utah and wrote her first book, La Petite: The Life of Louise de la Vallière, during two dark Scandinavian winters while her husband was working as a research fellow in Uppsala, Sweden. La Petite was followed by two other novels, The Marquis and The Nature of Witches. Sanders has also written poetry, one-act plays and short stories for various magazines, but she especially enjoys research about the people of Louis XIV's court. (Information from the jacket of Baneful Sorceries.)

1560. Baneful Sorceries, or The Countess Bewitched. Boston: Houghton Mifflin, 1969.

Another book I gave up on after 100 pages. It appears to be historic romance. May be of interest to those who, like the author, "love the gossip of other centuries," in which the first 100 pages of this work abound.

SAVAGE, Mary

1561. The Coach Draws Near (B). New York: distr. by Dodd, Mead, 1964; New York: Dell, 1967. (NUC 1956-67 100-110)

One really does not know what awaits behind the formula Gothic covers of a paperback book. I very much liked and was delightfully surprised by this philosophical novel about hard-boiled, hard-drinking, Madison Ave. journalist Marianne assigned the job of investigating a West Coast self-styled reclusive guru, Janus, who is predicting the world would end in one week. I found the philosophy congenial and the story gripping. But this book is in no way Gothic, neo-Gothic or romantically suspenseful!

Other works by this author, all distributed by Dodd, Mead and listed in the 1956-67 NUC are: Just for Tonight (1961), A Likeness to Voices (1963) and Tenderly, My Love (1960).

SAXON, Peter

1562. The Killing Bone: The Guardians #1 (C). New York: Berkley Medallion, 1969.

Exotic-horror Gothic which I found exceedingly dull. Much of the supposed horror in this tale was of the mind and Saxon lacked the skill to do much more than report it. The basic idea of the series, a group of talented folk, dedicated to challenging Evil, has possibilities.

SCHWEITZER, Gertrude 1909-

In addition to works listed here has written love stories and/or romances.

1563. The Ledge (B). New York: Delacorte Press, 1972. (NUC 1968-72 84-662)

Catherine takes a secretarial job with the reclusive and

notorious former Senator, Amos Kent, following the traumatic death of her financé. She becomes deeply involved with the complex and troubled Amos and his strange household. Better than average romantic suspense.

1564. The Obsessed. Greenwich, Conn.: Fawcett, 1950. (LCAC 1948-52 18-609)

1565. So Many Voices. Englewood Cliffs, N.J.: Prentice-Hall, 1964. (NUC 1956-67 101-388)

SCOTT, Antonia

1566. Falcon's Island ("A Ravenswood Gothic") (B). New York: Pocket Books, 1973.

Glory, what a gory story! Skillful narrative and interesting characters manage to sustain the tale through one harrowing experience after another in this hypermelodramatic but nonetheless entertaining Gothic tale. A bit much, but I enjoyed it.

SEARS, Ruth McCarthy

1567. Wind in the Cypress. New York: Nordon Publications (Leisure Books), 1974. Orig. title: The Grangerfjord Monks.

This little tale was obviously the effort of some precocious 12-year-old. A bald narrative with no attempt at description, mood or atmosphere, or any of the refinements of what we call "literature." There are gaps in the clumsy story that suggest large portions were deleted--or the author took long breaks during the writing and didn't reread before progressing at the next sitting. Karma Millay gets stranded at an old mansion and is kept captive by some weird monks. The whole thing is an absolute put-on.

SEELEY, Mabel 1903-

Another author whose work borders between mystery-detective and Gothic. From the books of hers I read, I feel her work is most properly classified as the former. I recommend The Chuckling Fingers (1941) and The Crying Sisters (1939) both published for the Crime Club by Doubleday.

SEILAZ, Aileen

1568. The Veil of Silence (C). New York: Ace (K209), 1966.

Maggie is companion to the invalid Christine, heiress to a great fortune. Suspicion is aroused as to the nature of Christine's disease when she happens to fall in love with the local G.P. Her step-brothers behave in a very suspicious manner. Some new wrinkles and competent writing help a very overused Gothic plot.

SELLERS, Mary

1569. The Cry of the Cat (C). New York: Warner Paperback, 1975.

In some ways an engaging and innovative "Mississippi Gothic" but greatly flawed by a slow pace and a large amount of irrelevant narrative.

1570. House on Black Bayou. New York: Warner Paperback, 1975.

SETON, Anya

Born in New York, New York and educated privately except for courses taken at Oxford University, England. She has written several novels that have had wide popularity and prefers to classify her books as "biographical" rather than "historical" romances. Dragonwyck (Houghton-Mifflin, 1944) is probably her best known novel. The only one I have found that is Gothic is:

1571. Green Darkness (A). Boston: Houghton-Mifflin, 1972. (NUC 1973 12-771)

There's something for everyone in this story. It seemed to me a very mature historical Gothic. Seton is a fine storyteller and handles an enormous cast of characters with great skill.

SHATTUCK, Dora (Richards)
(Richard Shattuck)

1572. The Half-Haunted Saloon (B), by Richard Shattuck. New York: Simon & Schuster, 1945. (NUC 1956-67 103-58)

Quite an entertaining whimsical Gothic--almost slapstick in places. A straight-laced middle-class American family inherit a "haunted" saloon, come under its spell and have their consciousnesses raised. Clever, amusing and even, at times, thought provoking.

1573. Said the Spider to the Fly, by Richard Shattuck. New York: Simon & Schuster, 1944. (NUC 1956-67 103-58)

1574. The Snark Was a Boojum, by Richard Shattuck. New York: Morrow, 1941. (NUC 1956-67 103-58)

1575. The Wailing Woman (D). New York: Warner Paperback (75-289), 1973.

A very disappointing tale after the expectations I had from

reading Saloon. There are several Gothic elements but the tale is so poorly written and so disjointed that I soon tired of the effort required to figure out what was going on.

1576. The Wedding Guest Sat on a Stone, by Richard Shattuck. New York: Colliers, 1963. (NUC 1956-67 103-58)

SHATTUCK, Richard (pseud.) see SHATTUCK, Dora (Richards)

SHEARING, Joseph (pseud.) see LONG, Gabriella

SHEED, Wilfred

Other novels include: A Middle Class Education, The Hack, Square's Progress and Office Politics. He is also film critic of Esquire, book review editor of Commonweal, and a frequent critic of contemporary fiction for the New York Times Book Review, The Atlantic and other magazines.

1577. The Blacking Factory and Pennsylvania Gothic: A Short Novel and a Long Story. New York: Farrar, Straus & Giroux, 1968. (NUC 1968-72 86-182)

The Blacking Factory does not appear to be Gothic. Pennsylvania Gothic is Gothic in mood and setting only and does not use other elements. It's an interesting story with a very abrupt ending. Could almost be a prologue to a traditional Gothic novel.

SHENKIN, Elizabeth ?-1975

1578. Brownstone Gothic: A Suspense Novel of the 1970's (B). New York: Holt, Rinehart & Winston, 1961. (NUC 1956-67 103-193). Pub. also as: The Secret Heart. New York: Paperback Library, 1964.

Although this tale had very few Gothic elements, it was well enough written to capture and sustain my interest for the entire story. More of a domestic drama and intrigue than a Gothic.

1579. Midsummer's Nightmare. New York: Rinehart, 1960. (NUC 1956-67 103-193)

SHEPHERD, Donald (Lee)
(Barbara Kevern)

Born 5/26/32 in Jackson, Michigan. Received A.A. from Los Angeles Harbor College and B.S. from California State Polytechnical University, 1966. He is married to Barbara Kevern (a literary agent) and they have three children. He has worked as a magazine and book editor and served in the U. S. Army from 1953-56. He has had his own literary agency since 1969. Also wrote Women in History (Mankind, 1973). (Contemporary Authors, Vol. 61-64, p. 502.)

1580. Dark Eden, by Barbara Kevern. New York: Pocket Books, 1973.

1581. Darkness Is Falling, by Barbara Kevern. New York: Pinnacle, 1974.

1582. The Devil's Vinyard, by Barbara Kevern. New York: Pinnacle, 1975.

1583. The Key (C), by Barbara Kevern. New York: Ballantine, 1974.

Well, all the elements of sentimental horror Gothic are present and they're not badly assembled. On the other hand, they are not well assembled either. A satisfactory tale for the inexperienced or unsophisticated but the more choosey reader will do well to try elsewhere.

SHEPHERD, L. P.

Born in St. Louis, Missouri. Received a B. S. from Kansas State Teachers College in 1961 and an A. M. in 1962 from Columbia University. Works as an English teacher and lives in Fitchburg, Massachusetts.

1584. Cape House (C). New York: Dell, 1974.

Good ghosts in this one but the writing style is very strange and, for me, hard to follow. The ending was disappointing, too.

SHERIDAN, Elsie Lee
(Elsie Lee)

In addition to Gothics has written homemaker-type books on plants, cooking, rocks and gems and so on.

1585. The Curse of Carranca, by Elsie Lee. New York: Lancer, 1966.

1586. The Passions of Medora Graeme, by Elsie Lee. New York: Arbor House, 1972. (NUC 1973 8-298)

1587. Prior Betrothal, by Elsie Lee. New York: Arbor House, 1973. (NUC 1973 8-298)

1588. Satan's Coast (B), by Elsie Lee. New York: Lancer (74-548), 1969.

Widowed Nell takes her stepson to Portugal to spend the summer in the old castle inherited from her husband. The local people resent her arrival and something is seriously amiss. A very satisfying tale in several respects. There's a castle, a heroine who has a lot on the ball, and supporting characters of depth. The suspense is low-key but the story sufficiently well done that one forgives.

1589. Silence Is Golden, by Elsie Lee. New York: Dell (07903), 1971.

1590. Sinister Abbey, by Elsie Lee. New York: Dell, 1973.

1591. Wingarden (A), by Elsie Lee. New York: Arbor House, 1971; New York: Dell (9742), 1971. (NUC 1968-72 86-274)

Chloe goes to the Virginia estate of Wingarden to check out an inheritance from her estranged grandmother and finds more than she bargained for. A very well written and most entertaining neo-Gothic with lots of snappy dialogue and a good story.

Other works by Sheridan include: Clouds over Vallanto; Dark Moon; Lost Lady; Mansion of Golden Windows and Season of Evil all by "Elsie Lee" and all published by Lancer.

SHOESMITH, Kathleen A.

1592. Cloud over Calderwood (C). London: Hale, 1969; New York: Ace, 1973.

A somewhat better than average sentimental Gothic of the "companion at the mansion" formula.

Also wrote: The Reluctant Puritan.

SHUBAEL, (pseud.) see PURDY, Jennie Bouton

SHULMAN, Sandra (Dawn)

Born in 1944 and now living in London, England. Has worked as personal assistant to the fiction editor of children's magazines and a free-lance journalist and film researcher. Contributor to children's serials and short stories to periodicals and historical novels.

1593. The Brides of Devil's Leap (A). New York: Warner Paperback, 1968.

Pure Gothic. Kate's marriage to Piers Eddington was arranged when she was three. Kate, under the pall of the recent murder of her father and brother, goes to Devil's Leap, a bastion of evil doings. A delightful tale, set in 19th-century England.

1594. Castlecliffe. New York: Warner Paperback, 1967.

1595. The Daughters of Astaroth. New York: Paperback Library, 1968.

1596. The Menacing Darkness. New York: Warner Paperback (64-715), 1966.

SIBLEY, Patricia

1597. High Walk to Wadlemere (A). London: Hodder & Stoughton, 1973. New York: Dell, 1974. (NUC 1974 15-371)
No Gothic elements in this fine love story. The paperback cover on the Dell edition is most misleading. I liked this story enormously. The characters are beautifully drawn, the descriptive parts are interesting and the author has something important to say about human relationships. I highly recommend the book, but don't expect a Gothic.

SIMMONS, Margaret Irwin (pseud.) see LANSING, Elizabeth C.

SIMMONS, Mary Kay

1598. Cameron Hill. New York: Dell (00970), 1972.

1599. The Captain's House. New York: Dell (01085), 1970.

1600. The Diamonds of Alcazar. New York: Dell, 1972.

1601. The Hermitage (C). New York: Dell (3628), 1975.
Andrea goes to The Hermitage to tutor ten-year-old Felicia, confined to a wheel chair since the auto accident that killed her parents. Andrea and Felicia are terrorized by ghosts and a series of accidents and tragedies. Formula plot but fairly well done and manages, for the most part, to sustain the reader's interest.

1602. Megan. New York: Dell (0554), 1971.

1603. The Willow Pond. New York: Dell (09625), 1972.

1604. The Year of the Rooster. New York: Delacorte Press, 1971; New York: Dell (09782), 1972. (NUC 1968-72 87-180)

SINCLAIR, Olga (Waters)

Born 1/23/23 in Watton, England. Education: in Norfolk, England. Home: Coltishall, Norwich, England. Career: writer.

Bank clerk 1940-42; justice of the peace 1966; district councillor. Has also written non-fiction for children, and novels not likely Gothic.

1605. The Man at the Manor. London: Gresham, 1967; New York: Dell, 1972. (NUC 1968-72 87-285)

1606. Night of the Black Tower. New York: Lancer (74-679), 1968.

SKINNER, June O'Grady
(Rohan O'Grady)

Born 7/23/22 in Vancouver, B.C., Canada. Education: High school and business college. Is married and has three children. Now lives in West Vancouver, B.C., Canada. Formerly a newspaper librarian, now a housewife and author. Skinner is the only author I've found who has formally listed herself as a "housewife."

1607. Bleak November, by Rohan O'Grady. New York: Dial Press, 1970. (NUC 1968-72 87-519)

1608. Let's Kill Uncle, by Rohan O'Grady. New York: Macmillan, 1963. (NUC 1956-67 104-470)

1609. O'Houlihan's Jest: A Lament for the Irish, by Rohan O'Grady. New York: Macmillan, 1961. (NUC 1956-67 104-470)

1610. Pippin's Journal: or Rosemary Is for Remembrance (B), by Rohan O'Grady. New York: Macmillan, 1962. Pub. also as: The Master of Montrolfe Hall. New York: Ace, 1962. (NUC 1956-67 104-470)

John Montrolfe returns to his ancestral home and finds it haunted. A good tale, well told.

SLOANE, Sara (pseud.) see BLOOM, Ursula

SMITH, Lady Eleanor Furneaux

Born in Birkenhead, Cheshire, England in 1902. Journalist and novelist and specialist in lore of the Gypsies. She died in 1945.

1611. Caravan. Garden City, N.Y.: Doubleday, 1943. (LCPC 1942-47 34-366)

1612. A Dark and Splendid Passion (A). New York: Ace (13831), [1941].

This is a real humdinger--the kind I hope for with each new book I open. Mary Rohen, while at the family estate awaiting her husband's return from WWII, discovers a hidden cache of documents and thereby the story behind a family legend. Be prepared to weep. But it's worth it. A fine story, beautifully told and employing every Gothic element in the list.

1613. Magic Lantern. Garden City, N.Y.: Doubleday, 1945. (LCPC 1942-47 34-366)

1614. The Man in Grey. Garden City, N.Y.: Doubleday, 1942.

1615. The Spanish House. Garden City, N.Y.: Doubleday, 1938. (LCPC pre'42 138-365)

SMITH, Frederick E(screet)
(David Farrell)

Born in 1922, he became a full-time writer in 1952 after working as a local government officer and cost accountant. Lives in Bournemouth, Hampshire, England.

1616. The Devil Behind Me. London: Hodder & Stoughton, 1962.

1617. The Grotto of Tiberius. London: Hodder & Stoughton, 1961.

1618. Laws Be Their Enemy. London: Hutchinson, 1955.

1619. A Killing for the Hawks. n.p.: Harrap, 1966.

1620. Lydia Trendennis (C). London: Hutchinson, 1957; New York: Warner Paperback, 1964.

In a field of much-used plots, this author picked one that doesn't wear well--the barren wife of the heir apparent whose mother-in-law plots to kill her. Fairly good job otherwise and worth reading for the somewhat surprising and melodramatic ending.

1621. Of Masks and Minds. London: Hutchinson, 1954.

1622. The Other Cousin, by David Farrell. London: Gresham, 1962.

1623. The Sin and the Sinners. London: Jarrolds, 1958.

1624. The Storm Knight. n.p.: Harrap, 1966.

1625. Strange Enemy, by David Farrell. London: Hale, 1966.

1626. Temptation Isle, by David Farrell. London: Gresham, 1962.

SMITH, Naomi Gladish

1627. Buried Remembrance (C). New York: Ace, 1976.

"Allyn Bourke came to Sheldon's Crossing to forget a tragedy that haunted her nights, and made sad shadows of her days. But before her scar could heal, tragedy struck again ... and again ... and again." This inside-the-cover blurb pretty well sums it up. Tragedy buffs may enjoy but I thought the events in the story unduly grim and the solution to the mystery failed to justify them.

SNOW, Lyndon (pseud.) see ANSLE, Dorothy Phoebe

SNYDER, Zilpha Keatley

Has written over ten Gothic juveniles but no adult fiction of which I am aware.

SOMERLOTT, Robert

1628. The Inquisitor's House (C). New York: Viking, 1968; New York: Avon, 1969.

A long and multi-faceted tale very much in the tradition of its 18th-century counterparts such as Melmoth the Wanderer.

SOMERS, Suzanne

1629. Image of Truth. New York: Avalon, 1963. (NUC 1956-67 105-601)

1630. Until Death (C). New York: Curtis, 1973. [© Norman Daniels].

In spite of a somewhat juvenile writing style, this story has an engaging plot and is particularly appealing because the author has her characters behave with such good sense. Nurse Jennifer, in desperation, agrees to a secret contract with dying Vincent's family that she will wed and take care of him in return for sanitarium treat ment for her tubercular mother. After the wedding, Jennifer discovers an evil plot. Romantic suspense.

SPEARE, Elizabeth George 1908-

Has written several works that appear to be Gothic juveniles.

1631. The Witch of Blackbird Pond (C). New York: Houghton, 1958; New York: Dell, 7th printing 1973.

A moderately entertaining little romantic suspense set in colonial times but lacking in depth or insight and therefore seeming rather juvenile.

SPECTOR, Robert Donald

Born 9/21/22 in Bronx, New York; Education: B. S. Long Island University, 1948; M.A. New York University, 1949; Ph.D. Columbia, 1962. Home: Brooklyn, New York. Career: Professor of English. Has also written several scholarly works related to his field.

1632. The Candle and the Tower. New York: Warner Paperback, 1974.

1633. Seven Masterpieces of Gothic Horror. New York: Bantam, 1963. (NUC 1956-67 106-414)

SPICER, Dorothy Gladys

Author of a large number of juvenile Gothics and some non-fiction on folk festivals and customs. Describes herself as "an ardent researcher into ESP." Born in New York City. Received an A.B. from Vassar College in 1916; an A.M. from Radcliffe in 1918 and pursued additional studies at Columbia, New York University, College of the City of New York and various European and Asian countries. Now living in Berkeley, California.

1634. The Humming Top (B). New York: Phillips, 1968; New York: Ballantine. (NUC 1968-72 89-317)

A story of a young girl gifted, or cursed, with ESP which gets her into a good deal of trouble but also helps her to solve both a long standing mystery and a murder, and to find love. Nicely done.

STANTON, Coralie (pseud.) see HOSKEN, Ernest Charles

STEVENSON, Anne

1635. The French Inheritance (B). New York: Putnam, 1974; Greenwich, Conn.: Fawcett-Crest, 1975. (NUC 1974 15-999)

David travels to France to claim a house he inherited upon his French mother's death. There he finds more than he bargained for and becomes a catalyst in the unraveling of an intrigue that began during WWII. Well conceived, written and plotted and a very entertaining story. Note: If this book had had the main character female, it would more than likely have been labeled "Gothic" by its publisher.

1636. A Game of Statues. New York: Putnam, 1972. (NUC 1968-72 90-256)

1637. Ralph Dacre. New York: Walker, 1967. (NUC 1956-67 107-523)

1638. A Relative Stranger. New York: Putnam, 1970. (NUC 1968-72 90-256)

STEVENSON, Florence

1639. Altar of Evil (C). New York: Universal-Award House, Inc., [1973].

Horror Gothic. Kitty Telefair, a contemporary member of an ancient line of sorcerers, confronts the supernatural. An acquaintance is cursed by her rejected sorcerer lover and the results are gruesome indeed.

1640. Bianca, with Patricia Hagan Murray. New York: New American Library (Signet T5434), 1973.

1641. The Curse of the Concullens (B). New York: World Pub. Co., 1970; New York: New American Library (Signet T4903), 1972. (NUC 1968-72 90-259)

Lucinda, one of 15 children of an English parson, goes to Ireland as governess to the O'Hagan children and meets the family ghosts, goulies and curse. Fast-paced, witty and fun. This should have been a longer and "meatier" tale, darn it.

1642. Dark Odyssey. New York: New American Library (Signet Q6223), 1974.

1643. Ides of November. New York: New American Library (Signet Q6370), 1975.

1644. Kilmeny in the Dark Wood. New York: New American Library (Signet T5711), 1973.

1645. Ophelia. New York: New American Library, 1968.

1646. A Shadow on the House. New York: New American Library (Signet Y6520), 1975.

1647. Where Satan Dwells. New York: Universal Pub. & Distr. (Award Books A883S), 1971.

1648. Witches' Crossing (D). New York: New American Library (Signet Y6813), 1975.

A second-rate love story with some spurious semi-supernatural effects thrown in just to qualify for "Gothic." Clarissa's parents die of the "grippe" when she's 20 and leave her penniless and in charge of her younger sister. Clarissa marries her fiancé's father after the fiancé jilts her ... and all that. There's a ghost and a curse and "voices," but they're just props.

1649. The Witching Hour. New York: Universal Pub. & Distr. (Award Books A868N), 1971.

STEWART, John Innes
(Michael Innes)

Has written dozens of mysteries and detective novels. The ones listed here are those which have, or may have, Gothic elements.

1650. The Bloody Wood, by Michael Innes. New York: Dodd, Mead, 1966. (NUC 1956-67 107-556)

1651. A Change of Heir (B), by Michael Innes. New York: Dodd, Mead, 1966. (NUC 1956-67 107-557)

A tale of a conspiracy to defraud by impersonation. Not Gothic but interesting in comparison with female oriented stories using the same formula.

1652. Christmas at Candleshoe (A), by Michael Innes. New York: Dodd, Mead, 1953. (NUC 1953-57 22-541)

Christmas is not a holiday in this delightful whimsical Gothic tale. I long for a leisured listener and the wit to speak such soul satisfying sentences as Michael Innes produces. The whole thing is great good fun.

1653. A Comedy of Terrors, by Michael Innes. New York: Dodd, Mead, 1940. (LCPC pre'42 143-7)

1654. A Family Affair, by Michael Innes. London: Gollancz, 1969. (NUC 1968-72 90-287)

1655. The Guardians. New York: Norton, 1957. (NUC 1953-57 22-541)

1656. Lament for a Maker (B), by Michael Innes. New York: Dodd, Mead, 1938; New York: Collier, 1961.

This has all the Gothic elements but on a very elegant level. It's a funny story. It's a mystery--and a tricky one at that. It's got a castle and a conspiracy and a wrong to be righted. It's also a bit long.

1657. The Last Tresilians, by Michael Innes. New York: Norton, 1963. (NUC 1956-67 107-557)

1658. The Secret Vanguard, by Michael Innes. New York: Dodd, Mead, 1941. (LCPC pre'42 143-7)

1659. What Happened at Hazelwood?, by Michael Innes. New York: Dodd, Mead, 1946. (LCPC 1942-47 35-420)

STEWART, Mary (Florence Elinor Rainbow)

Teacher, lecturer and writer born 9/17/16 in Sunderland, Durham, England. Received a B.S. with first class honors from the

University of Durham in 1938 and went on to obtain a diploma in theory and practice of teaching in 1939 and an M.A. in 1941. She is married and now lives in Edinburgh, Scotland. I do not, for the most part, consider Stewart's work Gothic but, as it has often been published as such, I am including most of it here.

1660. Airs Above the Ground. New York: Mill & Morrow, 1967; Greenwich, Conn.: Fawcet-Crest, [1965]. (NUC 1956-67 107-561)

A spy-suspense story. Not Gothic, but fairly entertaining.

1661. The Crystal Cave. New York: Morrow, 1970. (NUC 1968-72 90-291)

A cleverly written story of Merlin Pendragon and the Arthurian legend. Neither Gothic nor romantic suspense.

1662. The Gabriel Hounds (B). New York: Mill & Morrow, 1967; Greenwich, Conn.: Fawcett-Crest, 1968. (NUC 1956-67 107-561)

A fair-paced tale based on the legend of Lady Hester Stanhope. Very few Gothic elements, but suspense, intrigue, exotic setting and romance aplenty.

1663. The Hollow Hills. New York: Morrow, 1973. (NUC 1973 13-581)

1664. The Ivy Tree (B). New York: Mill, 1961; Greenwich, Conn.: Fawcett-Crest, 1963. (NUC 1956-67 107-561)

"The story of a perilous impersonation." Cleverly done and entertaining. Maybe neo-Gothic.

1665. Madam, Will You Talk? New York: Mill & Morrow, 1956. (NUC 1953-57 22-542)

1666. The Moon-Spinners (C). New York: Mill & Morrow, 1963; Greenwich, Conn.: Fawcett-Crest, 1964. (NUC 1956-67 107-561)

Nicole travels to Crete on vacation from a job at the British Embassy in Athens. There she becomes embroiled in murder and intrigue. A tale of adventure and romance and fairly well done with the exception of a weak conclusion and unduly conscientious descriptions of Cretan wildflowers and landscapes.

1667. My Brother Michael. New York: Mill & Morrow, 1960. (NUC 1956-67 107-561)

British Crime Writers Award, 1960.

1668. Nine Coaches Waiting. Greenwich, Conn.: Fawcett-Crest, [1958]. (NUC 1968-72 90-291)

1669. This Rough Magic. New York: Mill & Morrow, 1964. (NUC 1956-67 107-562)

Mystery Writers of America Award, 1964.

1670. Thunder on the Right. London: Hodder & Stoughton, 1957; Greenwich, Conn.: Fawcett-Crest, [1956]. (NUC 1953-57 22-542)

The author herself says of this book: "I detest that book ... I'm ashamed of it, and I'd like to see it drowned beyond recovery. It's overwritten. It was actually the second book I wrote, and for some strange reason I went overboard, splurged with adjectives, all colored purple" (Contemporary Authors, Vol. 1-4, p. 910). I agree fully.

1671. Touch Not the Cat (C). New York: Morrow, 1976; Greenwich, Conn.: Fawcett, 1976.

A smooth piece, overall, but nonetheless I found it tedious with its thin trickle of story wending through the descriptive passages which comprise the bulk of the book, and rather pretentious with all its quotes, poetry, and Greek and Roman references. In this book Stewart seems more a show-off than a storyteller.

1672. Wildfire at Midnight. New York: Appleton-Century-Crofts, 1956. (NUC 1953-57 22-542)

STOKER, Bram (i.e., Abraham) 1847-1912

Probably best known for his Dracula published in 1899 by Doubleday & McClure. His 20th-century works include:

1673. Garden of Evil. New York: Paperback Library, 2nd printing 1968; Orig. pub. as: The Lair of the White Worm. London: W. Rider, [1911]. (LCPC pre'42 143-246)

From a promising beginning, this developed quickly into a very stupid story. Tends to reach the outer limits of just how dumb one can get.

1674. The Gates of Life. New York: Cupples & Lion, [1908]. (LCPC pre'42 143-246)

1675. The Jewel of Seven Stars. New York & London: Harpers, 1904. (LCPC pre'42 143-256)

1676. Lady Athlyne. New York: Reynolds, 1908. (LCPC pre'42 143-246)

1677. The Lady of the Shroud (C). London: Heinemann, 1909; New York: Warner Paperback, 1966. (LCPC pre'42 143-246)

A legend and quest story. Rather corny by contemporary standards but keeps pace fairly well. Certainly Gothic.

1678. The Mystery of the Sea. New York: Doubleday, Page, 1902. (LCPC pre'42 143-246)

STONE, Elna (Burchfield)
(Elna Worrell Daniel)

A native of Gattman, Mississippi now living in Pensacola, Florida. Has been an employment counselor and teacher in addition to novelist.

1679. Dark Masquerade (B). New York: Lancer, 1973.
Tale of amnesia and mixed identity. Is the heroine Laurice or Merridith? How and why had Merridith supposedly died? Laurice comes to Dangerfield (!) in Florida to discover the answers. A fairly well placed and written tale. Romantic suspense with token Gothic elements.

1680. Ghosts at the Wedding. New York: Belmont-Tower (B75-2182), 1972.

1681. Secret of the Willows. New York: Belmont (B75-2077), 1971.

1682. Whisper of Fear. New York: Ballantine, 1973.

STORM, Virginia (pseud.) see SWATRIDGE, Irene

STUART, Alex (pseud.) see STUART, Vivian

STUART, Anne

1683. Barrett's Hill. New York: Ballantine, 1974.

1684. Cameron's Landing (C). Garden City, N.Y.: Doubleday, 1977.
From a promising and somewhat innovative beginning this competently written tale quickly turns into one of complete predictability. Disappointing.

STUART, V. A. see STUART, Vivian

STUART, Vivian (Finlay)
(Barbara Allen, Fiona Finlay, Alex Stuart, V. A. Stuart)

Romantic novelist and lecturer born 1/2/14 in Rangoon, Burma. Attended the University of London, University of Budapest and the Technical Institute of Australia. She is married, has four children and lives in York, England. There are 29 Alex Stuart books--romances, nurse and doctor stories; 5 Barbara Allen books appear to be the same sort of thing, as do the 20 or more V. A. Stuart books all listed in Contemporary Authors.

1685. Castle in the Mist. London: Mills & Boon, 1959.

1686. The New Mrs. Aldrich (C). New York: Pyramid Books, 1976. [© Charles Stuart-Vernon].

Tracey marries aristocrat Maurice after a brief courtship and moves with him to Renhope Manor after their honeymoon. Tracey begins to have some doubts about the marriage as she begins to discover some family history that Maurice never mentioned. Her husband may even be mad. Of course, it all works out happily for Tracey in the end, but she does have a bit of a bother. Not badly written, actually, and the characters are quite deft for their number and the brevity of the book.

1687. The Peacock Pagoda. London: Mills & Boon, 1959.

STUBBS, Jean

Born in Lancashire, England, in 1926, the daughter of a university lecturer. She claims to have written her first novel, The Rose-grower, on the subway on her way to work. Two earlier novels have been published in the U.S.: My Grand Enemy, based on the life of a real person, the 18th-century patricide Mary Blandy, and Eleanora Duse. (Information from the Bantam edition of Case.)

1688. The Case of Kitty Ogilvie. New York: Walker, 1971; New York: Bantam (Q8423), 1974. (NUC 1968-72 90-709)

This novel is based on an 18th-century murder case. I see no justification for the promotion of this book as "Gothic," or as being "in the tradition of Victoria Holt and Ann Maybury."

SUBOND, Valerie

1689. House over Hell Valley (C). New York: Ballantine, 1974. [© Valerie Grayland].

The unusual setting in the volcanic area of New Zealand is about the only plus for this otherwise routine, predictable, sentimental Gothic. A definite minus is the author's device of including the heroine's thought process in italics along with a perfectly adequate third person narrative.

SUMMERTON, Margaret
(Jan Roffman)

What I have read of this author I have enjoyed: Death of a Fox (Doubleday, 1964), also pub. as: Reflection of Evil (Ace, 1964); A Bad Conscience (Doubleday, 1972), and Quinn's Hide (Ace, 1964). They are, however, not Gothic or romantic suspense but mystery and detection. Her works are comprehensively listed in the NUC 1956-67 96-394.

SWANN, Francis

Born in Annapolis, Maryland in 1913. Studied at Princeton and Johns Hopkins. Currently living in New York City and has worked as an actor, musician, stage director and author, mainly of movie scripts.

1690. Angelica. New York: Lancer, 1973.

1691. The Brass Key (C). New York: Simon & Schuster, 1964; New York: Lancer (73-777), 1968. (NUC 1956-67 109-163)

Not a bad little romantic suspense about a young girl who goes to her dead father's home to vindicate him of a crime of which he was accused twenty-five years before.

1692. Day of Dark Memory. New York: Avon, 1970.

1693. Greenwood. New York: Lancer, 1965.

1694. Hacienda Triste. New York: Lancer, 1968.

1695. Hellgate Plantation. New York: Lancer, 1973.

1696. Hermit Island. New York: Lancer, 1967.

1697. House of Terror. New York: Lancer, 1968.

1698. Royal Street. New York: Lancer, 1966.

1699. You'll Hang My Love. New York: Lancer, 1967.

SWATRIDGE, Irene Maude Mossop
(Irene Mossop; pseuds: Fay Chandos, Virginia Storm, Jan Tempest; Theresa Charles--joint pseud. with her husband.)

The author and her husband farm on the south Devonshire coast, keeping a dairy herd and raising sheep. She has published a great number of romances under her maiden name and other pseudonyms as well as all those with her husband as "Theresa Charles."

1700. Castle Kelpiesloch, by Theresa Charles. London: Hale, 1973.

1701. Dark Legacy, by Theresa Charles. New York: Dell, n.d.

1702. The Distant Drum, by Theresa Charles. London: Longmans, Green, 1940.

1703. Fairer Than She, by Theresa Charles. London: Cassell, 1953.

1704. From Fairest Flowers, by Theresa Charles. London: Hale, 1969.

1705. House of Pines, by Jan Tempest. New York: Ace, 1975.

1706. House on the Rocks, by Theresa Charles. London: Hale, 1962.

1707. Man-Made Miracle, by Theresa Charles. London: Longmans, Green, 1949. (NUC pre'56 104-106--verified under pseudonym)

1708. My Enemy and I, by Theresa Charles. London: Longmans, Green, 1941. (NUC pre'56 104-106)

1709. No Through Road, by Theresa Charles. London: Hale, 1960.

1710. Nurse Alice in Love (B), by Theresa Charles. London: Hale, 1964; also pub. as: Lady in the Mist. New York: Ace (46889), 1964. (NUC 1956-67 21-317)

Alice takes a job as nurse-nanny for the precocious Fernie and finds that Fernie's life may be in danger. This is a fairly well written tale and the plot is solid and sufficiently innovative to make it better than average romantic suspense.

1711. Proud Citadel, by Theresa Charles. London: Hale, 1967.

1712. Return to Terror, by Theresa Charles. New York: Pocketbooks, n.d.

1713. The Shadowy Mind, by Theresa Charles. London: Hale, 1968.

1714. To Save My Life, by Theresa Charles. London: Longmans, Green, 1948.

TATE, Ellalice (pseud.) see HIBBERT, Eleanor Alice

TATE, Mary Anne (pseud.) see HALE, Arlene

TATE, Velma (Young)
(Francine Davenport, Valerie Taylor, Narcella Young)

Born in Aurora, Illinois 9/7/13. Attended Blackburn College 1935-37. Worked as a creator of display advertising 1959-68 and owner and operator of an editorial agency since 1961. The "Valerie Taylor" books have been banned in South Africa and the author writes: "as a worker for civil rights, [I] think this is a good place to be banned." She further comments: "My lesbian books are not lurid, nor are they meant to be pro-gay propaganda, but true to life." Tate speaks four languages and has lived in the Canary Islands for a time and hopes to return there. The Narcella Young pseudonym has been used for contributions of poetry and articles to magazines and journals. (Information from Contemporary Authors, Vol. 23-24, p. 410.)

1715. The Secret of the Bayou (C), by Francine Davenport. New York: Ace (G624), 1967.

A rather tame sentimental Gothic set in the American South. I think it will prove satisfactory to many who haven't already read two or three hundred that are just the same.

TATTERSALL, (Honor) Jill (Blunt)

This author has been employed during her earlier years as a giftwrapper, typist, photographic model, receptionist, film extra, horse trainer, nursery school owner and teacher. Born 12/18/31 in Tintagel, Cornwall, England, she now lives in Greenbanks, Tortola, British Virgin Islands and is married and has three children.

1716. Enchanter's Castle. London: Collins, 1966.

1717. Lady Ingram's Retreat. London: Collins, 1970. (NUC 1968-72 92-644)

1718. Lady Ingram's Room. New York: Morrow, 1971. (NUC 1968-72 92-644)

1719. Lyonesse Abbey. London: Collins, 1968. (NUC 1968-72 92-644)

1720. The Midnight Oak. London: Collins, 1967. (NUC 1973 14-193)

1721. Midsummer Masque. New York: Morrow, 1972. (NUC 1968-72 92-644)

1722. A Summer's Cloud. London: Collins, 1965.

1723. A Time at Tarragon. London: Collins, 1969. (NUC 1968-72 92-644)

1724. The Wild Hunt. New York: Morrow, 1974. (NUC 1974 16-459)

1725. The Witches of All Saints (D). New York: Morrow, 1975.

She has got to be kidding! And yet, I fear she's not. Tansy Tremayne goes to live with her aunt in early 19th-century England and gets involved in some pretty absurd situations with a cast of utterly absurd characters. Tansy is an ass and everyone else a caricature. But it's Gothic.

TAYLOR, Beatrice

1726. Journey Into Danger. New York: Ballantine, 1974.

TAYLOR, Mary Ann

1727. The Serpent Heart (C). New York: Pyramid, 1971.

Recent heiress, Marta, just married and honeymooning in Italy, is hit by a car and awakens in the hospital to confront a man she is sure is not her husband but who claims to be. Where is the real Ted and who is trying to kill her? Interestingly written story and very fast-paced. The author keeps a tricky plot quote logical. Romantic suspense.

TAYLOR, Phoebe Atwood 1909-1976

Has written a very large number of mysteries, many of them featuring Asey Mayo, a New England detective. Mentioned here mainly because some paperback editions have Gothic covers, for example:

1728. Octagon House. New York: Norton, [1937]; New York: Pyramid, 1970. (LCPC pre'42 146-254)

A beautiful young girl is accused of murdering her sister and engages her old acquaintance, Asey Mayo to help prove her innocence. Competently written with bright dialogue and an interesting plot. The house is incidental and the story is not Gothic.

TAYLOR, Valerie (pseud.) see TATE, Velma

TEMPEST, Jan (pseud.) see SWATRIDGE, Irene

TEMPEST, Sarah

1729. A Winter of Fear (D). London: Hurst & Blackett, 1967; New York: Pyramid, 1968, 1972. (NUC 1956-67 110-514)

Things ground to a creeping halt for me half-way through this clumsy little Gothic story about orphaned Vanessa who goes to stay with distant relatives until she comes of age and inherits a small fortune. The household she encounters is populated by unbelievable characters who behave absurdly and Vanessa herself emerges as a wishy-washy nonentity with no interests or character. Not even the promise of a haunted room, ghosts and a soon to arrive Lochinvar could make me care to finish this dreary tale.

THANE, Elswyth

Author of a wide variety of works which include novels, romantic and historical; non-fiction and plays. Thane was born in Burlington, Iowa in 1900 and married William Beebee, the naturalist and writer (now deceased).

1730. Tryst (B). New York: Harcourt Brace, [1939]; New York: Grosset & Dunlap, 1962. (NUC 1956-67 111-130)
Another of the "love affair with a ghost" tales and a thoroughly charming one. This theme could easily be worn out but Thane handles it with craft and delicacy.

THATCHER, Julia

1731. Home to the Night. New York: Ballantine, 1976.

1732. Inherit the Mirage. "Zodiac Gothic Series, Libra." New York: Ballantine, 1976.

1733. Nightgleams. "Sagittarius." New York: Ballantine, 1976.

1734. Tempest at Summer's End. New York: Ballantine, 1976.

THEROUX, Paul

1735. The Black House. New York: Houghton, 1974.
"The book might best be described as a hybrid composed of unequal parts of social satire, commentary on colonialism, anthropological insights, some randy sex and an inconclusive gothic tale...." (Michael Mewshaw, New York Times Book Review, p. 18. S 8 '74.)

THIMBLETHORPE, June Sylvia
(Sylvia Thorpe)

1736. The Devil's Bondsman, by Sylvia Thorpe. London: Hurst & Blackett, 1961. (NUC 1956-67 111-208)
Historical romance.

1737. No More A-Roving, by Sylvia Thorpe. London: Hurst & Blackett, 1970. (NUC 1968-72 93-483)

1738. Strangers on the Moor (A), by Sylvia Thorpe. New York: Pyramid, 1974; orig. pub. as: Smuggler's Moon. Arlington Books, 1955.)
If I were asked to pick one book to prove that the Gothic form was extant in the 20th century, this just might be the book. The plot was undoubtedly Radcliffian as well as being skillfully constructed and keeping the reader thoroughly engrossed. The characters are 3-D, and absolutely terrible or delightful. The prose was charmingly quaint, ever so delicately witty, and perfectly suited to this type of

literature. This is the kind of book I read dozens of others in hopes of finding.

THOMPSON, Ann

1739. House of Strange Music. New York: Avon, 1973.

THOMPSON, Anne Armstrong

1740. The Swiss Legacy (B). New York: Simon & Schuster, [1974]; New York: New American Library (Signet W6635), 1975.

Carolyn goes to England with her dashing financier husband on a business trip. When her husband is suddenly killed in a traffic accident, Carolyn is thrown into an intrigue of international high finance and murder. This is a very well done tale of romantic suspense. My only reservation was the recurring question of what would have happened to the poor heroine if she hadn't been so alluring as to compel assistance from all the males in the story.

THOMPSON, Estelle

1741. Three Women in the House (C). New York: Avon (15057), 1973.

Not a bad little tale though a bit too close to the plot of Rebecca for my comfort. Paula becomes the second wife of Bret and lives in the shadow of his deceased wife, Marion. Du Maurier wins on style and Thompson comes out ahead on a livelier plot.

THORPE, Sylvia (pseud.) see THIMBLETHORPE, June Sylvia

THUM, Marcella

Native of St. Louis, Missouri and author of several juvenile novels.

1742. Fernwood (B). Garden City, N.Y.: Doubleday (Crime Club), 1973; Greenwich, Conn.: Fawcett-Crest, 1975. (NUC 1974 16-657)

A very polished and competent treatment of one of the standard neo-Gothic masterplots--the young governess, the post-Civil War Southern U.S. mansion, a wrong to be righted, and a gentle touch of the supernatural. Nothing new but the author manages to breathe life into a type of story that seems, for some of us, to have an almost unfailing appeal.

THURBER, James 1894-1961

1743. The 13 Clocks (B). New York: Simon & Schuster, 1950;

London: Hamilton, 1966. (NUC 1956-67 111-435)

The inclusion of this adult fairy tale here is somewhat an arbitrary decision but many of these tales seem to include the Gothic elements even when used in a slightly different perspective. This little tale was fun and I believe those who enjoy whimsical Gothic literature would enjoy Thurber's story.

TIERNEY, Pat

1744. The Powers of Lismara (C). New York: Avon, 1972.

A good plot with many Gothic elements. Siobhan returns to the family castle in Ireland after her father's death. Flawed by a boring style of writing--moods are stated rather than created, for example.

TILTON, Alice (pseud.) see TAYLOR, Phoebe Atwood

TOOMBS, Jane (Jenke)

1745. A Topaz for My Fair Lady. New York: Ballantine, 1975.

1746. Tule Witch (B). New York: Avon, 1973.

Well, well. A great pleasure and relief to find a hero and heroine "of Color" in this lily-white literature called Gothic. Numerous other tales have used Black folklore of the supernatural but have maintained all the cliché roles. Nurse Bebe is haunted by her childhood life with her witch grandmother. A very puzzling emergency room case brings Bebe's problems and the lives of two doctors into crisis. A good story, simple but well told.

TORDAY, Ursula
(Paula Allardyce, Charity Blackstock, Lee Blackstock)

Most of Torday's work seems to lean more toward mystery and detection than Gothic. A few exceptions may be as follows:

1747. The Briar Patch, by Charity Blackstock. London: Hodder & Stoughton, 1960; published in U.S. as: Young Lucifer. Philadelphia: Lippincott, 1960. (NUC 1956-67 112-243)

1748. The English Wife (C), by Charity Blackstock. New York: Coward-McCann, 1964; New York: Macfadden, 1965. (NUC 1956-67 112-243)

The Macfadden edition describes this as "in the romantic tradition of Wuthering Heights and Rebecca--a haunting Gothic novel...." Very misleading! I would call it an historical romance and a very mediocre one at that. The theme: a spirited English girl's Great Love for a crumb.

1749. The Exorcism (B), by Charity Blackstock. London: Hodder & Stoughton, 1961; pub. in U.S. as: A House Possessed. Philadelphia: Lippincott, 1962. (NUC 1956-67 112-243)

An ancient house on Loch Ness, now taking tourists is the scene of this well wrought tale of human relations and how they can be influenced by ghosts from the past. There is a good deal to this story. Gothic elements are secondary but undoubtedly present.

1750. The Ghost of Archie Gilroy, by Paula Allardyce. London: Hodder & Stoughton, 1970. (NUC 1968-72 94-403)

1751. The Knock at Midnight, by Charity Blackstock. London: Hodder & Stoughton, 1966; New York: Coward-McCann, 1967. (NUC 1956-67 112-243)

1752. Miss Fenny, by Charity Blackstock. London: Hodder & Stoughton, 1957; pub. also as: The Woman in the Woods, by Lee Blackstock. Garden City, N.Y.: Doubleday (Crime Club), 1958; New York: Dell, 1959. (NUC 1956-67 112-243)

1753. Witches' Sabbath (B), by Paula Allardyce. New York: Macmillan, 1962. (NUC 1956-67 112-243)

Good handling of a tale of witchcraft in an English village.

TOWER, Diana

1754. Dark Diamond. New York: Ballantine, 1975.

1755. A Gleam of Sapphire. New York: Ballantine, 1975.

1756. Red Lion. New York: Ballantine, 1974.

TRAFFORD, F. G. (pseud.) see RIDDELL, Charlotte

TRAVIS, Gretchen

1757. The Cottage. New York: Putnam, 1973. (NUC 1973 14-530)

1758. She Fell Among Thieves. Garden City, N.Y.: Doubleday (Crime Club), 1963. (NUC 1956-67 112-459)

1759. 2 Spruce Lane (C). New York: Putnam, 1975.

Cy and Janet buy a house that brings tragedy into their lives. I did not particularly like this story. There is horror without anything to justify it. Technically, the book was more than competent.

TREVELYN, Julia

1760. Greythorne. New York: New American Library (Signet Q5868), 1974.

TRIMBLE, Jacquelyn W(hitney)
(J. L. H. Whitney)

Born 10/21/27 in Portland, Oregon. Education: B.A. University of Washington, 1951; M.L.S. 1959 and post graduate study. Lives in Seattle, Washington and works as a reference librarian.

1761. Guardians at the Gate, with Louis Trimble. New York: Ace, 1972.

1762. The Whisper of Shadows (C), by J. L. H. Whitney. New York: Ace (K200), 1964.
Ruth goes to a Canadian island for a six-month librarian job with the fabulously wealthy Stephen. Intrigue and murder follow. A hypermelodramatic plot, the outcome of which seemed all too apparent early on. Nothing new or different.

TROY, Katherine
(listed in the NUC under Anne Maybury)

1763. Farramonde. New York: McKay, 1968. (NUC 1968-72 62-248)

1764. Roseheath. New York: McKay, 1969. (NUC 1968-72 62-249)

TRYON, Thomas

1765. Harvest Home. New York: Knopf, 1973.
The first section of this three-part novel seemed dull as dishwater and a dip into the next was beyond bearing or caring. Tryon may have been leading up to something in the horror Gothic vein but he took too long getting there for my impatient nature.

1766. The Other. Greenwich, Conn.: Fawcett-Crest, 1977.

TURTON, Godfrey (Edmund)

Reporter, editor and writer born in Kildale, Yorkshire England in 1901.

1767. The Devil's Churchyard (B). Garden City, N.Y.: Doubleday, 1970; New York: Pocket Books, 1971. (NUC 1968-72 95-388)
A very engaging tale of deviltry in a small English village

where the new parson has big ideas for reinstituting some ancient ceremonies with the new teacher, the red haired and beautiful Kate, as the main attraction at the festivities. A bit of horror and whimsical Gothic combined.

UNSWORTH, Barry (Forster) 1930-

1768. Mooncranker's Gift. New York: Houghton-Mifflin, 1974.
Listed in Book Review Digest as Gothic but I see no justification for calling this psychological melodrama Gothic. It fits none of my criteria, at any rate.

UNSWORTH, Mair

1769. Wild Winds. New York: Ace, 1968.
A grossly misleading stock Gothic book cover encloses this purely adolescent romance. No Gothic elements.

UPSHAW, Helen

1770. Day of the Harvest. Indianapolis: Bobbs-Merrill, 1953. (NUC 1953-57 25-234)

1771. The Return of Jennifer (A). New York: Dodd, Mead, 1964; New York: Bantam, 1966. (NUC 1956-67 117-237)
Not a Gothic, as advertised, but a fine and gripping novel about love, pride and power. It is far more than a "love story," although that part is beautifully done.

VALDES, Ivy

Has also written several romances.

1772. Chase a Dark Shadow. New York: New American Library, n.d.

1773. Gift from a Stranger. New York: New American Library (Signet), 1972.

1774. Over My Shoulder. New York: New American Library (Signet P5216), 1972.

VALE, Rena M.

1775. The House on Rainbow Leap ("A Ravenswood Gothic") (F). New York: Pocket Books, 1973.
The author's endless fascination with descriptions of clothing

and furnishings, her poorly integrated tidbits of history and "local color," combined with a large cast of totally unbelievable characters, make this sentimental Gothic very close to unreadable and totally uninteresting.

VANCE, Ethel (pseud.) see STONE, Grace Zaring

VANDERGRIFF, Aola

1776. Bell Tower of Wyndspelle (C). New York: Warner Paperbacks, 1975.

A tale in the saga of Wyndspelle set in the pre-Revolutionary era and telling of Caryn, a Loyalist whose family is destroyed and who, in desperation, marries a Tory and moves to Wyndspelle. The author creates an interesting tension by having the heroine espouse a now unpopular cause. Not so good as some of her other works.

1777. House of the Dancing Dead (B). New York: Warner Paperbacks, 1974.

Christie allows herself to be talked into a very devious impersonation and finds herself trapped in a grim mansion with a household of very peculiar people. Not so polished as Wyndspelle, but nonetheless an entertaining and imaginative tale.

1778. Sister of Sorrow. New York: Warner Paperbacks, 1974.

1779. Wyndspelle (B). New York: Warner Paperbacks, 1975.

Andria flees from her Puritan foster home, accused of being a witch, and seeks refuge at Wyndspelle, reputed to be the "home of the devil." A wonderful, and truly Gothic tale in the Radcliffian tradition.

VANE, Norman T.

1780. The Exorcism of Angela Gray. New York: Belmont-Tower, 1974.

VAN HAZINGA, Cynthia

1781. The House on Gannet's Point (B). New York: Popular Library, [1974].

Angel leaves a stale life in New Mexico to visit an eccentric uncle on Cape Ann, Massachusetts. She arrives to find her uncle missing at sea, a fabulous mansion filled with a life-time collection of art and some very mysterious goings on. Skillful writing and a few new wrinkles make this a better than average story. A good example of a transitional story from Gothic to romantic suspense. Gothic elements are present but not dominant.

VICARY, Jean

1782. The Ice Maiden. New York: Avon, 1972.

1783. Saverstall (C). New York: Ace (75181), 1967.
Like so many of the mediocre books of the last two decades, this story lures the reader in with promises of a Gothic tale never fulfilled, a snowballing number of melodramatic events and no real plot or character development.

VIERECK, George Sylvester 1884-

1784. The House of the Vampire. New York: Moffat, Yard & Co., 1907. (LCPC pre'42 157-268)

VILLIERS, Margot

1785. The Serpent of Lilith (A). New York: Pocket Books, 1976.
A well written and gripping tale of 19th-century England and Jessica who discovers she has "the gift" but doesn't know quite how to deal with it.

VINCENT, Claire

1786. Garden of Satan (D). New York: Lancer (74-581), 1969. [© Miriam Lynch].
Teachers of creative writing might well use this book as a good example of how not to write a horror Gothic. The prose is stilted and immature, the plot is totally void of imagination, depth or insight and the characters are one dimensional and dull as doughnut holes.

1787. The Pink Castle. New York: Arcadia House, 1959. (NUC 1956-67 119-119)

VIVIAN, Evelyn Charles H.
(Jack Mann)

1788. Nightmare Farm, by Jack Mann. New York: Bookfinger, 1975.

VON CLEEF, Monique

1789. House of Pain. New York: Bantam (Y8087), 1974.

WADE, Joanna (pseud.) see BERCKMAN, Evelyn

WADLETON, Maggie Jeanne (Melody) 1896-

1790. Sarah Mandrake (A). Indianapolis: Bobbs-Merrill, 1946. (LCC supp. 41-103)

A very interesting book! It's Gothic and both close to and different from its 18th-century ancestors. It uses the prose, the story-within-a-story mode and many other Gothic devices including the supernatural. On the other hand, the setting is contemporary, the main character is a male, and the romance angle is all but absent. Sufficient proof that the Gothic novel is alive and well in the 20th century.

WAGNER, Sharon B.

Author of many juvenile novels, she was born in Wallace, Idaho in 1936 and is now living in Mesa, Arizona.

1791. Colors of Death. New York: Ballantine, 1974.

1792. Cry of the Cat. New York: Belmont-Tower, 1973.

1793. Dark Side of Paradise. New York: Ballantine, 1975.

1794. Dark Sun at Midnight. New York: Ace, 1972.

1795. Dark Waters of Death. New York: Ballantine, 1975.

1796. Echoes of an Ancient Love. New York: Ballantine, 1976.

1797. Haitian Legacy. New York: Avon, 1974.

1798. Havenhurst. New York: Ballantine, 1975.

1799. Maridu. New York: Lancer (74-714), n.d.

1800. Moonwind (B). New York: Lancer, 1972.

Rilla becomes tutor to Bonnie Moon who refuses to speak since the tragic death of her mother several months before. Rilla seeks to help Bonnie and discovers murder and danger. Romantic suspense.

1801. Satan's Acres. New York: Ace, 1974.

1802. Shades of Evil. New York: Ballantine, 1974.

1803. The Turquoise Talisman. New York: Ballantine, 1975.

WALKER, Harry (pseud.) see WAUGH, Hillary

WALKER, Irma Ruth (Roden)
(Ira Walker)

Born 8/2/21 in Cincinnati, Ohio. Married, with one child. Attended schools in Cincinnati. Home is now in Hawaii. Husband is in the Air Force and the family has traveled throughout the Orient.

1804. The Man in the Driver's Seat, by Ira Walker. London & New York: Abelard-Schuman, 1964. (NUC 1956-67 120-174)

1805. The Murdoch Legacy (B). Indianapolis: Bobbs-Merrill, 1975.
The publisher calls this a romantic suspense and I would say it qualifies as sentimental Gothic. Maura's husband attempts to murder her on their honeymoon and she flees to spend the next seven years under an assumed name trying to provide for the daughter conceived during her brief marriage. Things come to a crisis when she is offered a job with the wealthy Murdoch family on Stranger Island. An innovative, well written story.

1806. Someone's Stolen Nellie Grey, by Ira Walker. London & New York: Abelard-Schuman, 1963. (NUC 1956-67 120-174)

WALLACE, May Nickerson

Author of juvenile Gothics.

WALLACE, Pat

1807. House of Scorpio. New York: Avon (25601), 1975.

WALLRAPP, Lynn

1808. Murmuring Ever (F). New York: Manor, 1975.
Fourteen-year-old Sandra, two younger sisters and parents move from New York City to a 200-year-old haunted house in the country where Sandra becomes possessed. This is a sick little story. Although the style is juvenile, it certainly isn't suitable for the young, let alone anyone else who doesn't wish to be thoroughly disgusted. The book is poorly printed, too--full of typos--and should be classified as sick horror Gothic and pure junk.

WALPOLE, [Sir] Hugh Seymour

Born in Auckland, New Zealand in 1884. Began his literary career as a book reviewer and became a novelist and critic until his death in 1941.

1809. Above the Dark Circus, an Adventure. London: Macmillan, 1931. (LCPC pre'42 159-179)

1810. Above the Dark Tumult. Garden City, N.Y.: Doubleday, 1931. (LCPC pre'42 159-179)

1811. All Soul's Night; A Book of Stories. Garden City, N.Y.: Doubleday, 1933. (LCPC pre'42 159-179)

1812. The Blind Man's House. Garden City, N.Y.: Doubleday, 1941. (LCPC pre'42 159-180)

1813. The Bright Pavilions. London: Macmillan, 1940. (LCPC pre'42 159-180)

1814. Farthing Hall (B), by H. W. & J. B. Priestley. Garden City, N.Y.: Doubleday, 1929. (LCPC pre'42 159-181)

These authors had the clever idea of telling their story through a correspondence between two men, each author taking the part of one correspondent. They obviously enjoyed the whole thing enormously. The letters are witty and literate and crammed full of their lives and observations. Buried amongst all the chitchat is a rather low-key sentimental Gothic tale, but it does tend to get lost in the shenanigans. Whimsical Gothic, with the emphasis on the whimsy.

1815. The Fortress. Garden City, N.Y.: Doubleday, 1932. (LCPC pre'42 159-181)

1816. The Inquisitor. Garden City, N.Y.: Doubleday, 1935. (LCPC pre'42 159-182)

1817. The Killer and the Stain: A Strange Story. Garden City, N.Y.: Doubleday, 1942. (LCPC pre'42 159-183)

1818. Portrait of a Man with Red Hair (B). New York: Doran, [1925]; New York: Warner Paperbacks, 1967. (LCPC pre'42 159-183)

A nicely wrought tale of Harkness who helps rescue a damsel in distress and confronts the Powers of Good and Evil.

1819. Wintersmoon. Garden City, N.Y.: Doubleday, 1928. (LCPC pre'42 159-184)

Historical romance. Not Gothic.

I have been unable to find an imprint for The Green Mirror, said to have been printed in 1917 and to be Gothic.

WALTER, Dorothy Blake 1908-
(Katherine Blake, Kay Blake, Katherine Ross)

Free-lance writer with quite a varied career background.

Born in 1908 in Stroud, Oklahoma, she now lives in Wheaton, Maryland. Most of her novels seem to be romances and mysteries.

1820. Night Stands at the Door (D), by Katherine Blake. New York: Stein & Day, 1974.

Liesel marries the mysterious Frantz, against the wishes of her family, and moves to his castle in Germany. She is puzzled by the withdrawn behavior of the family and community and by her husband's strange behavior. A poorly written tale. The characters are shallow, the prose is plodding and the whole effort, although Gothic, is not worth the bother.

WALTON, Evangeline

1821. The Children of Llyr: An Adult Fantasy. New York: Ballantine, 1971. (NUC 1968-72 100-299)

1822. The Song of Rhiannon: The Third Branch of the Mabinogion. New York: Ballantine, 1972. (NUC 1968-72 100-299)

1823. Witch House. Sauk City, Wisc.: Arkham, 1945. (LCC supp. 1942-47 41-190)

WANDREI, Donald 1908-

1824. Strange Harvest. Sauk City, Wisc.: Arkham, 1965. (NUC 1956-67 120-310)

1825. The Web of Easter Island. Sauk City, Wisc.: Arkham, 1948. (LCAC 1948-52 22-550)

WARD, Arthur Sarsfield 1883-1959
(Sax Rohmer)

Author of a very large number of exotic adventure stories including a whole series of "Dr. Fu Manchu" tales. For works not listed here see LCPC pre'52 Vol. 159.

1826. The Bat Flies Low, by Sax Rohmer. Garden City, N.Y.: Doubleday (Crime Club), 1935. (LCPC pre'42 159-356)

1827. Brood of the Witch-Queen, by Sax Rohmer. Garden City, N.Y.: Doubleday, 1924. (LCPC pre'42 159-356)

1828. The Fire Goddess, by Sax Rohmer. Greenwich, Conn.: Fawcett, 1953. (NUC 1953-57 25-726)

1829. Grey Face (C), by Sax Rohmer. Garden City, N.Y.:

Doubleday, 1924. (NUC pre'42 159-357)

This book made me feel as I do when watching a 1935 exotic melodrama movie. It's a Gothic all right but of an age gone by and not sufficiently sophisticated for my tastes in the 1970's. The hero goes through some bizarre experiences before uncovering the plot behind some fake and some real occult intrigue. Certain thirteen-year-olds might still enjoy.

1830. Moon of Madness, by Sax Rohmer. Garden City, N. Y.: Doubleday, 1927. (LCPC pre'42 159-357)

1831. The Romance of Sorcery, by Sax Rohmer. London: Methuen, 1914; New York: Dutton, 1924. (LCPC pre'42 159-358)

1832. Sinister Madonna, by Sax Rohmer. New York: Fawcett, 1956. (NUC 1953-57 25-726)

1833. Tales of East & West, by Sax Rohmer. Garden City, N. Y.: Doubleday (Crime Club), 1933. (LCPC pre'42 159-358)

Subtitled: 13 little masterpieces of death, fear and terror.

1834. White Velvet, by Sax Rohmer. Garden City, N. Y.: Doubleday, 1936. (LCPC pre'42 159-359)

Secret service intrigue, drug smuggling and romance, seeming to me very much the forerunner of the spy stories of the 60's and 70's. Gothic only in lineage and very dated for today's tastes.

WARD, Dewey (Comstock)

1835. Reception at High Tower (C). New York: Dell (7277), 1969.

Maurie returns to her grandmother's house after six months in a psychiatric hospital suffering from a "nervous breakdown," only to find that her grandmother seems to be trying to get her recommitted by accusing her of bizarre behavior she didn't do--or did she? This is not too bad a tale, though a bit heavy on the paranoia theme for my taste and not really Gothic in spite of the formula paperback cover.

1836. The Unsheltered. New York: Random House, 1963; New York: New American Library (Signet P2957). (NUC 1956-67 120-402)

Maybe a psychological novel but not a Gothic. The story of Sare, a young girl living in a small fishing village on the East Coast of the U.S. She sets upon a course of vengeance against those she feels responsible for the death of her mad mother.

WARE, Judith

1837. The Faxon Secret. New York: Warner Paperback, 1966.

1838. Quarry House. New York: Warner Paperback, 1965.

1839. Thorne House (C). New York: Warner Paperback, 1965.
Karen goes to Thorne House with her orphaned nephew to meet his long-lost kin and runs into skulduggery and romance. A routine tale of romantic suspense, competent but hardly dazzling.

1840. A Touch of Fear. New York: New American Library, 1969.

Other works include: Detour to Denmark, The Fear Place.

WARREN, Paulette

1841. Caliban's Castle. New York: Berkley Medallion, 1976.

1842. Dark Shadows of Bitterhill. New York: Manor, 1976.

1843. Ghost of Ravenkill Manor. New York: Lancer (73-834), n.d.

1844. Night Falls at Bitterhill. New York: Manor, 1976.

1845. The Nurse of Brooding Mansion (B). New York: Lancer, 1967.
I'd call this a mystery rather than a Gothic. Well done in spite of the dopey title.

1846. The Shadowed Staircase (C). New York: Lancer (75-194), 1971. [© Paul Fairman].
Laura inherits a huge old house and moves there with her husband only to find some strange goings on. The house has been a meeting place for a witch coven and things get pretty grim. Not too bad, but nothing exceptional either.

1847. Some Beckoning Wraith. New York: Lancer, 1969.

1848. Storm over Bitterhill. New York: Manor, 1976.

Other works include: Horror House and Ravenkill (Lancer).

WATERS, T[homas] A.

1849. The Last Victim (B). New York: Random House, 1973. (NUC 1973 15-820)
Witty, fast-paced tale that is less than it should be due to a shallow, dull ending. Romantic suspense with a male lead.

1850. The Shrewsbury Horror. New York: Lancer (75-200), n.d.

WAUGH, Hillary Baldwin 1920-
(H. Baldwin Taylor, Harry Walker)

Bride is Waugh's 27th book according to the jacket and all of them appear to be mystery and suspense rather than Gothic.

1851. A Bride for Hampton House: A Gothic Novel (B). Garden City, N.Y.: Doubleday, 1975.

I don't think this is a Gothic. In terms of my criteria, I would call it romantic suspense. Not a bad one by any means. Though a bit verbose, it kept me reading and curious as to the outcome when journalist, Corrie, decides to investigate suspicious goings on in a prominent family by posing as the wife of the recently deceased heir.

WAY, Isabel Stewart

1852. Bell, Book and Candleflame. New York: Ballantine, n.d.

1853. The House on Sky High Road. New York: Belmont-Tower (B75-1096), 1972.

1854. Seed of the Land. New York & London: Appleton-Century, 1935. (LCPC pre'42 160-340)

Pastoral domestic romance. Not Gothic.

WEBB, Jean Francis
(Ethel Hamil, Roberta Morrison)

Born 10/1/10 in White Plains, New York. Education: B.S. Amherst, 1931. Married Nancy Bukeley, 1936. They have three children. Home: South Salem, New York; Career: free-lance writer since 1931. Webb has written hundreds of short stories for magazines, books on Hawaii with his wife, and dozens of romances and "nursie" stories under the name Ethel Hamil.

1855. Carnavaron's Castle. New York: Meredith, 1969. (NUC 1968-72 100-655)

1856. The Craigshaw Curse (B). New York: Meredith, 1968. (NUC 1968-72 100-655)

Book Review Digest (69:1378) rates this highly and I quite agree. Jill Heaton, secretary to a glamorous and powerful UN delegate, gets involved in mystery, intrigue and murder. This is an unpretentious but well written neo-Gothic in the best of the tradition.

1857. Roses from a Haunted Garden. New York: McKay, 1971. (NUC 1968-72 100-655)

1858. Somewhere Within This House (B). New York: McKay, 1973; New York: Popular Library, 1973. (NUC 1973 15-838)

Ellen goes to 19th-century Hawaii to find the truth behind her fiancé's reported suicide. A well told tale, essentially romantic suspense, but with some Gothic elements. Lots of information on Hawaii smoothly integrated into a fast-paced and entertaining story.

1859. The Tower in the Forest, by Ethel Hamil. New York: Bouregy & Curl, 1951. (LCAC 1948-52 23-16)

1860. Tree of Evil, by Roberta Morrison. New York: Paperback Library, 1966.

WELLES, Elisabeth

1861. Captains' Walk ("Grandview Series"). New York: Pocket Books, 1976.

1862. Fahnsworth Manor ("Grandview Series"). New York: Pocket Books, 1976.

1863. Seagull Crag ("Grandview Series"). New York: Pocket Books, 1976.

1864. Spaniard's Gift ("Grandview Series No. 4") (D). New York: Pocket Books, 1977. [© Lyle Kenyon Engel].

The main character of the Grandview Series is Jannine West who inherited her father's real estate business specializing in fabulous old homes. This book is about the sale of Spaniard's Gift, a Florida mansion, and the intrigue that develops around the transaction. A good idea, but, unfortunately, a poor execution. The plot is contrived and a good bit of it just doesn't make sense. The characters are uninteresting.

1865. Waterview Manor ("Grandview Series"). New York: Pocket Books, 1976.

WELLS, Herbert G(eorge) 1866-

1866. The Croquet Player (B). London: Chatto & Windus, 1936; New York: Viking, 1937. (LCPC pre'42 161-256)

A long short story and probably not Gothic but surely coming close. Should provide brief but thoughtful amusement to anyone interested in Good vs. Evil and the supernatural.

WELLS, John Jay (pseud.) see COULSON, Juanita

WELLS, Tobias (pseud.) see FORBES, Stanton

WELLSLEY, Julie

1867. The Castle on the Mountain (B). New York: Dell, 1972.

Geraldine befriends Philip Cavendish, a famous painter blinded in an accident, and takes him to the family castle in Wales to recuperate. Threats are made to their safety and supernatural forces convene. This is a fine little tale with lots of information of Welsh folklore and real ghosts.

1868. House Malign. New York: Lancer (73-674), 1967.

1869. The Wine of Vengeance. New York: Lancer (73-841), n.d.

WENTWORTH, Patricia (pseud.) see DILLON, Dora Amy

WESTMINSTER, Aynn

1870. Moon in Shadow (B). New York: Dell, 1974.
Claudia inherits Moonhall from a mother she thought long dead but who was recently killed in an auto accident. At Moonhall Claudia becomes entangled in a web of intrigue. A tightly written, fast-paced story. It's Gothic.

WESTON, Allen
(pseud. for works by Alice Mary Norton in collaboration with Grace Allen Hogarth.)

WESTON, Helen Gray see DANIELS, Dorothy

WETHERELL, June Pat
(Patricia Frame)

1871. Blueprint for Yesterday. New York: Walker, 1971. (NUC 1968-72 101-339)

1872. But That Was Yesterday. New York: Dutton, 1943. (LCC supp. 41-523)

1873. The Cottage at Avalanche (C). New York: Popular Library, 1972.
Connie goes to live with her last remaining relatives--two aunts--in their family cottage in a remote village in Washington State. She encounters adventure, romance and danger. A romantic suspense with some strong characterizations.

1874. Dead Center. New York: Dutton, 1946. (LCC supp. 41-523)

1875. Every Ecstasy. New York: Phoenix Press, [1941]. (LCPC pre'42 162-47)

1876. The House of Cabra. New York: Belmont, n.d.

1877. Run with the Pack, by Patricia Frame. New York: Arcadia House, 1942. (NUC 1968-72 101-339)

1878. A Touch of the Witch. New York: Lancer (74-576), n.d.

1879. Willoughby Manor. New York: Ballantine, 1974.

WHARTON, Althea

1880. The White Ghost of Fenwick Hall ("A Ravenswood Gothic") (F). New York: Pocket Books, 1974.
Dumb, dumb du-dumb dumb. Dumb dumb.

WHITE, Alicen

1881. Evil That Walks Invisible (C). New York: Dell (02354), 1973.
A very routine romantic suspense with few Gothic elements and little in the way of surprises. Dullsville for the experienced reader.

1882. Nor Spell nor Charm. New York: Lancer (74-753), n.d.

WHITE, Ethel Lina

Author of a large number of tame trite tales, many listed in LCPC pre'42 Vol. 162, pp. 303 ff. Examples:

1883. Fear Stalks the Village. New York: Harpers, 1942; New York: Warner Paperback, 1966. (LCPC pre'42 162-303)

1884. Midnight House (D). London: Collins (Crime Club), 1942. (LCPC pre'42 162-303). Pub. in U.S. as: Her Heart in Her Throat. New York: Harpers, 1942.
The U.S. title is a turn-off to begin with. Then the heroine is such an adolescent ass and the narrative so meandering that, as with certain numbers of these books, by mid-point all will to continue has been systematically extinguished by the author's failures.

1885. The Third Eye (D). New York: Harpers, 1937; New York: Warner Paperback, 1967. (LCPC pre'42 162-303)
Half-way through I gave up hope for this tedious tale of naughty women and silly conniving in a girl's school.

WHITEHEAD, Jane

1886. The House on the Hill (C). New York: Lancer (74-868), 1967.

Nancy goes to the Mississippi River town of Malinburg to find out the story behind her sister's sudden and mysterious death. There she encounters a wall of secrecy erected by the Malin family and the community they control. The author just managed to keep me reading, but this was a rather adolescent romantic suspense.

WHITNEY, J. L. H. (pseud.) see TRIMBLE, Jacquelyn

WHITNEY, Phyllis Ayame (Jahnke)

Born in Yokohama, Japan in 1903. Attended high school in Chicago and married L. F. Jahnke in 1950. They have one child. Has written numerous novels and mysteries for young people. Travels extensively to collect background for her books. Lived in Japan, China and the Philippines until she came to the U.S. at age 15.

1887. Black Amber (B). New York: Appleton-Century, 1964; Greenwich, Conn.: Fawcett, 1969. (NUC 1956-67 122-223)

Tracy goes to Istanbul to help Miles Radburn prepare a manuscript but also to learn more about her sister's sudden and mysterious death. A tight and interesting romantic suspense with a good deal of well integrated information on Turkey.

1888. Blue Fire. New York: Appleton-Century-Crofts, 1961. (NUC 1956-67 122-223)

1889. Columbella. Garden City, N.Y.: Doubleday, 1966; Greenwich, Conn.: Fawcett-Crest, 1967. (NUC 1956-67 122-223)

The plot and prospects for this story seemed so tediously evident after the first few chapters that I quit in utter boredom. If sagas of "wicked women" appeal, you might enjoy.

1890. Ever After. Boston: Houghton-Mifflin, 1948. (LCAC 1948-52 23-159)

1891. The Fire and the Gold. New York: Crowell, [1956]. (NUC 1953-57 26-231)

1892. The Golden Unicorn (D). Garden City, N.Y.: Doubleday, 1976.

Following the death of her adoptive parents, journalist Courtney Marsh goes in search of her real parents with only a golden unicorn pendant as a lead. The combination of Whitney's endless description of the minutest elements of daily living and her cramming down the reader's throat of her superliberated, ultratalented, gorgeous heroine seemed too, too much. The plot as it developed looked to hold few surprises worth enduring all that.

1893. The Highest Dream. New York: McKay, 1956. (NUC 1953-57 26-231)

1894. Hunter's Green. Garden City, N. Y.: Doubleday, 1968. (NUC 1968-72 101-484)

1895. Listen for the Whisperer (D). Boston: Hall, 1972; Garden City, N. Y.: Doubleday, 1971; Greenwich, Conn.: Fawcett, 1973. (NUC 1968-72 101-484)

Leigh goes to Norway after her father's death to meet her movie star mother, now a recluse, whom she has never before seen. She finds a troubled scene and a mystery regarding the long ago murder of a movie producer which ended her mother's career. A very slow-paced tale and not really much of a story in my view. The heroine is not a sympathetic character and the whole movie star, movie business theme I find a great bore.

1896. A Long Time Coming. New York: Dell, 1966. (NUC 1968-72 101-484)

1897. Lost Island. Garden City, N. Y.: Doubleday, 1970; Greenwich, Conn.: Fawcett-Crest. (NUC 1968-72 101-484)

1898. The Moonflower. New York: Appleton-Century-Crofts, 1958. (NUC 1956-67 122-223)

1899. The Quicksilver Pool. New York: Appleton-Century, 1955. (NUC 1953-57 26-231)

1900. Red Is for Murder (D). Chicago: Ziff-Davis, 1943; pub. in U. S. (New York: Warner Paperback, 1965) as: The Red Carnelian. (LCC supp. 41-600)

Linell, a copy writer at a large department story, discovers the murdered Michael Montgomery, the man who jilted her. A routine murder mystery. The first three chapters and the last one were plenty.

1901. Sea Jade (B). New York: Appleton-Century, [1964]. (NUC 1956-67 122-224)

Miranda, in a formula setting, straightens out the family turmoils. The characters are a bit extreme in this story but the writing is adequate and the pace good. I think Dorothy Daniels used this plot for The Pillars.

1902. Seven Tears for Apollo. New York: Appleton-Century-Crofts, 1963; Greenwich, Conn.: Fawcett-Crest, 1964. (NUC 1956-67 122-224)

1903. Silverhill. Garden City, N. Y.: Doubleday, 1967; Greenwich, Conn.: Fawcett-Crest (P2362), 1975. (NUC 1956-67 122-224)

1904. Skye Cameron (C). New York: Appleton-Century-Crofts, 1957. (NUC 1953-57 26-231)

More a romance than a Gothic. A well told story with little mystery or suspense.

1905. Snowfire. Boston: Hall, 1973; Garden City, N.Y.: Doubleday, 1973; Greenwich, Conn.: Fawcett (P2041), 1974. (NUC 1973 16-128)

1906. Thunder Heights (B). New York: Appleton-Century-Crofts, 1960; Greenwich, Conn.: Fawcett-Crest (P2143), 1973. (NUC 1956-67 122-224)

Solid, fast moving style kept me from skipping paragraphs or speed reading. A formula plot but handled innovatively. Camilla returns to her family and gets their troubles all sorted out.

1907. The Trembling Hills. New York: Appleton-Century-Crofts, 1956; Greenwich, Conn.: Fawcett-Crest (Q2414), 1973. (NUC 1953-57 26-231)

1908. The Turquoise Mask (C). Garden City, N.Y.: Doubleday, 1974; Greenwich, Conn.: Fawcett-Crest, 1975. (NUC 1974 18-362)

Average romantic suspense about Amanda who goes to her grandfather's house in New Mexico to try to clear up some mysteries in her family's past.

1909. Window on the Square (B). New York: Appleton-Century-Crofts, 1962; Greenwich, Conn.: Fawcett, 11th edition, 1970. (NUC 1956-67 122-224)

An intricate tale, cleverly conceived. Whitney creates a heroine who comes off as somewhat of a prudish prig. Nonetheless, quite an entertaining story.

1910. The Winter People. Garden City, N.Y.: Doubleday, 1969; Greenwich, Conn.: Fawcett-Crest, 1969. (NUC 1968-72 101-484)

WIDDEMER, Margaret 1897-

Author of a very large number of what appear to be sentimental romances (see LCPC pre'42, Vol. 163). There seems to be one important exception:

1911. The Red Castle Women (A). Garden City, N.Y.: Doubleday, 1968; New York: Popular Library, 1968. (NUC 1968-72 101-526)

A lovely, involved, true Gothic in the best of the tradition. Perdita's adventures from birth to motherhood involve her in an Indian maiden's curse, adventure and romance.

WILLIAMS, Charles (Walter Stansby) 1886-1945

Wrote a large and catholic group of works including literary studies, poetry and even a book on witchcraft.

1912. All Hallows' Eve. London: Faber & Faber, 1945. (LCC supp. 1942-47 42-53)

A rather mystical horror Gothic which reminded me very much of Arnold Bennett, E. F. Benson, and others of that ilk. This one, for me, did not come off so well. I found the characters hard to understand and the philosophy uncongenial. My view is that this work would be of interest only for scholarly comparisons.

WILLIAMS, Jeanne (Kreie)
(Jeanne Crecy, J. R. Williams)

Author of juveniles and westerns (under name J. R. Williams) who was born in Elkhart, Kansas in 1930. Now lives in Bodenham, Salisbury, England.

1913. The Evil Among Us (C), by Jeanne Crecy. New York: New American Library (Signet Y6812), n. d.

Kristen goes to her ancestral home in Norway to study the local architecture for her master's thesis. She finds her kin in trouble, learns a lot of Norwegian folklore and so forth. This book begins with great promise but rather fizzles out by the end. For all the talk of Norwegian supernatural phenomena, none really has much to do with the story. It's almost used to tease the reader along.

1914. My Face Beneath the Stone, by Jeanne Crecy. New York: New American Library (Signet Y6692), 1975.

1915. The Night Hunters, by Jeanne Crecy. New York: New American Library (Y6558), 1975.

1916. The Winter Keeper, by Jeanne Crecy. New York: New American Library (Signet Q6472), 1975.

WILLIAMS, J. R. see WILLIAMS, Jeanne

WILLIAMS, Lynn (pseud.) see HALE, Arlene

WILLIAMS, Rose (pseud.) see ROSS, William Edward Daniel

WILLIAMS, Wetherby
(Margaret Erskine)

Essentially a writer of mystery-detective fiction, a large number of which feature Inspector Finch, and many of which are sub-titled "Inspector Finch Gothics" such as:

1917. Case with Three Husbands (D), by Margaret Erskine. Garden City, N.Y.: Doubleday (Crime Club), 1967; New York: Ace (09223), 1967. (NUC 1956-67 122-558). "Inspector Finch Gothic No. 7."

The inspector is on vacation recovering from a bullet wound and a neighbor lady is murdered. I finally gave up and read the last chapter and wasn't a bit surprised. I fail to see the reason for the "Gothic" appellation. Seemed like a straight detective to me.

1918. The Family at Tammerton (B), by Margaret Erskine. Garden City, N.Y.: Doubleday (Crime Club), 1966; New York: Ace, 1965. (NUC 1956-67 122-558). "Inspector Finch Gothic No. 5."

Nurse Louise takes a case at Tammerton Hall and finds murder, intrigue and love. The only Gothic element seems to be the female main character. I'd classify as detective, and this one fairly good.

WILLIS, Maud (pseud.) see LOTTMAN, Eileen

WILSON, Barbara (pseud.) see JANIFER, Laurence

WILSON, Carolyn (Schisler) 1938-

1919. The Scent of Lilacs (D). New York: Ace (G603), 1966.

Another semi-Rebecca plot with the bride arriving at the family mansion only to find a hostile household, a suspicious death of the former mistress and a husband who behaves in a frightening and confusing way. I fail to understand the popularity of this particular formula and this author does nothing to enliven it.

WINCH, John (pseud.) see LONG, Gabriella

WINSLOW, Joan

1920. Griffin Towers. New York: Ace, 1966. [© Ware Torrey Budlong].

WINSTON, Daoma (Strasberg)

Novelist, born in 1922 and currently living in Washington, D.C. Has written poetry and the Bracken's World series in addition to works listed here.

1921. Carnaby Curse. New York: Belmont, 1967. Published with Virginia Coffman's Hounds of Hell.

1922. Castle of Closing Doors (D). New York: Belmont, 1967. Pub. with Genevieve St. John's Night of Evil.

Can't get much of a story into these short, double books. This one bears no relation to the title and is merely the bare bones of what might have been a good story with some character development, some atmosphere and a little less melodrama.

1923. Dennison Hill. New York: Warner Paperback, 1970.

1924. The Devil's Daughter (D). New York: Lancer, 1971; New York: Pocket Books, 1977.

Winston builds a fair "C" grade story and then blows it by condensing what should have been the second half of the book into the last two chapters. It has the effect of making the resolution silly and is very unfair to the reader.

1925. The Devil's Princess. New York: Lancer, 1971.

1926. Flight of a Fallen Angel. New York: Lancer, 1971.

1927. The Haversham Legacy. New York: Simon & Schuster, 1974. (NUC 1974 18-473)

1928. House of Mirror Images. New York: Lancer, 1970; pub. later as a trilogy (Lancer, 1973) with Trificante Treasure (Lancer, 1968) and Shadow on Mercer Mountain (Lancer, 1967).

1929. The Inheritance. New York: Avon, 1972.

1930. Kingdom's Castle. New York: Berkley Medallion, 1972.

1931. The Long and Living Shadow. New York: Belmont (B75-2098), 1971.

1932. Love of Lucifer. New York: Lancer (74-703), 1971.

1933. Mansion of Smiling Masks. New York: New American Library, 1967.

1934. Moderns. New York: Pyramid, 1968.

1935. Moorhaven. New York: Avon, 1973.

1936. Mrs. Berrigan's Dirty Book. New York: Lancer, 1970.

1937. Pity My Love. New York: Belmont, 1967.

1938. The Return. New York: Avon, 1972.

1939. The Secrets of Cromwell Crossing. New York: Lancer, 1965.

1940. Seminar in Evil (D). New York: Lancer (75-392), 1972.
Jennifer joins a college psychology seminar that turns out to be a pretty grim affair. A tale long on morbid melodrama and short on depth and skillful storytelling. It kept me reading, but I regretted doing so.

1941. Shadow of an Unknown Woman. New York: Lancer, 1967.

1942. Sinister Stone. New York: Warner Paperback, 1966.

1943. Tormented Lovers. New York: Monarch, 1962.

1944. The Trap. New York: Popular Library, 1973.

1945. The Unforgotten. New York: Berkley, 1973.

1946. Vampire Curse. New York: Paperback Library, 1971.

1947. The Victim (D). New York: Popular Library, [1972].
Jan marries Tim after a five-day love-at-first-sight romance and goes to the family mansion somewhere along the northeast U.S. coast. Jan is, it turns out, a look-alike of Rosamund, who disappeared a year before. Jan's life seems threatened from the moment of arrival. The style of this book seemed juvenile and there was too much rehashing of what already happened. Characters were shallow and there were few surprises in the plot.

1948. The Wakefield Witches. New York: Universal Pub. & Distr., 1966.

WINTHROP, Wilma

1949. Island of the Accursed. New York: Lancer, n.d.

1950. Tryst with Terror (D). New York: Lancer, 1965.
Distinguished by a unique style of archaic language ("The winged messenger from the law officer"--i.e., a bullet!) and a humor not intelligent enough to qualify as cynical, this silly story appears to have been written by some anonymous hack with a Thesaurus in one hand and a total lack of interest in or respect for the genre Gothic in particular or the English language in general.

WISSMANN, Ruth H.

Daughter of a writer and newspaperman, first turned to art and theater. After attending art schools and studying ballet for years, she danced professionally on both stage and screen. Then in 1963 she wrote her first book, the award-winning Summer Ballet Mystery. Since then she has written seven others. She now lives with her husband and family in San Marino, California in a haunted house. (Information from the jacket of Cypress.)

1951. The Claws of the Crow. New York: Paperback Library, 1974.

1952. Desert of Darkness. New York: Grosset & Dunlap, 1972; New York: Warner Paperback, 1972. (NUC 1968-72 102-373)

1953. Fear Waits on Cypress Road (D). Garden City, N. Y.: Doubleday, 1975.

Another tale of a contemporary haunted house and a generally unsatisfactory one. The book suffers greatly from a weak plot which comes to a hackneyed conclusion, from poor characterization and from a verbosity which allows pages to be skipped without the reader's missing a thing. Repetitive conversations abound in which the same information is told to different people.

1954. The Shadow of Sheila Ann. New York: Warner Paperback (75-369), 1974.

1955. To Hang a Witch. New York: Warner Paperback, 1974.

WITHERS, Julia

1956. Echo in a Dark Wind (C). New York: New American Library (Signet T5298), 1966.

Angela goes to England to design the renovation of an old castle. Her life is threatened and then her employer is murdered. A Gothic who-done-it, and not too bad.

1957. The Shuttered Room. New York: Dell (9883-1), 1971.

WOLFSON, Victor
(Langdon Dodge)

Novelist and playwright who T. S. Winslow in Book Week says is "one of the top writers of psychological horror stories." Born in New York City in 1910, he is married and has four sons. Still lives in New York City as of last report.

1958. The Eagle on the Plain. New York: Simon & Schuster, 1947. (LCC supp. 42-240)

1959. The Lonely Steeple. New York: Simon & Schuster, 1945. (LCC supp. 42-240)

"Psychological melodrama set in New England."

1960. Midsummer Madness, by Langdon Dodge (C). Garden City, N. Y.: Doubleday (Crime Club), 1950. (LCAC 1948-52 23-317)

Selina goes to Hawks Head as nurse and governess to the

five-year-old heir and finds his life in jeopardy through the devilish machinations of the incredible Zilla, companion to the aged lady of the manor. Neo-Gothic in form but the situation and Zilla are just too unbelievably melodramatic.

1961. My Prince! My King! London: Davies, 1962. (NUC 1956-67 123-387)

WOODWARD, Edward Emberlin
(Jane Grierson)

1962. A Dinner of Herbs, by Jane Grierson. London: Wright & Brown, 1935. (LCPC pre'42 165-503)

1963. Each Night We Die. London: Hutchinson, 1936. (LCPC pre'42 165-503)

1964. Fingers Before Forks. London: Selwyn & Blount, 1931. (LCPC pre'42 165-503)

1965. The House of Terror (B). New York: The Mystery League, 1930; New York: Warner Paperback, 1967. (LCPC pre'42 165-503)

Alicia inherits a country estate from a long-lost relative of ill-repute and moves there with friend, Veronica, only to find a conspiracy to get them to leave. Sounds like the same old thing but several innovations plus good characterizations and skillful narrative make this a very entertaining neo-Gothic tale.

1966. The Service of Love, by Jane Grierson. London: Wright & Brown, 1935. (LCPC pre'42 165-503)

1967. There Are Giants. London: Hutchinson, 1934. (LCPC pre'42 165-503)

1968. Windrack, by Jane Grierson. London: Wright & Brown, 1936. (LCPC pre'42 165-503)

1969. Winter Wheat. London: Hutchinson, 1932. (LCPC pre'42 165-503)

WOOLRICH, Cornell (pseud.) see HOPLEY-WOOLRICH, Cornell George

WYLIE, Philip 1902-

1970. Danger Mansion. New York: Popular Library, [1937].

This very dated pseudo-sophisticated little murder mystery is included here solely because of the gross misrepresentation of the paperback edition cover. It is in no way Gothic.

YATES, Alan Geoffrey 1923-
(Carter Brown, A. G. Yates)

English novelist whose works are primarily of mystery and detection. One exception may be:

1971. House of Sorcery, by Carter Brown. New York: New American Library (Signet Y6755), 1967, 1975. (NUC 1968-72 103-391)

YORK, Helen

Born 10/27/18 in Braddock, Pennsylvania. Graduated from Carlow College in 1941 and California State University in 1962. Was a public school teacher of English in Pasadena, California from 1957 to 1968. Malverne is her first novel.

1972. Malverne Manor (C). Garden City, N.Y.: Doubleday, 1974. (NUC 1974 18-744)

Claire goes to Malverne at the urgent request of her friend Amy who is visiting there prior to her marriage to the lord of the manor. Claire arrives only to be told that Amy had never been there and Claire decides to investigate. The author kept me reading in spite of a contrived plot and dim, unbelievable characters.

YORK, Jeremy (pseud.) see CREASEY, John

YOUNG, Narcella (pseud.) see TATE, Velma

ZUMWALT, Eva

1973. Masquerade of Evil (C). New York: Ace, 1975.

Slightly better than average "Louisiana Gothic." All the clichés are here but are handled with some skill and imagination.

INDEX OF TITLES

Radcliffe, Elsa
Gothic novels of the
twentieth century.

DATE DUE
